Overcoming Inertia in School Reform

R. Murray Thomas

Overcoming Inertia in School Reform

How to Successfully Implement Change

CORWIN PRESS, INC.
A Sage Publications Company
Thousand Oaks, California

Copyright © 2002 by Corwin Press, Inc.

All rights reserved. When forms and sample documents are included, their use is authorized only by educators, local school sites, and/or noncommercial entities who have purchased the book. Except for that usage, no part of this book may be reproduced or utilized in any form or by any means, electronic or mechanical, including photocopying, recording, or by any information storage and retrieval system, without permission in writing from the publisher.

For information:

Corwin Press, Inc.
A Sage Publications Company
2455 Teller Road
Thousand Oaks, California 91320
E-mail: order@corwinpress.com

Sage Publications Ltd.
6 Bonhill Street
London EC2A 4PU
United Kingdom

Sage Publications India Pvt. Ltd.
M-32 Market
Greater Kailash I
New Delhi 110 048 India

Printed in the United States of America

Library of Congress Cataloging-in-Publication Data

Thomas, R. Murray (Robert Murray), 1921-
  Overcoming inertia in school reform : how to successfully implement change / R. Murray Thomas.
     p. cm.
Includes bibliographical references (p.   ) and index.
  ISBN 0-7619-4591-1 (c) — ISBN 0-7619-4592-X (p)
  1. School improvement programs. 2. School management and organization. I. Title.
  LB2822.8 .T46 2002
  371.2—dc21
                            2002000164

This book is printed on acid-free paper.

02 03 04 05 10 9 8 7 6 5 4 3 2 1

Acquisitions Editor: Rachel Livsey
Editorial Assistant: Phyllis Cappello
Production Editor: Sanford Robinson
Cover Designer: Tracy Miller

Contents

Preface

This book is about why educational-development projects so frequently fail. Or, if projects don't fail completely, at least they often fall short of expectations. The descriptions of such projects in the following pages are organized around an analytical model called *inertia theory*, a model designed to identify conditions that prohibit the satisfactory implementation of planned educational change. The two purposes of discovering conditions that contribute to failure are (a) to warn educators of pitfalls they should avoid in the future and (b) to propose steps that might be taken to reduce or eliminate the problems suffered by a reform that has already been launched.

Gathering evidence about failed ventures—and particularly about the causes of failure—can be difficult, because powerful forces operate to hide what went wrong and why. Those forces are mainly people's desire to save face—their desire to absolve themselves of blame for failures in order to maintain the fiction that they have consistently behaved as efficient, well-intentioned, honest, wise, foresightful, generous, modest, and public-spirited professionals.

In view of the barriers to data collection that such forces erect, what, then, have been the sources of evidence for the failures described throughout this book? Those sources have been of three kinds—(a) published accounts of educational reforms that went awry, (b) my own experience during more than half a century in the education profession, and (b) what other people have told me about educational-development projects with which they were acquainted.

The first of these sources—published accounts—offers far more valuable information about successful projects than about failed ones, because people are more apt to publicize their triumphs than their failures. Furthermore, professional journals, newspapers, and book publishers are usually more willing to accept manuscripts describing projects that went well than ones that turned out badly. And even when a published account admits to blunders in the implementation of an educational reform, the explanation of what went wrong may well distort what actually happened, a distortion fashioned to protect the reputations of those at fault. Consequently, for the purposes of this book, published materials are useful, but only to a limited extent.

The second and third kinds of evidence—my own experiences and what others have told me about their experiences—are major sources of the cases described in this volume. The nature of my personal experiences, and of the sorts of people who have told me of theirs, can perhaps be best inferred if I describe the main kinds of educational settings in which I've encountered educational-development efforts. I began in the 1940s as a high school teacher in Honolulu, first at Kamehameha Schools and later at Mid-Pacific Institute. Subsequently I taught at universities in San Francisco (one year), upstate New York (Brockport, eight years), West Java (Pajajaran University in Bandung, four years), and 30 years at the University of California, Santa Barbara, including four years as dean of the Graduate School of Education. I also served as an educational-development consultant to the Indonesian Ministry of Education (periodically between 1965 and 1983), the American Samoa Department of Education (periodically between 1968 and 1975), and the University of Malaya's Ford Foundation Development Grant (1967 to 1972). These positions furnished a host of opportunities to observe, and to participate in, educational-reform projects in diverse contexts and at all levels of the educational ladder. They also provided the chance to talk with many kinds of educators and to hear their tales of development projects that had turned sour and listen to their explanations of why.

Finally, a word is in order about the nature of the cases of failure described throughout the book. Only rarely does a case identify the exact place and people who were involved in a project that went bad, because it's not my purpose to sully the reputation of any individual, group, or institution. My purpose is solely to illustrate what can go wrong with reform efforts, why, and what might be done to repair the damage. Thus, although the cases are all based on fact, in this book they assume the form of generic examples—types of situations common to many educational settings. As a result, the lessons to be learned from the analysis of the cases should be applicable to a wide range of the educational efforts of diverse people in diverse places.

Acknowledgements

The contributions of the following reviewers are gratefully acknowledged:

Roberta E. Glaser, Ph.D.
Assistant Superintendent
St. Johns Public Schools
St. Johns, MI

Sue Godsey
Educator
Carl Junction High School
Carl Junction, MO

Karen K. Coblentz
Elementary Principal
Dassel Elementary
Dassel-Cokato Schools
Dassel, MN

Robert B. Amenta, Ed.D.
Director of Educational Administration
School of Education
California Lutheran University
Thousand Oaks, CA

Betty J. Alford, Ph.D.
Associate Professor
Secondary Education/Educational
    Leadership
Stephen F. Austin State University
Nacagdoches, TX

I also wish to thank a pair of Corwin Press editors, Rachel Livsey and Sanford Robinson, for their valuable guidance in the production of this book, and Phyllis Cappello of the Corwin staff for her efficient support.

About the Author

R. Murray Thomas (PhD, Stanford University) is an emeritus professor at the University of California, Santa Barbara. His experiences as a teacher, researcher, teacher educator, and administrator range from the nursery school through the university. Over a period of 50 years, he taught junior- and high-school students, conducted research in preschools, prepared elementary- and secondary-school teachers, and served as a university administrator. Books he has written, coauthored, or edited that are related to the content of *Overcoming Inertia in School Reform* include *Ways of Teaching in Elementary Schools, Judging Student Progress, Decisions in Teaching Elementary Social Studies, The Puzzle of Learning Difficulties, Politics and Education: Cases from 11 Nations* (editor), and *Encyclopedia of Human Development and Education* (editor).

Part I

The Role of Inertia Theory in Education

The principal conviction on which this book is based is that inertia theory offers a useful vantage point from which to analyze attempts at educational development and reform. The purpose of Part I is to explain the nature of the theory in order to prepare readers for the host of applications described in the remaining four parts of the volume.

1

Inertia Theory in Education— Why Things Don't Change

The concern throughout this book is the partial or complete failure of efforts to improve education. At first glance, a project aimed at exposing failures may look like a pessimistic, destructive venture. But such is not the case, because something that's broken cannot be fixed until the fixers discover what went wrong and why. Thus, the book's contents concern not only why things don't change but also how damage to planned change might be repaired.

Among Sir Isaac Newton's contributions to physical science are his three laws of motion. The first of these postulates—the law of inertia—asserts that a body at rest or moving at a constant speed in a straight line will remain at rest or will continue moving in a straight line at constant speed unless acted upon by a force. In the following pages, I propose that the concept of inertia can profitably be transferred from the field of physics into the social sciences as a perspective from which to interpret cases of planned social change, including the sort of change known as educational development, educational reform, or educational innovation. In effect, inertia in an education system is the complex force that resists change—that fosters "business as usual."

Although the single phrase "why things don't change" describes the general focus of this volume, the book's theme is more accurately represented by five interrelated phrases:

- Why things don't change
- Why things don't change enough
- Why things change, but in the wrong direction
- Why things change simultaneously in both good and bad ways
- Why things change, and then retrogress to their former state

My interest in the role of inertia in education derives from the observation that many attempts to change educational operations or to change the objects of education—the learners—either fail entirely or enjoy very limited success. Hence, key inertia questions become:

- Why is it so often difficult to alter the way people act or the way things have traditionally been done?
- What conditions and forces thwart attempts to direct educational activities or people's lives into new paths?
- Why does an educational innovation or reform that's been put in place sometimes revert to a version of its pre-change condition?

The term *inertia theory*—or the more informal *inertia metaphor*—identifies a formally organized way to answer such questions by focusing on the dark side of educational development. By concentrating on resistance to change, the theory highlights factors that might be overlooked or minimized when a proposed educational change is viewed only from the vantage point of a typical educational-development theory.

The six purposes of this opening chapter are to

- Sketch the main components of an education-system model. The model is intended to help educators identify which components of their present education system may frustrate efforts to produce the sort of better education they envisage. Each of the book's remaining chapters, 2 through 12, focuses on significant subcomponents of the model, (a) illustrating how faulty handling of the subcomponents can frustrate the implementation of an intended educational change and (b) suggesting ways to avoid or correct obstacles to educational reform. The contents of Chapters 2 through 12 are organized around generic cases of educational reform that illustrate flawed attempts to alter an education system.
- Analyze planned educational change from the viewpoint of inertia theory.
- Consider conditions that determine whether a planned change is a good idea or a bad idea.
- Offer a sample of propositions about the education-system model that influence the inertia that must be overcome if a desired change is to occur.
- Describe the nature of the book's remaining chapters.
- Suggest ways that readers might wish to use the book.

An Education-System Model

As Figure 1-1 shows, an education system can be understood as consisting of the teaching/learning process along with two support systems that significantly influence what students learn and how well they learn it. This model is admittedly a much simplified version of the way education within a society actually functions, in that the model identifies only a limited number of the components affecting how planned learning occurs. However, a more ambitious model that attempted to identify every sort of influence on the teaching/learning process would be far too cumbersome for the intent of this book. Hence, I have adopted this scaled-down version as sufficient for the purpose of illustrating the operation of inertia in the conduct of education.

Figure 1-1

An Education-System Model

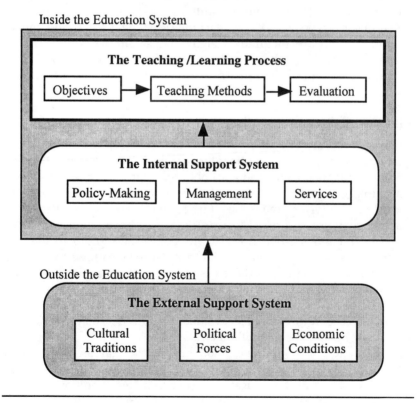

The center of an education system is the teaching/learning process (instructional procedures), which is composed of three chief components: (a) learning objectives (intended learning outcomes), (b) teaching methods, and (c) evaluation procedures that are designed to show how well learners have mastered the objectives. The teaching/learning process depends for its content and operational efficiency on two support systems—one internal and the other external.

The components of the internal support system are within the education system itself and can be described as functions that undergird and serve the teaching process. The three functions portrayed in Figure 1-1 are those of (a) setting policies that guide the teaching/learning process, (b) managing the school system (coordinating, communicating, establishing authority relationships), and (c) offering services to students, to the personnel who operate the education system, and to the society within which the education system is embedded.

The external support system is outside the education system and consists of such components as the society's (a) cultural traditions, (b) political forces, and (c) economic conditions.

The major components of the teaching/learning process and the two support systems are pictured in Figure 1-1 as simple boxes. In later chapters, each simple box is redesigned as a complex unit consisting of subcomponents whose condition may complicate and frustrate attempts at educational reform.

Planned Educational Change

Changes in an education system can occur either intentionally (planned change) or unintentionally (unscheduled change). Three examples of planned change in a school are: establishing a course in sex education, assigning an assistant principal to prepare the school budget, and altering the school-bus routes. Three examples of unplanned change are: fire destroying the auto shop, parents of school-age children moving out of the town because of rapidly rising real-estate prices, and a wealthy philanthropist bequeathing the school a million dollars. Although the focus of this book is on planned change, it seems obvious that planned change is often a response to unplanned change—the auto shop must be rebuilt, adjustments are required because of the decrease in the school's enrollment, and a decision must be made about how best to use the million dollars.

An estimate of the kind and amount of inertia that an intended educational change will generate can be based on a comparison between the present condition of the education system and the condition that will exist if the planned change succeeds. Our simple education-system model can aid in producing that estimate by drawing attention to which components need to be altered.

At any given time, the components pictured in Figure 1-1 assume a particular pattern. Therefore, if a proposed innovation is to succeed, then the existing pattern must be changed in certain respects. Envisioning the difference between the model's existing pattern and the newly intended pattern enables us to identify what changes will be needed in order to implement the proposed innovation. Consider this example of a very simple, ordinary change—the adoption of a new textbook for a high school American history class. In this case, several of the components of the model will need alteration if the new text is to result in students understanding American history better than they would have with the old text. For instance, changes will likely be required in (a) some of the specific *learning objectives* (students' knowledge and skills), (b) the *teaching methods* (lecture content, students' activities, class discussion topics, videos, charts, use of the Internet), and (c) *evaluation techniques* (test items, homework assignments). Introducing the new textbook may also require changes in the internal support system, such as in the *policies* regarding how often new textbooks can be adopted, who pays for the texts (the school or the students), and certain of the textbooks' contents (the portrayal of ethnic groups, of religious groups, of the two genders, of sexual behavior, of political parties, of labor unions). The school's *services* may also be affected by changes required in how the new texts are obtained and distributed to students. In addition, features of the external support system may need to be revised as well. *Political groups* (ethnic, religious, socioeconomic, gender, sexual-orientation, political-party) may object to the contents of the new text and attempt to block the book's adoption. Or publishers of other American history texts may seek to have their books replace the proposed text. And if parents are expected to pay for the textbooks, then the society's *economic condition* may influence families' ability to afford new books. In summary, inertia generated within different components of the education-system model can serve to diminish the success of a proposed educational improvement .

As Figure 1-2 illustrates, a further variable crucial to the success of an innovation is the nature of the learners. A teaching/learning innovation can succeed only to the degree that it is compatible with such characteristics of students as those listed in Figure 1-2. *Skills* are the behaviors learners need in order to profit from teaching procedures. In the case of the American history textbook, the principal skill needed is reading ability. *Knowledge* consists of the information and beliefs students bring to their task of understanding the contents of the textbook. Learners' *interests* and *motives* influence how much attention students devote to studying the text. Their *study habits* affect how efficiently they pursue their reading assignments. Finally, a variety of factors in their *home background* influence how much learners will gain from the new book. For instance, barriers to students' profiting from the textbook include the exclusive use of a foreign language in the home (so there is no chance to practice English at home), lack of parental respect for academic achievement, or a heavy load of chores borne by the student (child care, meal preparation, housekeeping, outside job).

As suggested by the arrow extending from the external support system to the learner in Figure 1-2, students' characteristics that affect their performance in school can be significantly influenced by the broader society in which they live. Widespread prejudice against a pupil's ethnic or religious group may cause the pupil to hate school as a result of classmates' taunts. An economic recession that causes a girl's parents to lose their jobs can reduce the parents' ability to provide their daughter satisfactory clothing, food, and study facilities. The spread of illicit drugs in the community may cause a boy to adopt a cocaine habit, thereby damaging his ability to complete school assignments.

Figure 1-2

Education-System and Learner Interactions

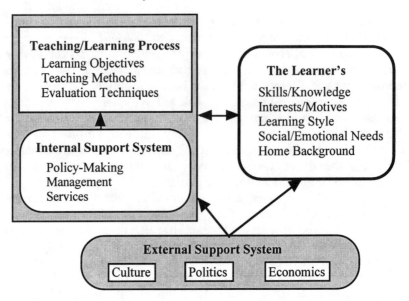

In summary, students can differ from each other in all of the ways listed in the *Learners* box in Figure 1-2. Those differences pose the teaching/learning system's most demanding challenge. I assume that the ideal goal of any education system is to ensure that each person performs at the maximum of his or her potential. However, it's apparent that such an ideal can never be reached, because the task of accommodating all of the influential differences among learners is impossibly daunting. The most that can be hoped for is that changes in the education system can effect ever-closer approximations to the ideal. Inertia theory is intended to aid with that pursuit by proposing ways of identifying obstructions to learners' success.

When Is Change a Good Idea Rather Than a Bad Idea?

It's apparent that nearly any proposal about changing an educational practice will generate both advocates and opponents. Some people consider the intended change a good idea while others consider it a bad idea. Perhaps the most powerful cause of this conflict of opinion is the difference among individuals in how they expect the change will affect their own welfare. A working mother may welcome the proposal of a longer school day, since it will reduce her after-school childcare costs. A high school teacher may oppose a plan that requires individualized homework assignments for students because the plan will substantially increase his workload.

In some cases, people's judgments of an intended innovation are influenced by their concern for others' welfare rather than their own. A teacher may approve of an after-school tutoring plan because she thinks it will result in children learning more effectively, even though it will cause her more work and bother. A father may object to a school district's adding a required high school class titled Personal-Social Adjustment because he fears the class will reduce his daughter's opportunity to take "enough of those hard-core courses needed to get her into a first-rate college." A legislator may support an innovation, such as statewide achievement testing, because he thinks it will enhance his state's public image in comparison to the image of other states. A school board member may oppose a plan to reduce class size because she believes it's too costly and thus an additional burden on taxpayers.

In other cases, people's attitudes toward a proposed development are formed by multiple concerns—their own welfare, students' welfare, the peace and efficiency of the broader society, and the society's ability and willingness to finance schooling. For instance, a third-grade teacher may oppose placing mentally disabled children in regular classrooms because she believes such mainstreaming (a) increases the complexity of her teaching tasks and places the mentally slow child in unfair competition with more able agemates, even though mainstreaming (b) saves the cost of special education facilities and teachers, and it may help the mentally apt pupils learn to get along amicably with people whose intellectual abilities are less than their own.

In summary, there is no absolute, objective criterion to apply in judging whether a proposed change in educational practice is a good idea or bad idea. Rather, individuals base their judgments of innovations on their personal values and their expectations of how a reform would likely work out. Therefore, in most—if not all—cases of proposed educational improvement, conflicts will arise over the desirability of the suggested change.

Inertia theory is of use to both the advocates and opponents of a proposed educational-reform project. For proponents of an innovation, the theory can help identify (a) the components of the education system that will need to be changed, (b) the conditions that maintain the system in its traditional form, and (c) what will be required to alter traditional conditions in ways that support the innovation. In contrast, for critics of an intended change, inertia theory can help identify (a) which conditions of a traditional educational activity serve to resist change, and (b) how to sustain and encourage those conditions. Thus, for both the supporters and foes of a proposed project, a principal issue addressed by the theory is: What causal factors produce inertia in the conduct of education? In other words, what factors account for educational activities continuing in their usual fashion in the face of efforts to introduce change?

With the education-system model on page 5 in mind, we next consider a series of propositions about conditions that affect the success of planned educational change.

Dimensions of Educational Change

The amount and source of resistance to change can be influenced by various conditions that can be cast as dimensions or scales. Six illustrative dimensions are introduced here as a preview to similar propositions about educational change that appear throughout the book. The six are identified by the labels (a) quantity of components, (b) organizational complexity, (c) extent of change, (d) time period, (e) incentives, (f) expense, and (g) communication accuracy.

At first glance, the six may appear to be no more than truisms—statements so self-evident that they're not worth mentioning. However, observations of educational reforms in action suggest that the six are often ignored in practice, thereby increasing the inertia that must be combated when reforms are introduced.

Quantity of Components

Proposition: The greater the number of components within an educational operation that must be altered so as to effect a proposed change, the greater the inertia that must be overcome in order to carry out the change.

Few components   Many components

For a contrast in the quantity of components, consider the following two examples.

Few Components. Two general-science instructors in a junior high school decide to add a Socratic questioning style to their array of techniques for leading class discussions. The style will involve organizing discussion questions about a scientific phenomenon (gravity, air pressure, plant growth, and more) in a sequence that leads students to a logical conclusion. The intention of the Socratic approach is to encourage students to adopt logical patterns of reasoning rather than simply to accept the explanations that their teachers habitually have offered in the past. To effect this instructional improvement, the two instructors only need to discover how to order their questions in a sequence that guides the learners to inevitable conclusions.

Many components: In this same junior high school, the principal intends to introduce computer–literacy classes for all eighth-graders. If the plan is to succeed, two classrooms must be wired so that each room accommodates 35 computers in a network connected to printers and the Internet. In preparation for this innovation, a survey must be conducted of the available types of computers; and the ones best suited to the school's needs must be purchased and installed. A similar survey of software is also necessary, and the selected software must be purchased. Teachers must be trained in computer-literacy instruction, and new lesson plans must be purchased (perhaps in the form of a workbook) or created by the teachers to furnish a well-organized course for the students. Technicians must be hired (or students trained) to keep the computer system in proper working order. And funds must be found to finance the entire plan and to maintain the program in the future.

It's clear that there are far more potential barriers to the success of the computer-literacy plan than to the Socratic-questioning proposal.

Organizational Complexity

Proposition: A simple innovation involves establishing few new relationships among components in an education system. A complex proposal involves changes in many relationships among components. The greater the number of new relationships, the greater the inertia that must be overcome. In other words, the more complex the system of connections among components of an educational operation, the greater the resistance to change.

Few new relationships   Many new relationships

Few new relationships: Our earlier example of the plan to adopt a new American history textbook involved a limited number of new connections among components of the education system. For example, links would be necessary between newly adopted objectives, teaching procedures, and evaluation techniques. However, traditional connections among most objectives, teaching methods, and evaluation techniques could remain unchanged. Also unchanged would be the existing system of purchasing textbooks and delivering them to students.

Many new relationships: A county that maintains a standard curriculum throughout the public schools intends to replace the existing practical mathematics program with a conceptual mathematics plan that stresses students' understanding the nature of mathematics rather than the application of mathematics in solving problems met in common, everyday situations. Implementing the plan requires altering a multitude of relationships between the county education office and such entities as school districts, individual schools, individual teachers, textbook publishers, and inservice and preservice teacher-education programs. The complexity of the plan offers the possibility that a seemingly infinite number of coordination problems will diminish the hoped-for success of the innovation.

Extent of Change

Proposition: The more drastic the alteration required in a component of an educational operation, the greater the inertia that must be overcome.

Slight change   Drastic change

Slight change: In a school district that transports many of its students to school by bus, officials decide to change the places that students will be picked up and to change the times that a bus will arrive at those locations. The change is being introduced in order to ensure that all students arrive at school in plenty of time for their first class.

Drastic change: As the Spanish-speaking population of a small city has rapidly increased, political pressure exerted by the Hispanic community convinces the school system's policy-makers to institute bilingual instruction in elementary schools. According to the plan, teaching in all kindergartens and in the first three primary grades must be in both English and Spanish. Furthermore, in grades 4 through 6, where English is the dominant medium of instruction, clarifying explanations in the Spanish language must be available to students who need such help. This plan requires changes in teachers' language skills, new instructional materials, the amount of money needed for purchasing them (books, periodicals, audiotapes, videotapes), and changes in how classroom instruction is organized to accommodate different pupils' language skills.

Planned Time Period

Proposition: The expected development period for a proposed educational innovation is judged by the length of time from the first stage of the project to the date that the innovation is securely in place. The more complex and massive the intended change, the longer the time required to overcome the inertia.

Short time   Long time

Problems in implementing educational-improvement projects often result from planners underestimating how long it will take to establish a new program in its complete operating state. Underestimates frequently result from planners failing to recognize all of the ways that components must be altered in order to bring about the intended reform. Hence, planners can find themselves in trouble with their superiors in the educational hierarchy (school boards, superintendents, state education departments), with users of the education system's services, and with political activists whenever educational innovations are not in proper working order by the end of the predicted time period.

Brief project: A high-school registrar intends to revise the student-registration process so that students can sign up for classes via the Internet rather than having to stand in line in the gymnasium during a two-day period in order to record their names on class lists and receive class-period assignments.

Lengthy project: The directors of a county library system that services the schools intend to abandon their traditional card catalogue in favor of making records of all the library's holdings—past, present, and future—available on a computer network.

Expense

Proposition: The cost of a proposed reform can be estimated in terms of funds, time, and bother. The greater the cost, the greater the force required to implement the reform, that is, to overcome inertia. And among innovations that are already in place, the greater a reform's continuing cost, the more vulnerable it is to being eliminated.

Low cost   High cost

Low cost: In a socially and economically disordered district of a large city, daily life for many teens was marked by bullying, gang fights, heavy use of alcohol and illicit drugs, vandalism, robbery, theft, intimidation, family alienation, unhealthy dietary practices, and illness. For many students, school attendance was erratic. In class they often paid little attention to the lesson and frequently failed to complete assignments. In an effort to improve these conditions, an English teacher in the district's central high school created a peer-counseling class in which students learned how to counsel agemates who suffered personal/social problems. To gain practical experience at the same time that they were helping members of the community, class members counseled both their fellow students and youths in the community at large. Their teacher served not only as the instructor of the peer-counseling class but also as the supervisor of how peer counselors managed their cases.

There was no opposition from any source—within the school or within the wider community—to the introduction of the peer-counseling program. The school's administrators, in particular, welcomed the innovation because it provided a new service and engaged counseling-class members in socially constructive activities at no cost to the school district (Diver-Stamnes, 1995).

High cost: An example of an earlier innovation whose continuation was threatened by its high cost is the case of a high school childcare course. Eight years earlier, an early childhood education course was introduced into the county's high schools as part of the school system's career-and-technology offerings that were intended to "train students in professions that are occupationally viable." To implement the program, each high school was equipped with a nursery school for three- and four-year-old children, thereby providing a laboratory in which high school students in the childcare course could gain direct experience educating and caring for the young. The expense of operating a nursery school (suitable room and playground, equipment, salaries of early childhood specialists as teachers, liability insurance) made the program considerably more expensive than the facilities needed for a typical school class.

Recently, a committee of local business leaders and educators was assigned to assess all of the school system's vocational programs. The committee's report to the county school board recommended that the childcare course be dropped from the schools' offerings.

Despite the fact that the course is one of the most popular programs (with 110 students currently enrolled in the class at Evans High), the early childhood course does not fit the school system's mission to train students in professions that are occupationally viable. The expected pay for childcare workers is $10,433 annually, which is not even minimum wage if calculated on 40 hours per week for 52 weeks. A question that arises is this: Are we doing our students a service by preparing them for minimum wage or sub-minimum wage occupations? The program is costly, and the money saved by eliminating it could be better invested in preparing students for professional careers that yield higher financial returns. (Hall, 2001)

Communication Accuracy

Proposition: Inertia increases in proportion to the difficulties proponents of a change experience in communicating clearly to the program's participants the goals and procedures required to effect the change.

Accurate communication   Garbled communication

A study conducted under the aegis of a nationwide language arts association reported that the teaching of poetry in the schools had been seriously neglected in recent decades. In an effort to revive interest in poetry, a committee of the association proposed that a four-week unit of study focusing on poetic forms and on poetry's functions be included in middle school language arts programs. The following examples illustrate the way that two school districts sought to implement the proposal by means of instructions provided for classroom teachers.

Inaccurate communication: In District A, the instructions to classroom teachers consisted of the following paragraph taken from the language arts association's report on the teaching of poetry.

Studying poetry for approximately 45 minutes a day over a four-week period furnishes students ample opportunity to gain a multifaceted appreciation of verse forms, of the contributions poetry can make to their lives, and of how to distinguish between high-quality and low-quality poems.

Accurate communication: In District B, the instructions to teachers were created from detailed descriptions extracted from the language arts association's report. The descriptions identified particular aspects of poetry that students might profitably study, including poetry's (a) patterns (limerick, rhymed couplet, quatrain, Rubaiyat, sonnet, ballade, epigram, haiku, and more), (b) feet (such as iambic, trochee, anapest), (c) meters (such as trimeter, tetrameter, pentameter), (d) functions (epitomize a truth, depict scenes, describe people, amuse, and more), and (e) emotions (joy, sadness, regret, optimism, contentment, fear, guilt, and more). The titles of poems that illustrate these features were also included in the instructions, along with suggestions about ways of presenting poetry (teacher reads aloud, students read aloud, videotaped excerpts of poetry are accompanied by scenes and music). A proposed set of rating scales was also in the packet, with each scale representing a suggested criterion or standard by which a poem's quality could be judged (such criteria as meter consistency, aptness of similes and metaphors, rhyming accuracy, and clarity of meaning).

Conclusion

The above six illustrative propositions are only a sample of ones that can be generated within inertia theory. And, as shown in later chapters, all such propositions are conditional, in the sense that none is absolutely true in all cases of planned change. Rather, the propositions interact, so that in any particular case of change, the significance and function of one proposition will be influenced by the condition of other propositions that bear on the case. For example, it is typically more difficult to communicate accurately to participants when making drastic changes in a multitude of components than when making modest changes in a single component.

The Book's Structure

As the table of contents shows, Chapters 2 through 11 are organized in terms of the education-system model presented earlier in this chapter. Because the success of every component of the model depends on the efficiency of the people who carry out that component's functions, Chapter 2, "System Participants," describes cases of attempted educational change that suffer from inertia produced by individuals failing to fulfill their assigned roles satisfactorily. Then the subsequent chapters—3 through 11—feature cases in which educational reforms are frustrated by difficulties arising in each of the nine major components of the education-system model. The book's final chapter, "Applying Inertia Theory to Education," suggests ways the theory can be put to practical use in diagnosing and treating problems of inertia that arise during planned educational change.

Every chapter, 2 through 11, is organized in the same pattern. Each begins with the chapter's central component depicted in terms of constituent subcomponents. The nature of each subcomponent is then illustrated with a case in which the unsatisfactory handling of the subcomponent has hindered the effort at educational change. Each case is presented in five stages: (a) the subcomponent is described , (b) a proposition relating to the subcomponent is offered, (c) one or more typical problem cases are described, (d) causes of the inertia problems in each case are estimated, and (e) potential ways to reduce the inertia are analyzed.

In summary, inertia theory is composed of four principal elements:

(1) a model of the education system that consists of major components,

(2) subcomponents of each major component,

(3) propositions about how conditions of the subcomponents may contribute to inertia (that is, the complete or partial failure of an attempt to alter the education system), and

(4) potential remedies for reducing the resistance to the intended change.

Using the Book

There are several ways this book can be used. Perhaps the most obvious is that of reading it from start to finish for a sequential view of the theory and its applications.

Another way is to begin by studying this opening chapter, then hopping around to chapters whose subject matter seems of particular interest. For instance, Chapter 2 concerns problems that participants' characteristics can pose for proposed reforms, and Chapter 10 inspects the influence of political groups on educational change.

A third way to use the book consists of selecting problem cases from Chapters 2 through 11 as the focus of group discussions about the suitability of different attempts to solve the inertia problems reflected in those cases. To foster this activity, each chapter—2 through 11—closes with "Discussion Topics" on which a group can focus its debate about the matters addressed in that chapter.

A fourth use of the book involves adopting the theory and its education-system model as a guide to identifying potential sources of inertia in projects of educational change contemplated by members of a school's curriculum committee or by a board of education. A process for conducting this fourth type of inquiry is described in Chapter 12.

2

System Participants

Throughout this book, the word *participants* refers to three types of people:

- The ones who operate the education system (teachers, principals, counselors, custodians, secretaries, technicians, bus drivers, and more)
- Individuals in the schools' external support system (parents, textbook publishers, legislators, ethnic-group activists, newspaper columnists, and more)
- Students—the learners whose welfare the education system is designed to promote

Participants are obviously key factors within all of the components of the education-system model described in Chapter 1. Each type of participant has particular characteristics important for the success of planned change. Consequently, the significant characteristics of teachers will not be identical with the significant features of students or of people outside the school system. In order to highlight those differences, the three types of participants will be discussed separately. First are educational personnel, second are individuals and institutions in the external support system, and third are the students.

Educational Personnel

For the purpose of estimating the effect on inertia exerted by individuals within the education system, I have selected six personal characteristics that I believe are particularly influential. The six are obviously not the only traits of educational personnel that affect the success of a proposed innovation. For example, additional personal characteristics that influence individuals' engagement in educational reform include participants' (a) interpersonal-relations habits (ways they interact with colleagues, students, and parents), (b a residue of background experience that impinges on the way they interpret educational proposals, and (c) energy level (the amount of vigor available to invest in their work). However, the following six attributes should be sufficient to illustrate ways individuals' characteristics can contribute to inertia.

Educational Personnel Characteristics

- Skills and knowledge
- Interests and motives
- Commitment
- Comprehension
- Perceived risk
- Compatibility

Skills and Knowledge

Obviously, the people occupying each position in an education system must command particular skills and knowledge if the system is to operate efficiently.   Nearly all educational-improvement projects call for some degree of change in the skills and knowledge needed for implementation. This observation leads to the following proposition.

Proposition: The greater the discrepancy between the skills and knowledge of available personnel and the skills and knowledge required for a proposed innovation, the greater the resistance to change.

The term *available personnel* refers to three kinds of people: (a) ones already filling a role (such a role as that of classroom teacher or school principal) in the present system, and that role is the same as one in the envisioned innovation, (b) people who can be transferred into the envisioned program from other roles in the present system (a teacher is selected to become a counselor), or (c) individuals imported from outside the system.

Problem case A: In an effort of improve classroom instruction by making the Internet readily available to teachers and students, a school district supplied each classroom with five computers, all of them connected to the Internet. In addition, each secondary school was furnished a computer laboratory—a classroom equipped with thirty-two personal computers for use in teaching computer skills to all members of a class at the same time. To prepare teachers to use computers and the Internet for enhancing instruction, the district provided each teacher with the manual *Guidebook to Computers in the Classroom* and conducted a two-day training workshop that every teacher and administrator was obliged to attend.

Six months after the computer project had been launched, members of the district's instructional-technology staff interviewed teachers and selected students to discover in what ways and how frequently computers and the Internet were used for improving learning. The survey revealed that in most classrooms the computers were rarely used, and no more than 20 percent of classes had ever taken material from the Internet. The main reasons that the computer project had had so little effect on teaching methods were that (a) teachers did not feel confident using computers for searching the World Wide Web, (b) they believed that too much time and effort would be needed to acquire skill in using the Internet, and (c) they felt far more confident staying with their traditional instructional techniques than trying to adopt new ones.

As a result of the survey, district officials concluded that the computer project, at least during its first six months, had essentially failed.

Remedy options: The following four options are ones the district could attempt for reducing the inertia that the computer project suffered.

Incentives: Rewards—in the form of bonus money or special certificates or recognition ceremonies—could be offered to teachers who developed lessons that involved computers and the Internet.

Roving consultants: One or two members of the district's technology staff could work with individual teachers in developing specific lessons that the teachers could use in their instructional programs. The lessons would be designed to take advantage of computers and the Internet.

Inservice workshops: Periodic workshops in using computers to improve instruction could be offered, with teachers required to attend.

Student experts: The district could adopt the *Generation www.Y* program for training student experts in computer applications to teaching. The program involves establishing a special secondary-school course in which students are trained in computer skills—that is, trained to explore the World Wide Web, to use digital cameras, to create websites and audiovisual presentations, and to work successfully with teachers in developing lesson plans for each teacher's subject matter field. During the course, each student in the class works with one teacher in the secondary school or in a nearby elementary school to create one or more lessons for that teacher's class. In this partnership venture, the teacher serves as the education expert and the student as the computer-use expert, thereby relieving teachers of the necessity to master computer skills before using computer technology in their teaching (Harper, Hardy, & Thomas, 1999).

Among the above options, the student-experts approach would likely result in the greatest gain in reducing resistance to the computer project. However, the student-experts option would also be more expensive and more complex to implement than would any of the other alternatives.

Problem case B: A school district received a large government grant to test the value of an experimental program designed to "mainstream" various types of disabled pupils. Specifically, the project would place autistic, deaf, and limited-sight children in regular classrooms alongside nondisabled pupils. The program staff included (a) planners, who formulated the ways pupils would be integrated into regular classrooms; (b) trainers, who aided teachers in accommodating the disabled; and (c) an evaluator responsible for assessing the strengths and weaknesses of the program. The evaluator was a nephew of the president of the school board, who had urged the director of the program to hire the young man. In the middle of the school year and at the end of the year, reports of the program's success were to be submitted to the government agency that funded the experiment. However, by the end of the fourth month of the program, it was clear that the project evaluator's skills were completely inadequate. When he was asked to prepare tests to measure the disabled children's academic progress, he took an inordinate amount of time to furnish the tests and the final tests were badly flawed. When asked to prepare rating scales for recording observations of the children and for guiding interviews with the children and their teachers, the evaluator was completely baffled. Thus, it was clear to the program's director and staff members that the needed evaluation reports would not be forthcoming and, as a result, the government agency would stop funding the project.

Remedy options: The following are among the options the program's director might attempt for rescuing the program.

Discharge and replace: The incompetent evaluator could be fired and a replacement hired. However, the director did not consider this a feasible option, because he feared that the evaluator's uncle, who was rumored to be a headstrong and vindictive man, would scuttle the mainstreaming project.

Transfer: The evaluator could be moved to some other part of the school system and given a prestigious title but no important responsibility. Although this might be politically safe, it would be economically undesirable, for it involved paying an unproductive employee.

Duplicate: A second evaluator who commanded the required skills could be hired to work along with—and to guide and train—the incumbent. Again, this might be politically safe but would be economically wasteful.

Redefine: The responsibilities of the evaluator could be redefined so as to eliminate the actual evaluation tasks, which would then be transferred to another member of the project staff.

Interests and Motives

Interests, as the term is intended here, are the topics and activities in which people willingly invest their time and effort. *Motives* are forces that that give direction and energy to the pursuit of interests. For example, a classroom teacher is interested in becoming a school principal, with that interest motivated by a desire for a higher salary and greater authority and prestige.

> *Proposition:* The less that a proposed innovation appeals to the interests and motives of a person who is expected to participate in that innovation, the less energetically that person will support the change and, consequently, the greater the resulting inertia.

Problem case C: In a medium-sized school district, a science education consultant arrived from the state department of education to visit elementary-school classes and to review "teachers instructional plans in order to judge the nature of pupils' opportunities to study science." She concluded that, in grades 1 through 4, there was little or no systematic teaching of science. To correct this neglect, she recommended that the schools adopt the Direct Science Experience Program, which consisted of a series of textbooks, workbooks, and teachers' manuals. The program also offered a science kit containing equipment and supplies useful for conducting experiments and making observations (a microscope, a telescope, a magnifying glass, magnets, chemicals, and the like). The teachers' manuals explained how to guide pupils in carrying out the hands-on activities described in the texts and workbooks. School officials, convinced of the desirability of regular science instruction in the early grades, adopted the recommended program for all primary classes.

Six months after the science plan was put in place, the consultant returned to learn how well it was being implemented. Her visits to a variety of classrooms revealed a mixed result. Some teachers did, indeed, systematically apply the program. Others, however, taught science only sporadically, and a few rarely used the textbooks or engaged children in the workbooks' activities. Typical of the teachers who paid little attention to the adopted program was one who explained that

> I really can't get excited about science in the early grades. I'm more of a humanist—more interested in children learning about the diverse people in the world and how to get along with them. I'm also interested in children learning self-expression—to express their humanity and individuality in story telling, creative dramatics, art, and music. We do a lot of those things

in our class. It's not that I object to teaching science. It's just that I'm not interested in it, and I don't see why my pupils would be interested either.

Remedy options: If school district officials wish to ensure that the primary-grade science program is adhered to in all elementary schools, then the following trio of corrective measures could be attempted.

Lessons schedule: Rather than allowing teachers to arrange the school day in whatever pattern they wished, the district could specify when during the day different subjects would be studied (arithmetic, reading, writing, science, physical education, music, and more). However, the main problem with this solution is that it prevents teachers from organizing children's studies in a pattern that accommodates the conditions existing in a given classroom, such as the range of individual differences among children (how patient they are, how long they can concentrate on an activity, their fund of background knowledge, their ability levels) and a teacher's skill in managing classroom routines.

Monitoring teachers' behavior: Two ways principals might try for discovering how closely teachers adhere to the science program are: (a) making frequent, unannounced visits to classrooms and (b) requiring teachers to report which units in the science program had been covered during the current week. However, the animosity that such surveillance might generate on the part of teachers—and the extra work that classroom visits would require of principals—might render the monitoring plan counter productive.

Testing pupils: Tests covering the contents of each grade's science content could be administered to pupils, with the pupils' test scores interpreted as reflecting how consistently teachers have been applying the science program. Two problems with this solution are that (a) it's difficult to prepare paper-pencil tests that accurately assess what primary-level children have learned about science and (b) pupils' success on tests is not simply the result of a teacher's instructional skill but is influenced by a variety of other variables as well (children's ability levels, their home backgrounds, their mental and physical health, their attitudes toward school, and more).

Commitment

Commitment is an individual's strong conviction that one particular way of managing educational affairs is more constructive than are other possible ways. In the following words, C. E. Beeby, long-time head of New Zealand's education system, explained the significance of commitment for educational-reform proposals.

There is one thing that distinguishes teaching from all other professions, except perhaps the Church—no change in practice, no change in curricula has any meaning unless the teacher understands it and accepts it. . . . If a young doctor gives an injection under instruction, of if an architect as a member of a team designs a roof truss, the efficiency of the injection or the strength of the roof truss does not depend on his faith in the formula he has used. With the teacher it does. If [the teacher] doesn't understand the new method, or if he refuses to accept it other than superficially, instructions are of no avail. At best, he will go on doing in effect what he has always done, and at worst he will produce some travesty of modern teaching. (Beeby in Whitehead, 1997, p. 42).

Proposition: The more strongly an intended participant in educational change is committed to the existing way of doing things (rather than to a proposed innovation), the greater the inertia the innovation will face.

Problem case D: In a city school system, the recently appointed supervisor of language arts curricula sought to "modernize and streamline" the teaching of grammar in secondary schools by substituting "functional grammar" for the "formal grammar" that traditionally had been part of the curriculum. The functional approach, as explained in the recommended workbook, required students to learn only those aspects of grammar and syntax that were commonly misused. For example, students would practice when to use *who* and when to use *whom* but would not be required to learn about verbs, predicate nominatives, prepositions, objects of verbs, objects of prepositions, or the like. To reduce errors of communication, students would be taught to place pronouns close to the pronouns' referents but they would not learn how to diagram sentences. In order to monitor the implementation of the functional-grammar program, the supervisor of language arts required teachers to fill out periodic reports indicating which portions of the new program had been covered. Even though the reports were often late in arriving at the supervisor's office, they did suggest that the program was working well. However, when the language arts supervisor made surprise visits to secondary-school English classes and later talked with students, he discovered that a substantial number of students were being taught parts of speech and how to diagram sentences, which had been the practice before the functional-grammar innovation. In effect, some teachers had falsified the required monitoring reports and had continued to teach in their usual fashion, because they were not convinced that the functional-grammar approach was as effective as their traditional method of teaching written and spoken English.

Remedy options: Methods that the language arts supervisor might try for overcoming the inertia that his innovation suffered could include:

Inservice workshops: Teachers would be required to attend sessions during which the supervisor would explain the time-saving advantages of functional grammar and would demonstrate appropriate teaching methods. However, the effectiveness of such workshops was questionable, in view of the teachers' strong convictions about the superiority of formal grammar over functional grammar.

Threatened sanctions: The supervisor could threaten teachers with the disapproval of their superiors (principals, central office staff); and he could caution teachers that he would put critical remarks in their personnel records if they persisted in teaching traditional grammar. He could warn them that those critical remarks could damage their chances for promotion and pay increases. However, the problem with making such threats is that there was little possibility the supervisor could carry them through, because school principals were prone to trust teachers whose amount of classroom experience was greater than that of the supervisor.

Comprehension

In the present context, *comprehension* refers to how well the intended participants in an educational-development project understand (a) the ways their skills and knowledge must change in order to implement their part of the project, and (b) the specific steps they must take to effect the required changes. As Michael Fullen (1991) has proposed, teachers often resist a change, not because of an intrinsic antagonism toward it, but because they don't understand how to cope with it.

Proposition: The more complex the process of changing a participant's behavior, the greater the resistance to the educational innovation that requires such a change.

Problem case E: Traditionally, when learners have been taught as a group, rather than tutored individually, everyone in the group has received the same sort of instruction—the same lecture, the same homework assignment, the same textbook. However, it is apparent that differences among the learners (in ability, in background knowledge, in diligence, in learning style) significantly affect their mastery of the objectives. Frequently, teachers design their instruction to suit the "average learners," meaning those students who achieve the objectives at a moderate rate. In such classes, faster learners can be bored and slower ones can be left behind when they fail to master the current objectives before the teacher moves ahead to new ones.

A school district sought to cope with this perennial problem of individual differences by adopting a Tri-Level Instructional Plan. The plan involved three sets of instructional activities. The first set, called *basic activities*, consisted of learning objectives that every student in the class would be expected to achieve by the end of the current study unit (with each unit lasting between two and four weeks). All class members would engage in the basic activities (lectures, demonstrations, textbook readings, homework assignments). And throughout the unit, the teacher would be assessing how well the different students were progressing. These periodic assessments would reveal that some students mastered the goals faster than did most of their classmates. Those adept learners would then be provided with *enrichment activities,* so that, as they waited for their classmates to achieve the basic objectives, they would not be bored and waste their time. Instead, they would have a chance to extend their learning into areas beyond the basic program. In addition, the teacher's periodic appraisals of student progress (by means of tests, assignments, observations) would also reveal which class members were having difficulty managing the basic objectives. To help such students catch up with the bulk of the class, the teacher would provide *remedial activities* which repeated the basic instruction by means of simpler or more varied methods and materials. In summary, the intent of the tri-level plan was to keep the class more or less together in studying a given unit of work by adjusting instruction to the needs and talents of both the faster and slower learners before the class moved ahead to a new unit.

The school district's central office of instructional management sent an explanatory bulletin to teachers in all subject matter fields and at all grade levels. The bulletin first described the purpose of the plan and explained the general nature of the basic, enrichment, and remedial activities. Then it urged teachers to adopt such an approach in their classes.

During the school year, instructional consultants from the district's central office visited classrooms to discover how well the tri-level program was working. To their dismay, most teachers were still operating in their traditional manner. Those teachers who had already been adjusting to learners' individual differences before the tri-level plan was introduced (adjusting by means of ability grouping within the class, differentiated assignments for different students, remedial aid) continued to do so. Those who had been providing a single program for everyone were maintaining that pattern as well. The consultants concluded that the program had failed. They discovered that teachers did not understand exactly how to manage a tri-level approach because they did not know precisely how to prepare enrichment and remedial activities, and teachers felt they lacked the classroom management skills that would enable them to conduct the program even if suitable activities were available.

Remedy options: To render the tri-level plan more practical, the school district might adopt the following measures.

Enrichment and remedial packets: For as many grade levels and subject-matter fields as possible, the district could purchase published workbooks and activity books and could distribute those materials to teachers in the form of instructional-support packets.

Activity-preparation workshops: It is unlikely that enough appropriate activities to meet the district's needs would already be available in published form. Therefore, the district could profit from conducting workshops at which teachers constructed enrichment and remedial activities that would be distributed to the schools.

Classroom management seminars: Inservice seminars for teachers could be conducted to illustrate ways the tri-level plan could be implemented in classrooms at different grade levels and in various subject fields. The seminars would likely be more effective if illustrated with videos of classrooms in action than if offered solely in the form of lectures and advice.

Perceived Risk

In planned change projects, perceived risk is the threat a participant believes the proposed change poses for her or his welfare. Hence, how willingly participants support a proposed change depends—at least partially—on the extent of risk they think is involved. The issue here is not how much threat the intended change *actually* poses but, rather, how much danger participants *assume* they would face.

> *Proposition:* The more serious the perceived risk of an innovation for the welfare of participants, the greater the participants' opposition to the innovation. Individuals' sense of risk may not be constant throughout the conduct of a reform effort but may change from time to time, thereby resulting in their resisting the project more at one time than at another.

Problem case F: In an effort to accommodate the needs of students who did not adjust readily to life in a typical high school, a city school system maintained two alternative schools that featured more flexible curricula and more attention to individuals' learning styles than were available in the city's existing high schools. However, there were still students who were unable—or unwilling—to adapt themselves to an alternative school's program, so they attended only sporadically or dropped out entirely. A few members of one alternative school's faculty attempted to help remedy the dropout problem by providing materials for students to study on their own at home. The faculty members hoped that such an arrangement could prepare dropouts to pass tests that earned them the equivalent of a high school diploma. However, this practice of teachers providing home-study materials was no more than an informal arrangement that reached only a few of the dropouts. Because a growing number of students were leaving high school without graduating, the district's officials followed the lead of other school systems by establishing a home-study program that would furnish systematic guidance for dropouts who did not perform satisfactorily in either a regular or an alternative school. The guided-study plan would parallel the school system's visiting-teacher service, which was designed for pupils whose illness or injury prevented them from leaving home to attend school. However, rather than teachers going to students' homes, the guided-study plan required participants to meet a study-supervisor once a week at an alternative school to report their progress, to get help with problems they faced in completing their lessons, and to receive new assignments for the coming week.

The principal of one of the alternative schools was selected as the director of the new program. To obtain additional financial support from outside the school district, the principal planned the venture as an innovative experiment, with novel features not found in typical home-study programs. Whereas the learning materials in most other guided-study programs consisted of self-instructional units or contracts that students worked through week after week, the principal proposed that the materials in this project be individualized, based on a diagnosis of each student's learning style. In effect, the activities (readings, problems to solve, videos to watch, projects to complete) in which each participant engaged would be determined by the analysis of that student's most effective mode of learning. In order to formulate a precise description of the plan that could be submitted to an outside funding agency, the principal needed an expert in learning-style diagnosis and curriculum design. The assistant director of the school district's curriculum-development division appeared to be the sort of knowledgeable and inventive woman who could do the job properly, so she was asked to take the task on. She would devote 80% of her time to the experimental program and 20% to her usual responsibilities in the curriculum-development office.

In deciding whether to accept the principal's offer, the curriculum specialist was obliged to consider the risk involved. According to *risk theory*, decisions of this sort are made by balancing the personal gains to be expected against threats to the individual's welfare. The greater the perceived risks, the less willing a person is to take on the task in question. Such decision making involves a somewhat imprecise form of mental algebra, with the person weighing expected advantages and disadvantages against each other to arrive at a decision (Anderson, 1991; Arrow, 1971; Thomas, 2001a). This decision-making process appears to be a mixture of conscious and intuitive considerations—some factors are deliberately analyzed, while others are only vaguely sensed. In the instance of the curriculum expert, she was intrigued by the challenge the new venture offered (a positive factor) and she imagined that the project, and her own role in it, would be publicized through the news media, at professional conferences, and in professional journals (a second positive factor). For working on the project, she would also receive such fringe benefits as travel expenses to conferences and visits to other school systems (a third positive factor). In contrast to these advantages were such potential negative forces as those of entering the uncharted waters of an experimental program, of having difficulties in diagnosing students' learning styles, and of losing control of some of her existing projects in the curriculum-development office (all negative factors). However, in weighing the perceived rewards against the perceived dangers, she decided that the challenge was worth the risk, and she accepted the position as the chief formulator of the guided-study methods and materials.

A philanthropic foundation agreed to finance the plan that the principal submitted, and the curriculum expert launched into the work with enthusiasm, spending even more than 80% of her time on the project. A vigorous campaign to recruit students for the guided-study program yielded encouraging results. Among the most avid students were people in their twenties and thirties who, as teenagers, had dropped out of high school but now regretted that move and wished to earn their high school diplomas while still holding their present jobs.

Over the next two years, the following events caused the curriculum expert's sense of risk to change dramatically, with the result that she spent increasingly less time on the guided-study project. First, the task of diagnosing students' learning styles and matching them with suitable learning methods and materials proved very difficult. Second, progress in adapting and creating suitable learning activities was far slower than she had envisioned.

Third, after the first few months, the number of students in the program dwindled rapidly because the more adept and dedicated ones completed the program and graduated, while the less apt failed to study consistently and eventually dropped out. It became apparent that most of the students who could not succeed in regular or alternative school were not good candidates for studying at home on their own. If they were to do the required work, they—even more than most youths— needed the systematic direction of classroom teachers and the model of classmates who were truly dedicated to studying. The principal sought to salvage the experiment by sending letters to the parents of alternative-school students, inviting them to enroll their offspring in the home-study program. However, those parents had found their teenagers difficult to raise and therefore wanted them to attend school regularly where they would be under the surveillance of teachers rather than out on the streets getting into trouble. Thus, the principal's letter failed to accomplish its purpose.

Fourth, the curriculum expert feared that her further participation in the program threatened her career. She thought the educational community would see her as one of the prime movers behind a doomed experiment. And by participating so little in the district's curriculum-development office over the initial year of the experiment, she had weakened her political power there. She felt that her curriculum-development colleagues saw her as a self-serving opportunist who had abandoned their ship. Consequently, during the second year of the project she asked for a heavier work schedule in the curriculum office, volunteered for committee assignments, attended staff meetings regularly, and sought to engage colleagues in cooperative curriculum-enhancement projects. This increase in her curriculum-office activities reduced her participation in the guided-instruction project and thereby contributed further to the project's decline and a resultant loss of outside funding for the program. By the third year, she had transferred back to the curriculum office full time, and the home-study venture limped along with a small number of students studying from the same textbooks as those used in the alternative school's classes.

This case illustrates how a change in an individual's perception of risk affected the inertia that the innovation suffered. As the curriculum expert initially saw little or no risk in the experiment, she happily contributed to the project's success. But as the experiment began to fail, her perception of risk caused her to distance herself from the program and, in doing so, to hasten the program's collapse. It was an instance of conditions first changing in the direction of the proposed innovation, but subsequently reverting to their original state.

Remedy options: There was nothing effective that could be done to eliminate two of the most important negative factors contributing to the demise of the program: (a) the inability of most school dropouts to work effectively on their own at home, and (b) parents' belief that their recalcitrant offspring were better off in school than being left to their own devices.

Pilot study. A good deal of energy and money might have been saved if the principal had set up the home-study program as a small pilot study rather than a full-blown program. Before submitting a plan to a foundation in order to obtain financial backing, he could have asked the curriculum-department assistant director to spend a limited amount of time helping him conduct a modest tryout of his idea, using four or five typical dropouts as the subjects. The miniature project likely would have informed the principal of the problems such a program faced—of difficulty in recruiting students, of parents' attitudes, of dropouts' unwillingness to "stay the course" over time, and of matching learning materials and methods to individuals' learning styles. On the basis of knowledge derived from the pilot study, the principal could have decided whether such a home-study plan was viable and, if so, the form it might best assume.

Compatibility

In educational-reform projects, *compatibility* refers to how amicably participants work together without their efforts hampered by disrespect, jealousy, and antagonism. Incompatibility is clearly one of the most common contributors to inertia.

Proposition: The greater the disrespect and antipathy among participants whose cooperative effort is required for a reform to succeed, the greater the inertia the reform will suffer.

Problem case G: With the intention of "integrating and modernizing" the required eighth-grade social studies and English classes in a city's three middle schools, the city's central curriculum-development department devised a social-problems-centered program that required team teaching. According to the plan, the traditional separation between social studies and English classes would be eliminated, with each social studies instructor paired with an English instructor to teach a dual-period class focusing on a series of social issues. The program was dubbed The Composite Plan, ostensibly a novel invention but clearly reminiscent of core, correlated, and integrated curricula of past decades. The social studies content of the program drew heavily on anthropology, history, political science, sociology, and social psychology. Students' speaking, reading, and writing skills that formerly had been the chief province of English classes were now to be taught in relation to the social problems that the new program addressed. The literary selections that students studied would concern the social issues.

To effect the transition from the old curriculum to The Composite Plan, the curriculum office prepared an outline of the social problems on which the course would focus and suggested teaching methods and materials. Teachers were obliged to attend a day-long inservice-education session at which curriculum-office personnel and two outside consultants introduced the plan. The middle schools' principals were responsible for deciding which social studies teachers would be paired with which English teachers.

Compatibility problems began at the outset of the new program and continued at various levels of intensity throughout the school year. Although some teachers liked the partners they were assigned and enjoyed team teaching, others were somewhat unhappy, and a few were very displeased. Those who objected to the arrangement had a variety of complaints, with some of their objections voiced openly and others expressed only in private to their intimates or else reflected merely in a lack of willing collaboration between partners. The compatibility difficulties were of various kinds. Some teachers disagreed with their partner's teaching style—with their partner's "talking down" to students, giving vague assignments, wandering away from the topic, failing to prepare adequately, or giving lengthy and boring lectures when the students would be better off actively discussing—or writing about—a social issue. Some teachers resented their partner's suggestions about the division of responsibility between the pair or about how to assesses students' progress or how to handle disruptive class members. Some considered their partner lazy or ill informed about the social issues. Some differed politically or philosophically with their colleague. Some didn't even like the idea of team teaching and much preferred to operate independently, as had been the practice before The Composite Plan was introduced.

In summary, in a number of the dual-period classes, incompatibility between teaching partners impaired the success of the composite program.

Remedy options: Which remediation approach will reduce the inertia caused by incompatibility obviously depends heavily on the personalities and relationships of the people involved in each case—the teaching partners, the school principals, and the curriculum-department staff members. Hence, an attempted remedy that meets some with some success in one case can fail in another, depending on the individuals involved.

Intimidation: When a principal learns of a disagreement between teaching partners that threatens the success of The Composite Plan, the principal can use explicit or implied threats of sanctions against the partners if they fail to work together harmoniously. Such threats can include those of sending unfavorable reports to higher authorities in the school system (curriculum director, assistant superintendent), assigning the teacher to unattractive duties (more lunchtime playground supervision, after-school monitoring of students on detention), delaying a salary increase, or reprimanding a teacher in the presence of colleagues.

Intimidation is most successful with people who are sensitive to being censured in front of others, are in fear of losing their jobs, or are especially subservient to people in authority. It is least successful with people who can be openly rebellious, who are willing in public to expose a principal's mistakes or misbehavior, who have friends in positions of authority, or who appear to comply with a principal's orders but still exert passive resistance and adopt tactics that undermine the principal's plans.

Direction: A principal or curriculum-center staff member can seek to ameliorate a conflict between teaching partners by discovering the nature of the disagreement and then offering specific directions about how the conflict might be resolved.

Providing direction (training, materials, information) works best when the incompatibility has resulted from a lack of the information or skill needed for succeeding with the plan.

Mediation: Sometimes the teaching partners can profit from meeting with a mediator who helps them define the source of their disagreement, generate potential solutions, select from those options the ones to which the partners can agree, and set up specific steps for adopting the solutions. All three participants—the partners and the arbitrator—are expected to suggest solutions and assess them. But the final decision about how to resolve the problem is the responsibility of the partners, not the mediator.

Mediation is useful whenever the partners are angry or disgusted with each other and the arbitrator is skillful at calming the antagonists and guiding them toward rationally explaining their disagreements and proposing ways that their difficulties might be resolved.

Separation: Sometimes the dissent between partners is so great and heavily laden with bitter feelings that the best solution, from the standpoint of students' welfare, is to have the pair operate separately. The two remain a "team" in name only. Hence, a social studies teacher would independently handle one half of the dual period and an English teacher the other half. Any linkages between the two sessions would be achieved solely by the schedule of topics provided by the curriculum-development center. That is, both teachers would focus on the same social issue during the same period of time.

Rearrangement: Rather than assigning the pairings of teachers, the principal could have teachers select their own partners. If there are individuals left without a partner, the principal could then negotiate with them to arrange the additional partnerships.

Members of the External Support System

The members of the external support system are individuals and organizations that will be affected by—or that believe they will be affected by—an anticipated educational reform. The types of participants that compose the external support system can differ from one kind of reform to another. For example, a change in the science curriculum in a single secondary school will affect different individuals and organizations than will an increase in school fees or the adoption of a national law specifying English as the only acceptable language for instruction in schools. Furthermore, members of the external system can support a proposed innovation or else resist it by favoring the traditional way of doing things. For purposes of illustration, I've selected four characteristics of members that can influence the strength of the inertia faced by a planned change.

> **External Support System:**
> **Members' Characteristics**
>
> • Skills and knowledge
> • Interests and motives
> • Political power
> • Perceived risk

Skills and Knowledge

Two kinds of skills and knowledge that can affect the inertia an intended educational reform faces concern (a) the detailed nature of the reform and (b) effective techniques for blocking the implementation of the reform.

Proposition 1: The greater the skills and knowledge that opponents of a proposed change command in the area of education that the change involves, the greater the inertia that must be overcome to produce the change.

Proposition 2: The greater the skills and knowledge that opponents of a proposed reform have for exercising political power, the more difficult it is to execute the reform.

Problem case H: A single case can illustrate both of these propositions. In a North American university, a proposal to establish a department of Chicano studies was submitted to the faculty council, which was the body responsible for deciding on changes in the institution's organizational structure. Three Hispanic faculty members (one from the history department, another from foreign languages, and the third from education) were the proponents who presented the virtues of the proposal before the faculty council. The three professors were supported in their endeavor by two sets of proponents outside the university: (a) local and statewide Hispanic political activists and (b) Hispanic professors in other universities that already had established Chicano studies departments. However, the proposed innovation faced significant resistance. Opponents within the university included several members of the faculty council and a variety of other faculty members. These campus adversaries were supported by two groups outside the university: (a) organizations that feared the growing power of the state's Hispanic political movement and (b) professors in other universities who held a low opinion of the existing Chicano studies departments in their own institutions.

The pro-Chicano-studies political forces outside the university supported the proposed department by: (a) newspaper articles and radio and television interviews that publicized the value of such a department, (b) letters sent to state legislators and university officials, urging the creation of the department, and (c) help in financing and organizing on-campus student demonstrations. Professors in other universities attempted to aid in the campaign by sending information to the three Hispanic faculty members who presented the initiative to the faculty council. The information included descriptions of Chicano studies courses, examples of publications by faculty members in such departments, and testimonials from students who majored in Chicano studies.

The proposal's antagonists outside the university also publicized their opposition via newspaper articles, letters to the editors of newspapers, and radio and television interviews. In addition, professors from other campuses sent (a) testimonials that cast Chicano studies in a poor light, (b) statistics showing low enrollments in such departments, and (c) negative assessments of the quality of research and publication coming out of Chicano studies departments. The publications were often characterized as political rather than scholarly. Furthermore, opponents contended that the same goals that advocates of Chicano studies set for such a department were already being achieved through existing departments that taught courses on Hispanic topics in such disciplines as anthropology, art, education, foreign languages, history, music, and sociology.

After all of the evidence from both sides of the issue had been presented to the faculty council, no clear decision was forthcoming. Those council members who voted in favor of the department numbered nearly the same as those who voted against it. Other council members abstained, saying they wanted to investigate the matter in greater detail. Consequently, the proposal for setting up the department was tabled. Too much inertia had been generated by the opponents' skills and knowledge of the field of university scholarship as buttressed with the efforts of off-campus political forces. The proposed innovation—at least for the present—had been defeated.

Remedy options: In preparing for presenting their proposal to the council on a future date, advocates of the new department might strengthen their case in two ways.

Stronger research and teaching evidence: To counteract their opponents' claims that publications emanating from Chicano studies groups were political diatribes that did not fit a traditional conception of scholarship, supporters of the proposed department could (a) compile a larger fund of publications from other universities' Chicano studies departments that did, indeed, fit an established scholarly tradition and (b) illustrate the political nature of studies from non-Chicano departments to show that much respected scholarship had a political cast. Additional testimonials from students who had taken Chicano studies courses in other institutions (including supportive statements from non-Hispanic students) might help counteract the adversaries' claims that the teaching in Chicano studies classes was often of a political rather than scholarly nature.

Greater political pressure: Increased political pressure could be exerted on the university's administration (particularly on the president and the board of governors) by letters from state legislators and prominent Chicano business leaders. The letters could mention that a Black studies department was already operating in the university and that denying Hispanics their own department was a blatant exhibition of ethnic prejudice.

Interests and Motives

Individuals and groups outside of the education system can be expected to resist system changes that appear contrary to their own welfare or that appear harmful to the common good or to some group they favor.

Proposition: The stronger the motivation of opponents of an intended educational improvement, the greater the inertia.

Problem case I: The Chicano studies case illustrates the potential influence on planned change of the interests and motives of individuals and groups outside the education system. The chief supporters of the Chicano studies initiative were Hispanics who were interested in enhancing the importance of their ethnic group's status and power in both the academic community and American society in general. Aiding the Hispanics in this effort were non-Hispanics who believed that ethnic groups which did not trace their culture to European origins deserved greater recognition in an American society whose dominant cultural background was European. Therefore, such non-Hispanic individuals, motivated by an ideal of equity and fair play, would endorse the Chicano studies proposal.

The opponents of a Chicano studies department included both academic conservatives and political groups outside the university. The academic conservatives felt that altering the traditional departmental structure of the university would weaken the quality of both teaching and research. The political opponents were motivated by the fear that the expansion of Hispanic influence in both academia and general American society threatened their own status and power.

In effect, the strength of interest on both sides of the Chicano studies debate appeared to be similar, leading to what was—at least temporarily—a deadlock that prevented the adoption of the plan. The future of the plan would depend to an extent on the comparative strength of motivation on the part of the pro- and anti-Chicano studies activists—on how persistent each side would be in pursuing their objectives.

Remedy options: Chicano studies advocates' strength of motivation would be reflected in how vigorously they pursued the remedies suggested above for enhancing the skills and knowledge they would bring to a future submission of the proposal.

Political Power

Throughout this book, the expression *political power* refers to the effect that one entity—a person, a group, an institution—has on the behavior of another entity. Power is measured by the extent to which one entity's behavior is influenced by the presence and actions of another entity. If each entity behaves in the same way whether or not the other entity is present (physically or only mentally), then neither entity has any power over the other. And the more radically Entity A's behavior is altered as a result of Entity B's presence, the greater the power of Entity B over Entity A.

> *Proposition:* The stronger the political force that can be mustered in opposition to a proposed educational innovation, the greater the inertia that must be overcome.

Problem case J: A class titled "Modern American Life" was taught as an elective course in all three of a small city's high schools. In two of the schools, the teachers in charge of the class recently began inviting gay and lesbian activists to speak to the students about homosexuality in America and in the world at large. When students reported this innovation to their parents—and mentioned that the visitors' had lauded homosexuality as a desirable alternative lifestyle to that of heterosexuality —the city newspaper's letters-to-the-editor page was filled with blistering criticism of school officials. In response, letters from the gay community and from advocates of freedom of speech claimed that high school students had a right to learn the beliefs of people of different cultural backgrounds, religions, and sexual orientations.

Three months later, in a city election that included four contested positions on the seven-member school board, the homosexual community ran four candidates against four others who were openly critical of gay and lesbian speakers appearing in school classes. The four antigay candidates won the election. In the first meeting of the board following the election, a resolution was passed forbidding the presentation in schools of homosexuality as an acceptable way of life or even as a topic of discussion. Thus, the two "Modern American Life" teachers' innovation failed because political forces outside the school system gained control of decision making at the top of the system's administrative hierarchy.

Remedy options: There was nothing immediate that the two teachers could attempt for reinstating their innovation without jeopardizing their own jobs. Therefore, the most that they and the gay community could do would be to try gaining favor with the public by publicizing the contributions to society of gays and lesbians—past and present—in the hope that positive images of homosexuals would enable them in the future to elect school board members who were in sympathy with their cause.

Perceived Risk

Similar to people within the education system, those on the outside may attempt to block an innovation if they believe it will harm individuals or institutions they value.

Proposition: The more serious the perceived risk of an innovation for the welfare of concerned individuals outside the education system, the greater those individuals' opposition to the innovation.

Problem case K: In an upper-middle-class suburb, six eighth-grade teachers in a middle school were prompted to launch an experiment to help settle the debate over the influence of homework on young adolescents' academic, social, and emotional well-being. The experiment, scheduled to be conducted for a period one semester, would include classes in English, social studies, mathematics, and science. In each of these subject fields, half of the eighth-grade classes would be given homework assignments, while the other half would not. During the semester and at the end, appraisals would be made of students' *academic progress* (test scores, work completed, quality of class participation), *social life* (activities reported on a questionnaire filled out by students and parents), and *emotional life* (students' feelings as reported on a questionnaire). The school had traditionally required homework in most subject fields, so the teachers recognized that eliminating homework might attract opposition on the part of some parents. Thus, in order for students to be in a class that required no homework, the school would be obliged to get parents' written permission. In response to the school's solicitation, less than 15% of the parents agreed to have their daughter or son in a non-homework class. The reasons parents gave for opposing the plan was that they feared their children's academic progress would suffer if homework were eliminated. In other words, parents believed that the purported advantages of the experiment were not worth the perceived risk.

Remedy options: In order to salvage their experiment, the teachers might try the following.

Reduce the scope of the project: If there are only enough students to form no more than a single no-homework class (which perhaps would be a rather small class), then the teachers would need to limit their study to comparing that one class with the rest of the eighth-grade classes. Such a limitation would apparently decrease the kinds of generalizations that could reasonably be drawn from the results of the study.

Appeal to parents: The teachers might prepare a brief brochure to send to parents who had withheld permission. The intent of the brochure would be to alleviate parents' fears of potentially negative effects of no homework. The appeal might include evidence from studies reported in the professional literature attesting to the advantages of no-homework programs.

Students

Whereas educational personnel can be shifted around (persuaded, trained, reassigned, fired, or hired) to suit the needs of a planned change in the education system, students must be accepted as they are. Hence, if an intended improvement is to succeed, its form must be adjusted to the learners' characteristics rather than vice versa.

Students' Characteristics

- Skills and knowledge
- Interests and motives
- Learning style and study habits
- Social-emotional needs
- Home background

Skills and Knowledge

Students' skills and knowledge are capabilities they need if they are to succeed with an innovation such as an unfamiliar teaching method (language immersion in a foreign language class), a new textbook, or a new instructional aid (a computer and the World Wide Web).

Proposition: Each innovation introduced into the teaching/learning process requires particular skills and knowledge on the part of the learners. The weaker the requisite skills and knowledge that students command, the greater the inertia experienced in implementing the innovation.

Problem case L: In the elementary school classrooms of a county in the Southwestern United States that specialized in fruit and vegetable crops, classroom enrollments frequently changed during the school year. The changes were the result of children of migrant-labor families accompanying their parents whenever their parents moved into or out of the community as a result of local farm-labor demands rising or declining with the area's planting and harvesting seasons. Such shifts in enrollment affected the success of a new series of social studies books that were introduced into the county's schools. The series had been designed to focus children's attention on their own community in first grade, then gradually shift that focus at each grade level through an expanding sequence of social environments (state, region, nation, neighboring nations, the world). The reading difficulty of the books in the series was arranged to suit the average reading ability of children at the different grade levels, as determined by a nationwide study of children's reading skills at ages five through twelve.

The nature of the inertia that the new textbook series faced can be illustrated with the example of a fourth-grade class in which the textbook focused on the study of the history and culture of the United States. During the school year, less than half of the pupils attended class the entire time from September to June. In other words, more than half entered school late in the year or left early as a result of their parents' transitory employment schedule. Thus, many children's schooling was fragmentary rather than cumulative and consistent. Furthermore, the majority of the families were originally from Mexico and still spoke Spanish at home. Without a continuing model of spoken English at home, children often came to school with no more than a faulty grasp of English that left them ill equipped to understand the social studies textbook when they tried to read the book on their own.

The teacher's manual that accompanied the textbook recommended that social studies instruction consist of pupils' reading a chapter in the book, then participating in class discussions and projects that enabled the pupils to apply—and that helped the teacher assess—what the pupils had studied in the text. In this fourth grade, the recommended approach worked successfully for only the few students who were adept readers—ones who spoke English at home and were permanent residents of the community. The rest of the class members were confused by the reading assignments and, as a result, were often inattentive, apathetic, or into mischief. The same difficulties that were suffered in the fourth grade appeared in the other grades as well. In short, the new social studies program, in its recommended form, failed. The fourth-grade teacher, like most of her colleagues, abandoned the textbook approach and reverted to her traditional method of teaching social studies. That method consisted of her giving illustrated lectures, reading aloud to the class, showing films or videos of historical and cultural events, and guiding children in carrying out projects (drawing maps and pictures, constructing cardboard villages, preparing dioramas, creating playlets based on historical events).

Remedy options: The following are techniques the fourth-grade teacher might adopt in order to incorporate the textbook more successfully into the class's social studies program.

Oral reading—Teacher: To help ensure that pupils understood the content of the textbook, the teacher could read aloud each chapter—or each segment of a chapter—while students followed the reading in their own textbooks. Such an approach would enable the teacher to interrupt the recitation periodically to explain difficult concepts and to ask students questions about the meaning of passages.

Oral reading—Students: The class could be divided into small groups, with a skilled reader assigned as the leader of each group. The leader could read portions aloud while group members followed in their own books. Group members could also take turns reading segments aloud. The teacher could equip leaders with questions to ask the group so as to check on the members' understanding as the lesson advanced.

Pre-reading preparation: Before pupils silently read the day's assigned portion of the text, the teacher could write potentially difficult words on the chalkboard and have pupils discuss the words' meanings. In addition, the teacher could offer a brief summary of the sort of information the assigned passage contains so that the pupils would be oriented ahead of time to the nature of the material they were about to encounter.

Pretest preparation: The teacher could introduce the upcoming reading assignment by giving the pupils a pretest covering key concepts and words used in the text. When the students completed the test, the teacher could answer questions about words whose meanings were unclear, and the students could then silently read the passage to discover answers to the questions that had been posed in the test. In this way the list of test questions would serve as a study guide to the reading material.

Partners: To help pupils whose grasp of English is weak, the teacher could assign each such child a partner (an aide) who is at least moderately fluent in both English and Spanish. The aide could help the less adept partner by listening to the partner read passages aloud and by explaining the meaning and pronunciation of words that the partner found difficult.

Interests and Motives

As parents and teachers often painfully realize, they can't teach something to a person who doesn't want to learn it. Students must be willing to invest their attention and energy in an innovative practice in order to profit from it. Hence, the educational psychologists' adage: Interest is the sine qua non of learning.

Proposition: The less a student's motivation (willingness) to accept an innovation, the greater the inertia that the innovation must contend with.

Problem case M: A high school English teacher proposed to offer a new creative writing class as an elective subject for juniors and seniors. The school principal agreed with the proposal, so the class was scheduled for the following semester. The nature of the class was described in an article in the school newspaper and was advertised on placards displayed on bulletin boards in the school corridors. However, at the beginning of the next semester, when students registered for courses, only six selected the new class. And because six students was deemed too few to warrant holding the class, the envisioned creative writing course was dropped. It had failed before it began. Students were simply not interested—or at least not interested enough to forego other elective classes in favor of creative writing.

Remedy options: In an effort to revive the ill-fated class, the English teacher might try the following.

Sample unit: In the sophomore English classes that he usually taught each year, the teacher could include a three-week unit on creative writing during which students would be assigned to write stories, essays, and poems. The teacher could then read aloud to his classes some of the more successful of the students' creations, thereby providing a public display of the youths' creative talents. The three-week sample of what a creative writing class was like might generate enough interest to convince students to choose creative writing as an elective in their junior or senior year.

Publication: From the sophomores' three-week creative writing unit, the teacher might choose some of the more successful stories, essays, and poems to publish in a booklet bearing some such title as *Bright Minds* or *The Writers' Corner.* The booklet, produced in the professional-looking format made possible with computer desktop publishing, would be available free to anyone who wanted a copy. A copy would also be sent to the city newspaper for whatever publicity the editors wished to give it. The intent of the booklet, other than to give recognition to creative students, would be to stimulate interest in enrolling in a creative writing class.

Learning Styles and Study Habits

The expression *learning style* or *cognitive style* refers to the thought processes by which individuals acquire skills and knowledge. Or, in Entwistle's words,

> Cognitive style is the term used to describe different ways in which people process information, including perception, storage, transformation, and utilization of information from the environment. It describes habitual processes of perceiving and thinking which are qualitatively distinct. (Entwistle, 1985, p. 810)

Study habits are the typical acts in which individuals engage when they purposely attempt to add to their skills and knowledge.

People often differ from each other in their learning styles and study habits. Such differences are apparently the result of both genetic and environmental factors. For example, children's learning styles can be affected by their sight and hearing acuity, the neural circuitry of their brains, and the manner in which they have been taught in the past. Such differences among individuals bear important implications for educational innovations, because a newly introduced teaching method or textbook may be better suited to some learning styles than to others.

Proposition: The greater the discrepancy between a teaching/learning method and students' learning styles, the greater the inertia an innovation must face.

Problem case N: In a large city high school, a chronic problem experienced by foreign language instructors was that too few students became fluent enough to converse in the foreign language they studied. Therefore, as a means of fostering students' ability to speak French and to understand spoken French, the high school's foreign language department introduced a class titled "Conversational French," which would enroll students who had already completed two semesters of "Beginning French." Instruction in the class was designed around a commercially produced course that involved three kinds of activities:

- Students, equipped with individual headsets, would listen to audiotapes of conversations, and would practice speaking the phrases they heard in give-and-take exchanges between two people. Each brief exchange would first be given in English, next repeated in French, and then a pause was inserted in the tape to allow the student to repeat the French phrase aloud.
- The teacher would utter a phrase in French, and the class would respond aloud with an appropriate phrase that they had learned from the audiotapes.

- Students would be paired up to practice the conversations they had learned.

During the early weeks of the new class, the teacher was distressed to discover that some students progressed very well, whereas others who had succeeded well in their year of beginning French were experiencing a great deal of difficulty. It appeared that the class's instructional method suited some students' learning styles but not others'. For those others, the class was a discouraging failure. In order to improve their progress, several of the students who could not keep up with the pace of the class asked the teacher if they could copy the commercial tapes so they might listen to the conversations at home, and they could also produce written versions that they could study on their own. The teacher reported that copyright laws prevented them from copying the tapes. The students, in effect, wished to revert to their traditional method of studying French visually rather than aurally.

Remedy option: During the two semesters of beginning French, the method of teaching had included (a) students' reading in a textbook and taking written tests that evaluated their grasp of French vocabulary and grammar, and (b) the teacher demonstrating the pronunciation of French words and phrases, then having students practice saying those phrases aloud together as a class and as individuals. But in order to emphasize the aural nature of conversational French, the commercially developed course materials used in the conversational French course included no printed version of the tape-recorded conversations. The absence of a printed version was explained in the course's brief teacher's handbook in this fashion.

> In all societies, children become fluent conversationalists in their early years by copying what they hear their family members and friends say. This complete dependence on oral examples is dramatically demonstrated in nonliterate cultures where no written language exists, yet nearly everyone—before reaching adulthood—masters the meanings and pronunciation nuances of highly sophisticated, complex languages. In like manner, students who hope to gain conversational skill in a foreign language can profit from a method of instruction that focuses entirely on the spoken word.

The teacher concluded that some of her students were primarily *visual learners* rather than *aural learners* and therefore depended more on what they saw than on what they heard. To help the visual learners succeed in the conversational French class, she could—with the students' aid—cast the conversations in written form, thereby making available a printed version that might help all students master the vocabulary and grammar. Producing a printed version of the vocabulary seemed particularly important for a class in French conversation, since the correct spelling of words in French is not as easily determined by hearing the words spoken as it is in the cases of such languages as Spanish and Italian. If copyright laws prevented the teacher from producing an exact printed version of the conversations, she could transcribe the words, then recast the sentences into ones that were similar to those of the original but not direct copies.

Social-Emotional Needs

The emotional distress that students suffer often distracts them from concentrating on learning tasks. Anxiety during a test or when speaking in front of the class may cause a student to perform poorly. Worrying about a parent's illness or a family financial crisis may prevent a child from paying attention to the teacher's explanation of how to solve math problems. And frequently the distress students suffer is related to concern about social relationships—about breaking up with a boyfriend, hearing damaging rumors spread by jealous rivals, or being criticized by a teacher in the presence of classmates.

In addition, as the following case illustrates, the advent of an attempted planned change may also cause students emotional distress if they interpret the change as a threat to their self-confidence or self-image.

Proposition: The greater the social-emotional distress that learners experience with the introduction of a new teaching/learning procedure or a new student-behavior regulation, the greater the inertia the innovation will experience.

Problem case O: A high school history teacher enrolled in a four-week college summer session workshop that bore the title "Independent Thought and Action." The aim of the workshop was to encourage participants to depart from their traditional ways of thinking in order to devise new ways of viewing life. To accomplish this aim, the instructor first illustrated ways of departing from established thinking patterns by identifying the curious modes of thought of creative individuals in the past—scientists, inventors, novelists, poets, composers, painters, sculptors, dancers, entrepreneurs, and more. Then the instructor urged workshop participants to free themselves from their usual patterns of thought by carrying out a series of assignments that required them to produce novel interpretations of—or reactions to—public events and to works of art, music, and literature.

The high school teacher was so impressed by her workshop experience that she decided to include the independent-thought-and-action technique in teaching her high school world history classes the coming semester. In her adaptation of the approach, students would be assigned to interpret—or react to—historical events in novel ways. They could write essays that furnished new versions of historical figures or incidents, draw or paint unusual pictures of people and episodes, dramatize historical scenes, create dioramas, write poetry, compose music, choreograph dances, or build models. Whereas some students took to the assignments with great enthusiasm, others were disturbed. They felt that the approach "wasn't real teaching and not real history, where you learn what really happened." Unsure of what kinds of interpretations qualified as acceptable independent thought and action, the insecure students continually asked the teacher for more specific directions about how to complete the assignments. And when a new idea did occur to them, they felt compelled to ask the teacher's opinion before they were willing to pursue that idea further.

After the first semester of her innovation, the teacher concluded that the experiment had been only partially successful, because numbers of students were clearly disturbed by the assignments. She believed that their emotional distress limited their ability to succeed and caused them to dislike the class. Their disturbance, she felt, was a result of their having been taught over the years that any deviations from established ways of thought and action were inherently wrong. Therefore, they found that being asked to deviate intentionally from tradition was emotionally upsetting.

Remedy option: To illustrate the process of independent thinking, the history teacher had engaged the entire class in "brainstorming sessions" that consisted of class members proposing as many different ways as possible of viewing, or reacting to, a particular historical figure or event. At the opening of each session, students were instructed to avoid scoffing at classmates' suggestions, no matter how odd or ridiculous those notions appeared at first glance. The purpose of this rule of was to prevent students from rejecting seemingly weird proposals which, upon close inspection, might prove useful in expanding their views of life. However, one problem with the brainstorming was that the discussions were dominated by the most mentally agile and assertive class members. Other students, less adept at divergent thinking or else afraid of being laughed at, remained passive observers. One way the teacher might stimulate these passive individuals to think more creatively could consist of her collecting a few of them into a subgroup to engage in brainstorming among themselves. As the teacher led the small-group session, she would praise even the slightest deviations from traditional thought so as to further the participants' progress toward independent thought. The hope would be that such treatment might reduce the students' emotional distress at being asked to break with their past convictions about the impropriety of departing from established modes of thought.

Home Background

Two important ways that children's and youths' home backgrounds influence their school performance are by the models of behavior their families offer and by the ways families support students' learning efforts. Influential models that families offer for students to copy consist of varied behaviors in language usage, modes of social interaction, study habits, forms of recreation, dining etiquette, financial planning, and more. Ways that families can support students' efforts to succeed in school include those of supplying study facilities, monitoring homework assignments, providing school supplies, furnishing appropriate clothing, arranging transportation, and ensuring regular school attendance.

Proposition 1: The less the models of behavior provided at home are well suited to a planned innovation, the greater the inertia that confronts the innovation.

Problem case P: A junior high English teacher's repertoire of instructional methods included the practice of engaging class members in verbal confrontations in which the teacher would argue one side of an issue while a class member, without prior preparation, would be expected to argue the opposite side. The purpose of such a method was to furnish students with experience in identifying flaws in an adversary's logic and in responding successfully to the adversary's line of reasoning. Some students found this confrontational approach stimulating, and they enjoyed the chance to argue with an adult under conditions that would involve no retaliation. Others, however, were disturbed by the method and found themselves unable to react effectively to the teacher's arguments. The teacher, when speaking privately with several such students, learned that those students tended to be from families in which openly disagreeing with parents, or "talking back" to people in authority, was a punishable offense.

Remedy option: For some of the class members, the habit of always yielding passively to adults may have been so deep seated that nothing the teacher attempted would enable those youths to openly expose adults' fallacious arguments. However, a method that he might try would be that of meeting individually with such reticent class members in order to try a mild form of the confrontation technique. The encounter would be cast as a game in which (a) the teacher offered a flawed argument, and (b) the student identified the flaw and gave a persuasive rebuttal. If the student found this task difficult, the teacher could suggest a rebuttal that the student could try. By repeating this process a number of times, the student might be able to more readily offer rebuttals and perhaps later be able to apply the process in class.

Proposition 2: The less positive support the family furnishes for promoting students' success with an educational innovation, the greater the resistance to the innovation.

Problem case Q: The teacher of a seventh-grade general science class attempted to expand his students' access to scientific news and information by teaching a three-week unit called "Surfing the Web." The purpose of the unit was to demonstrate how to use a personal computer to search the Internet and its World Wide Web for science information. The method of instruction consisted of the teacher projecting a computer image onto a large screen at the front of the classroom, thereby enabling him to carry out a step-by-step searching procedure as the class members watched and took notes. The teacher also provided students with a set of written instructions on how to conduct a search. Each student was then assigned to conduct five searches for science information and to print out the results. Because there were only four personal computers in the classroom, the amount of time that any one student could spend doing the assignment at school was very limited. However, more than half of the class members had computers available at home and could pursue the assignment as homework. But, this put the remaining class members at a disadvantage unless they could use a computer at a friend's house. In effect, students whose families could not furnish a computer were handicapped in their efforts to locate scientific information. Consequently, they had to depend chiefly on such traditional sources as textbooks and library reference books for information.

Remedy options: The following are steps the teacher might take to make computers available after school hours for students who do not have a computer at home.

Computer laboratory: The teacher could arrange to have the school's computer laboratory open after school and in the early evening during the weeks of the science class's unit on "Surfing the Web." A member of the school staff, or perhaps a high school student (a computer expert), could be present to guide class members in using the equipment.

Donated computers: Advances in the development of personal computers are so rapid that a machine can be out of date before it is two years old. As a result, many business firms as well as individuals purchase new computers when their existing ones are still in good operating condition. The seventh-grade teacher could inform such people of his students' needs and ask them to donate their discarded but still usable computers to the school so those machines could be distributed to students who lacked a computer at home.

Internet access: Because the school district served as its own ISP (internet service provider), the district could arrange for students (at little or no cost) to use that ISP for connecting to the Internet at home without their having to pay the fee charged by commercial providers.

Conclusion

The purpose of this chapter has been to illustrate a number of attributes of people that can affect the kinds and strength of inertia faced by educational reforms and innovations. It should be apparent that the attributes selected for attention throughout the chapter represent only a limited number of personal characteristics that influence the success of planned educational changes. It should also be obvious that the problem cases chosen to illustrate the nature of inertia in specific educational settings form no more than a miniscule sampling of the great host of problem cases found in education systems around the world.

Discussion Topics

1. Five student attributes proposed in this chapter as influences on the inertia a schooling reform faced were students' (a) skills and knowledge, (b) interests and motives, (c) learning styles and study habits, (d) social-emotional needs, and (e) home backgrounds. Can you think of additional characteristics of learners that could affect the resistance that a reform faced? If you can, then describe each characteristic, create a problem case illustrating how that characteristic could contribute to the inertia affecting the reform the case involves, and suggest one or more remedies to reduce or avoid the inertia.

2. In problem case J (pages 38-39), two middle school teachers invited members of the gay and lesbian community to their "Modern American Life" classes. For a school district with which you are well acquainted, estimate how likely it is that a junior-high or senior-high teacher in the district would be permitted to have such speakers in class. Describe evidence you use to support your opinion. Furthermore, what arguments might opponents offer for prohibiting such speakers from appearing in a class, and what arguments might be presented by people who would permit such speakers to appear?

3. For problem case L (pages 41-42), five remedy options were described. Which of those options (or which combination of two or more) do you believe would likely be the most successful, and why?

Part II

The Teaching/Learning System

The model introduced in Chapter 1 places the teaching/learning process at the heart of the education system. That process has been portrayed as a three-stage sequence that advances from learning objectives through teaching methods to evaluation techniques.

Learning objectives are the answer to the question: "What is worth teaching? Or, what is worth learning?" When the process of education is seen as analogous to taking a trip, the question becomes "Where are we going?"

Teaching/learning methods are the answer to: "By what procedures can the objectives be most effectively achieved or mastered?" Or, in the case of taking a trip, the question becomes: "How can we best get to where we're going?" The phrase *teaching/learning process* is sometimes substituted for *teaching methods* in recognition of the fact that the active participation of students is necessary if learning is to occur. As the age-old maxim proposes, "You can't teach them if they don't want to learn." Furthermore, students often learn on their own, without direct instruction or continual monitoring. Such is the case when a teacher assigns a learning task that students are expected to complete without specific directions or direct supervision—to write a short story, to carry out a science project of the student's choice, to plant and tend a garden, to organize a group discussion.

Evaluation, as the third element in the process, is the answer to "How successfully did the learners master the objectives?" Or, in the case of a trip, "How close have we come to our destination?"

The three chapters that comprise Part I inspect causes of inertia that are associated with learning objectives, teaching/learning methods, and evaluation.

3

Learning Objectives

A variety of terms are used for labeling the desired results of education
—*objectives, goals, aims, purposes, intended outcomes.* Some people distinguish among these terms. For instance, they may use *goals* when referring to general, more abstract results of schooling, then use *objectives*
when referring to detailed, more specific results. Therefore, a general
goal could be *good citizenship,* and a specific objective under that goal
could be *the individual votes in all elections that he or she is qualified to vote
in.* However, throughout this book, no such distinction is made among
these terms. All expressions that refer to the hoped-for results of education are considered to be synonyms.

Three subcomponents under *learning objectives* have been selected for
attention in this chapter.

Learning Objectives

- Objectives' Specificity
- Learner suitability
- Social acceptability

Objectives' Specificity

Statements of learning objectives are issued at all levels of an education system's hierarchy, ranging from national and state legislatures at
the top of the system down to the individual classroom at the most basic
level. The higher in the system that an objective is proposed, the more
often the statement will be general, broadly encompassing, and abstract.

For example, a state legislature or department of education may declare that the aim of schooling should be to teach students to become (a) good citizens and diligent workers, (b) fluent speakers, readers, and writers of the society's dominant language, and (c) well versed in mathematics, history, the physical and social sciences, and health practices. It then becomes the task of agents at descending levels of the hierarchy (a city's board of education, a school district's curriculum office, an individual school's faculty, an individual classroom teacher) to translate those aims into more precise objectives, ones stated in sufficient detail to guide teachers' decisions about exactly what to teach each hour of the school day.

One problem that can arise during this process of moving from general to specific objectives is that when people higher in the school system cast learning goals only in general terms, there can be many different ways that people lower in the system will define those objectives for the purpose of classroom teaching. And the originators of the general objectives may not always approve of how the general aims are translated into classroom practice. Consider, for instance, an objective stated by a state's department of education as "Students become good citizens." There are many kinds of behavior that this broad aim can include. Hence, if the broad aim is not delineated more precisely at the state level, people lower in the hierarchy will do the necessary defining. One classroom teacher may decide that an important attribute of citizenship is that of "obeying all laws without question," whereas another may believe that a good citizen is one who "resists laws that fail to give equal rights to people of all ethnic, religious, and socioeconomic groups." Thus, pupils in the first teacher's class will learn somewhat different good-citizenship behaviors than will pupils in the second teacher's class. And the state education officials who decreed "good citizenship" as an important aim of schooling may not be pleased with the detailed form of that aim in certain classrooms.

The foregoing observations about the specificity of learning objectives also apply to educational reforms. Every proposed innovation that is intended to improve students' learning involves objectives. Whenever those objectives are cast only in broad terms, the people who are expected to implement the innovation are obliged to translate the general goals into highly detailed objectives. It then becomes a question of whether those translations will produce the learning outcomes that the creators of the innovation had in mind. Hence, from the perspective of people who plan to introduce a reform, the importance of objectives' specificity is found in the following proposition.

Proposition: The more general and abstract the statement of objectives, the less likely the proposed educational innovation will produce the outcomes that the proponents of the innovation had hoped to achieve.

Problem case A: A state department of education issued a new statement of the learning goals to be pursued in public schools. Among the aims was that of "Understanding modern science and applying that understanding in daily-life situations." The task of defining the constituent specific objectives under that broad goal was then left up to individual school districts. In certain districts, the task was assumed by a curriculum committee composed of science teachers. Other districts solved the problem by adopting a particular series of science textbooks, so that the authors of the textbooks were the ones who had specified the learning objectives, as reflected in the content of their books. Still other school districts left the delineation of detailed objectives to individual classroom teachers.

Consider, now, what occurred in two junior high school classrooms in which teachers were free to determine the precise meaning of "Understanding modern science and applying that understanding in daily-life situations."

In Classroom A, the teacher's translation of the modern science aim resulted in the following specific statement of what students would be expected to believe and to apply in daily life.

There are two principal sources of truth about the world. One is the Christian Bible. The other is modern science. The Bible tells the history of the Jewish and Christian peoples and explains how people should act toward each other and toward God. Modern science tells about how the physical world is organized and how it operates—about weather, the human body, the nature of matter and space, the chemical composition of objects, the health value of different foods, and much more. In most cases, there is no conflict between the truth from the Bible and the truth from modern science, because the Bible and modern science are designed to explain different things about life. However, in a few cases, the Bible and modern science offer different explanations of the same event, such as how the world began or how humans came to be the way they are today. In these cases, the explanation given in the Bible is the one that is correct, because the Bible is the word of God, and He created and continues to control the universe. An important characteristic of the Bible is that its truth does not change with the passing of time.

In contrast to such a translation of the state department's general objective is the interpretation of the general objective by the Classroom B teacher, who set the following specific beliefs as ones students would be expected to adopt and apply in their lives.

The words *modern science* refer to a way of making decisions about what is true in life—a way that is guided by several principles of scientific thinking. Here are two of those principles:

1. Beliefs about what the world is like—both the physical/biological world and the world of human relations—should be founded on empirical evidence, that is, on evidence derived from the study of events as they happen or evidence as reported by trustworthy observers (past and present). Those reports should be supported by the kinds of empirical evidence that the reporter used to draw his or her conclusions. The reports should not be accepted simply because someone said or wrote that they are true.

2. All conclusions about the nature of the world are tentative and subject to revision as the result of additional empirical evidence and its logical analysis. Consequently, from the viewpoint of modern science, no answers to questions about either the physical/biological or social world should be considered final and definitive. Each answer is assumed to be no more than an approximation of the truth, an approximation that requires further evaluation and refinement on the basis of better evidence and more convincing analysis.

Remedy option: It is apparent that the students in Classroom A would be acquiring a somewhat different understanding of modern science than would those in Classroom B. If the officials in the state department of education who had proposed the modern science goal preferred one of these two interpretations of their general objective over the other, they would have done well to define their intended objective in more precise terms than those in which they issued their directive (rather than leaving the specific meaning up to classroom teachers).

Learner Suitability

A useful distinction can be drawn between existing abilities and needed abilities. *Existing abilities* are the skills, knowledge, and interests that learners already possess. *Needed abilities* are the skills, knowledge, and interests that learners must have in order to achieve the objectives of an intended educational reform.

Proposition: The greater the discrepancy between learners' existing abilities and the abilities required by an educational reform, the greater the inertia the reform will face.

Problem case B: In a state whose public school students scored lower on language and mathematics tests than did students in many other states, the state department of education—at the insistence of the governor and legislature—instituted an annual state wide achievement-testing program for pupils in all public elementary and secondary schools. To motivate teachers in low-performing schools to raise students' scores in language (reading, writing) and mathematics, schools' scores would be publicized in newspapers and magazines as well as on radio, television, the Internet. As a further incentive, schools whose test scores during the current year were at least 10% higher than their scores the previous year would receive cash bonuses to be distributed among the teachers.

The state's schools that had the lowest average scores came in for particular criticism from the governor's office and the department of education—criticism widely reported in the public press. Such phrases as "get those teachers in order" and "make them clean up their act" appeared in critics' estimates of the causes of low achievement in such schools. Over the first three years of the testing reform, the schools that had scored highest during the first year showed little subsequent improvement, since they were already doing well. Some schools that had moderate or low scores the first year did improve during the second and third years, with the more successful ones earning bonuses. However, a good many of the first year's lowest-scoring schools continued to do poorly the second and third years. In such cases, the testing program had not raised achievement to what state political leaders and much of the general public regarded as satisfactory. Thus, from the viewpoint of the testing program's purpose, the innovation had failed in those schools.

Critics of the way the testing program was administered charged that a significant factor contributing to the score differences among schools was the nature of the learners. Students in the different schools—and, indeed, within any given school—did not all have the same ability to master the objectives that were being assessed by the test items. Nor did their home conditions and earlier experiences in life equip all of them to succeed equally well on the tests. In other words, teachers' skills and motivation were not the only variables—and not even the most important variables—affecting students' test scores. The abilities of students—as determined by their inherited potential, previous learning opportunities, motives, and interests—were more important.

Remedy option: Analyze the causes of students' ostensible underachievement. In the ideal instructional program, the objectives (what a student is expected to learn) would be matched precisely to that student's present ability to achieve those objectives. However, it seems clear that this ideal is rarely reached, especially in the typical school setting where students are taught in groups rather than individually. The ideal can be approximated only when instruction is provided by individual tutoring, apprenticeship, or self-instruction. Inevitably, holding the same expectations (as reflected in test questions) for all students of a given grade level throughout an entire state will result in a great many mismatches between objectives and learners' capabilities.

In our example of a statewide testing program, there appears to be no adequate immediate remedy for the mismatches. As is often true of politicians when confronted with a complex social problem, a single simplistic solution was proposed. That solution was the statewide testing program which ignored the multiplicity of factors that affect students' achievement. In suggesting such a naïve policy, the legislators and officials in the state education department appeared to be operating from a "one size fits all" mindset. They expected that the problem of students and schools being "below average" or "not up to standard" would be solved by requiring all students to take the same achievement tests. Then the test scores would be publicized and money would be offered for annual score improvements. The embarrassment suffered by low-scoring schools was expected to motivate those schools' teachers and students to do better in the future. In addition, one obvious implication behind the plan was that teachers were the ones mainly at fault for the low scores, so the teachers should be responsible for raising all students to an acceptable level. Apparently that level would be the state or national average or, as state legislators hoped, even higher. (It's curious to note that some people who make judgments about students' achievement—parents, legislators, business executives, school-board members, and more—are shocked to learn that half of the students score below the group average on tests.)

In keeping with the foregoing observations about individual differences among students and about the complexity of the causes of those differences, one remedy option for the testing program's shortcomings would be to use each student's test results as only one part of the evidence needed to estimate (a) which learning objective's would be reasonable ones to expect the student to pursue at the present time, and (b) what might be done to help the student succeed up to his or her estimated potential. Therefore, a key aim of diagnosing the causes of a student's academic performance would be to set realistic learning objectives for each learner and no longer expect all students at a given age level to master the same objectives.

Social Acceptability

The expression *social acceptability of learning objectives* refers to the willingness of the public—or a significant portion of the public—to endorse the aims of an intended change in an education system.

> *Proposition:* The more that the objectives of a proposed innovation appear to violate the values held by an influential segment of society, the greater the inertia that confronts the innovation.

Problem case C: The board of education in a rural American public school district sought to improve the behavior of youths in their community by passing a resolution requiring that the biblical Ten Commandments be posted in every classroom and that students be obliged to recite the commandments at the beginning of each school day. The students had already been reciting the pledge of allegiance to the United States each morning. The Ten Commandments would simply be added to that ritual.

Hardly a week had passed before the school district's central office began receiving phone calls from parents and other members of the community who complained that the Ten Commandments directive violated the U. S. Constitution's separation of church and state. On the editorial page of the local newspaper, opponents of the newly introduced practice charged that such an act was an illegal endorsement of a particular religious tradition (Judeo-Christian-Islamic). In response, supporters of the practice stated that the commandments were a foundation stone of American democracy. When the school board refused to change its directive, a group of citizens filed a lawsuit to force the board to rescind its original resolution. The board's attorney, after reviewing the fate of similar lawsuits in other communities in their state, concluded that the board would likely lose in court, so the board members reluctantly withdrew their resolution, and the commandments were no longer posted or recited in classrooms.

(Periodically, state legislatures have changed their laws governing public declarations of the Ten Commandments. In 2001, the Oregon state senate voted to prohibit posting the biblical Ten Commandments in public schools, while the North Carolina senate voted to permit such posting [Robinson, 2001].)

Remedy option: One way that the schools might still teach the Ten Commandments without risking a lawsuit would be for a social studies class—probably in the junior or senior high school—to include a unit of study titled "Comparative Religion" or "Moral Principles Across Cultures." The objective of the course would not be to convince students of the rectitude of a single religion's moral principles but, rather, to inform them of likenesses and differences among various philosophical persuasions. Such a purpose would not violate the Constitution's policy of separating church and state. The following four examples illustrate the nature of doctrines that students could compare: the biblical Ten Commandments, Gert's secular moral rules, typical Confucian maxims, and tenets from the Hindu epic *Mahabharata.*

The Ten Commandments: People should not: (1) worship any gods other than Jehovah, (2) carve idols of gods, (3) use Jehovah's name lightly, as in cursing, (4) do work on the Sabbath day, (5) dishonor or disobey their parents, (6) kill, (7) steal, (8) lie about other people, (9) commit adultery, or (10) yearn for their neighbors' possessions. (Exodus 20:3-17)

Gert's secular set of rules: (1) don't kill, (2) don't cause pain, (3) don't disable, (4) don't deprive of freedom or opportunity, (5) don't deprive of pleasure, (6) don't deceive, (7) keep your promise, (8) don't cheat, (9) obey the law, and (10) do your duty. (Gert, 1970)

Confucian maxims: (1) If you are unflinching, bold, simple, natural, and un-hurried, you approximate humans at their best.
(2) If you are humble, you will not be laughed at.
(3) If you are magnanimous, you will attract many to your side.
(4) If you are sincere, people will trust you.
(5) If you are diligent, you will be successful.
(6) If you are gracious, you will get along well with your subordinates.
    (Ware, 1955, pp. 88, 94, 111)

Hindu tenets: Twelve virtues are: truth, self-restraint, self control, scholar-ship, tolerance, shame for vices, patience, absence of jealousy, sacrifice, charity, courage, and calmness.

Twelve vices to be avoided are: wrath, greed, delusion, too much desire for worldly pleasure, lack of compassion, jealousy, shamelessness, sorrow, desire, envy, and disgust. (Shastri, 1994, p. 18)

Conclusion

This chapter has illustrated three characteristics of objectives that can influence the inertia faced by an innovation. Those three have been objectives' specificity, learner suitability, and social acceptability. Other features of objectives that may also affect inertia are:

- *Objectives' sources.* Who has proposed the new learning goals?
- *Objectives' replacement.* Which existing objectives must be eliminated from the curriculum in order to accommodate the new ones?
- *Objectives' educational appropriateness.* Is it reasonable to expect schools to attempt to adopt a particular proposed objective? For example, should the school be expected to provide drug abuse treatment or to ensure that children eat a nutritious breakfast and lunch?

Discussion Topics

1. Problem case A (pages 55-56) showed how rather different specific objectives could be defined under the broad science education aim of "Understanding modern science and applying that understand-ing in daily-life situations." To demonstrate further how general

objectives can be interpreted differently at the classroom level, describe how two classroom teachers might define quite different specific objectives for each of the following general aims.

- Students appreciate music.
- Students adopt constructive social behavior.
- Students understand our nation's history.

2. In problem case B (pages 56-58), only one remedy option was suggested. Can you suggest other options that might permit the continued use of statewide achievement tests and still adjust objectives to the ability of students to reach the objectives?

3. Problem case C (pages 59-60) concerned the inertia that the introduction of new objectives can face as a result of the objectives being unacceptable within some segments of the society. To illustrate this point further, suggest (a) who might oppose the introduction of the following objectives and (b) what reasons they might give in support of their opposition.

- Students cite the advantages that a benevolent dictatorship form of government has over a representative democracy form.
- Students learn the appeal that crack-cocaine has for teenagers.
- Students identify the advantages of couples cohabiting rather than getting married.

4

Teaching Methods and Materials

As proposed in the introduction to Part I, teaching methods are the instructional procedures used to help students master learning objectives. Teaching materials are the supplies and equipment employed in those instructional procedures. Typical labels used for identifying different teaching methods include *lecture, class discussion, question-answer session, excursion, demonstration, experiment, student report, homework assignment,* and more. Supplies and equipment often used in conjunction with teaching procedures are *textbooks, pencils, notebooks, maps, charts, pictures, films, videos, television receivers, computers,* and others. As noted earlier, the combined term *teaching/learning process* is sometimes substituted for *teaching methods* in recognition of the fact that the active participation of the student is necessary if learning is to occur.

Six factors that affect the success of newly introduced teaching methods and materials are inspected in this chapter.

Teaching Methods and Materials

- Teachers' preparation
- Learners' preparation
- Method complexity
- Equipment/supplies availability
- Reasonable expectations
- Time constraints

Teachers' Preparation

Throughout this chapter, the terms *innovative teaching methods* and *teaching-method reforms* are not intended to imply that such methods and reforms are entirely new to the teaching profession. Indeed, nearly every teaching technique has been used by someone, someplace, at some time. Thus, such terms are used here to mean methods that are new for a particular school or a particular teacher. The nature of the human life span and of the teaching profession results in the same instructional techniques being newly introduced to one generation of teachers after another generation in an unending chain. Veteran teachers who have already mastered instructional techniques will retire from the classroom and be replaced by novices who must start from the beginning to acquire the techniques anew. Thus, the following pair of illustrative cases concerns two instructional methods—role-playing and individualized learning plans—that are new to the teachers who are involved in the cases.

Proposition: The more preparation a teacher needs in order to employ a new instructional method, the greater the inertia encountered in adopting that method.

Problem case A: The faculty members of an elementary school were obliged to attend a Friday afternoon inservice education session at which an educational consultant introduced role-playing as an instructional device.

The consultant began by explaining that role-playing—known also as *sociodrama*—required students to act as if they were some imagined individual who was involved in a social-problem situation. She pointed out that role-playing differed from formal dramatics in that participants' speech and actions were not dictated by a script they had memorized. Rather, the only two things defined for students prior to the conduct of a sociodrama were (a) the social problem that the dramatization would represent and (b) the kinds of characters involved in the problem situation. After the social situation was explained to a class and pupils were chosen to assume the several roles, pupils would be expected to act their assigned parts spontaneously, saying and doing what they thought their portrayed character might normally say and do under the described circumstances.

Using an overhead projector, the consultant displayed a list of educational advantages that role-playing offered.

- Participants in a sociodrama not only gain the intellectual experience of seeing which sorts of social interactions among individuals either solve or intensify social problems, but they also experience emotions that people feel in similar real-life encounters.

- Taking part in a sociodrama enables pupils to try solutions to problem situations before pupils are confronted by such situations in real life.
- Role-playing is often a better device for catching and holding the attention of a classroom of pupils than are such teaching techniques as lectures and class discussions.
- Sociodramas are useful for simulating the interaction of the complex factors that influence social behavior in real life.
- Role-playing offers children the chance to try diverse roles and to experience the feedback that those roles are likely to elicit from other people in daily-life situations.
- Role-playing promotes greater social understanding among pupils by placing them for a time in other people's shoes, enabling them to view life from others' perspectives.

To demonstrate the conduct of a sociodrama, the consultant posed a problem that involved the parents of a fifth-grade pupil meeting with the child's teacher in the presence of the school principal to complain about the teacher's accusing the pupil of bullying classmates. Four members of the inservice session's audience were asked to assume the four individuals' roles and act out the scene in front of the group. The consultant handed each actor a printed description of the attitude and feelings of the character that the actor was to portray—mother, father, teacher, principal. The consultant then described the setting in which the four participants met, told the nature of the accusations the teacher had made about the pupil, and asked the four actors to carry on from that point, spontaneously creating dialogue that they imagined would fit the circumstance.

At a point in the ensuing drama that the participants arrived at either an agreement or a stalemate, the consultant stopped the play and asked members of the audience for their reactions to such questions as: Was the scene played realistically? What alternative ways might the four actors have responded? How might events have worked out differently if those responses had been used?

Following the discussion of the initial sociodrama, the consultant described another social-problem situation in which a sixth-grade teacher spoke with three students after two of them had made insulting comments about the third student's ethnic origins. Members of the audience were then selected to portray the four roles as defined on slips of paper that the consultant handed the actors.

The second sociodrama was followed by a group discussion, and the inservice session ended with the school principal urging the teachers to adopt role-playing as an instructional technique. She particularly emphasized the desirability of applying sociodrama in grades 3 through 6.

Two months later, the consultant was invited back to the school to interview teachers and pupils about the ways that sociodrama had been used in their classrooms. The visit revealed a diversity of experiences in grades 3 through 6. Three teachers had used the method with good results and thus intended to continue using it. Several others who had tried role-playing on a single occasion and had decided, for various reasons, to abandon further attempts. Their reasons included (a) pupils acted silly, with the result that the class went out of control, (b) some pupils refused to take part, (c) the post-sociodrama discussion elicited no worthwhile comments from class members, (d) the teacher could not find suitable social problems on which the dramas would focus, and (e) the role-playing sessions consumed more class time than the results seemed to warrant. Other teachers had not yet tried role-playing, apparently because they felt insecure using the technique and didn't want to risk making fools of themselves in front of their pupils by appearing incompetent.

In summary, the principal's effort to incorporate role-playing as a standard tool among the school's instructional methods fell well short of her expectations. It seemed that one brief inservice education session had been inadequate for equipping the bulk of the faculty with the skills and motivation needed to make role-playing a popular instructional procedure.

Remedy options: Attempts to overcome teachers' resistance to role-playing include the following alternatives.

Live demonstrations involving pupils. During the inservice education session, the first incident that the consultant had used to illustrate role-playing had involved only adults, and the social problem was limited to an adult issue—a confrontation between parents and school personnel. Likewise, the audience consisted solely of teachers. Those conditions were far different than the ones in which classroom sociodramas are performed. Therefore, in order to illustrate role-playing under more typical circumstances, a teacher skilled at directing role-playing could conduct a series of sociodramas—perhaps in a school auditorium or activity room—using pupils as both actors and members of the audience. During such a session, the teacher in charge could demonstrate and explain ways of coping with problems that arise—children acting silly, actors who don't know what to say, and those who decline to participate.

Recorded demonstrations involving pupils. Videotapes of role-playing sessions with children in normal classroom settings might be even more effective than live demonstrations as a way of showing how to conduct sociodramas with different groups of children, with different types of social encounters, with the different problems that teachers face, and with the problems' solutions.

Mentoring. Skills in using role-playing can be disseminated throughout a school by means of the each-one-teach-one process that has been widely employed in adult literacy campaigns. One teacher who has become proficient at guiding sociodramas can be assigned to spend time in a second teacher's classroom to demonstrate role-playing with the second teacher's pupils. Then the second teacher gradually takes over the conduct of sociodramas until he or she feels confident in using the technique. When the second teacher has become adept, she or he can work in a third teacher's classroom to train the third teacher in directing role-playing sessions.

Written descriptions. In lieu of live demonstrations and videotaped incidents, teachers may profit from detailed written directions that (a) describe the typical stages of a role-playing session, (b) suggest social encounters that can be the focus of role-playing incidents for students of different age levels, (c) identify problems teachers often face in role-playing sessions, and suggest ways to solve those problems, and (d) illustrate the give-and-take that occurs among role-playing participants by quoting segments of dialogues from representative sessions.

Problem case B: In Kentucky, the commissioner of education, Gene Wilhoit, complained that in 2001, after 10 years of experimentation following the Kentucky Education Reform Act, many of the state's schools—especially middle and high schools—were still using outdated teaching practices. He said the state's most successful schools were individualizing instruction by adopting practices tailor-made for each student, but too few secondary school teachers were designing lessons to suit each student's learning style and stage of progress (Cooper, 2001). The traditional teaching methods to which Wilhoit objected were apparently those of instructing an entire class as a single group by means of lectures, textbook reading assignments, and general class discussions.

Observers noted that at least part of the difference between elementary and secondary schools in the frequency of individualized learning plans derived from the greater number of students that secondary school teachers typically face each day. The task of individualizing instruction for a third-grade teacher who has the same 30 children all day is far less demanding than the task of a high school history teacher who meets 150 or more in a day.

Remedy options: As the following three techniques illustrate, attempts to match instruction to individual students' present knowledge and interests vary from slight changes in traditional classroom instruction to extensive changes.

Slight change—individual projects. The most popular way that teachers attempt to accommodate students' individual differences is to assign occasional projects focusing on individually chosen topics in addition to assigning the usual tasks that all class members must complete in common—such tasks as everyone solving the same problems in the math textbook or everyone reading the same novel. Individual projects can obviously assume many forms—book reports, term papers, essays, experiments, stories, poems, drawings, constructions, excursions, interviews, and more.

Extensive change—diagnostic teaching. An instructional approach sometimes referred to as *diagnostic teaching* involves a teacher first (a) evaluating students' present skills, knowledge, and apparent learning styles in relation to the learning task at hand, then (b) assigning each student the kinds of learning activities that seem best suited to promoting that student's progress, and finally (c) evaluating what each student has learned. Diagnostic teaching, in effect, reverses the usual sequence of instruction that involves learners first (a) studying a topic (by hearing a lecture, viewing a demonstration, reading a book, completing workbook exercises) and then (b) being evaluated (by means of a test, discussion, report, or performance).

There are two principal purposes behind diagnostic teaching. First, the diagnostic approach informs the teacher at the outset of a unit of study (such as a two-week or four-week period during which students focus on a given topic) about what each student already knows about the upcoming topic. On the basis of this information, the teacher can avoid (a) boring advanced learners by requiring them to suffer through instruction focusing on objectives they have already mastered, and (b) confusing less adept learners by confronting them with tasks they are ill prepared to perform. Students who, in the diagnostic evaluation at the outset of a study unit, show that they already command the skills and knowledge (or at least substantial parts) that the class is going to study can be given enrichment activities to pursue while the rest of the students are acquiring the unit's basic skills and knowledge. Also, students who, in the diagnostic phase, show that they lack some of the foundational preparation for the unit, can be helped acquire that preparation by means of remedial activities. The remainder of the class members, who have the foundational preparation but have not yet mastered the content of the study unit, can be furnished with learning activities suited to their levels of current progress.

It should be apparent that diagnostic teaching (matching learning experiences to each student's current knowledge, motivation, and mode of learning) is an ideal to be pursued, but one that can never be fully achieved, for the individual differences among students are too varied for teachers to suit instruction exactly to each student's needs and abilities. There simply is not enough time, nor are there enough facilities (suitable books, computer programs, worksheets, assigned tasks), for teachers to flawlessly match learning methods to students' characteristics.

Intermediate change—partial individualization. Between the extremes of slight change (occasional personal projects) and extensive change (heavy application of diagnostic teaching) are ways of adjusting instructional methods to learners' needs, such as assigning more frequent personal projects, dividing a class into smaller groups whose members study together, pairing students so they can tutor each other, enlisting parents as teacher aides who assist individual pupils, and adopting computer programs designed to teach the skills and knowledge needed by particular students.

Learners' Preparation

It's apparent that the inertia encountered by a teaching/learning method can vary from one student to another. Whereas one youth learns very efficiently under a particular method, another will fail when taught in that same way. Therefore, the use of a given method often yields a mixed results—among the students there will be some instances of dramatic learning progress, some instances of modest progress, and some instances of failure.

> *Proposition:* The less adequately prepared students are to succeed with a new instructional method, the greater the inertia that method will face.

In the present context, the term *adequately prepared* refers to how well students' current skills, knowledge, and motivation equip them to satisfactorily perform the learning tasks required by the content and instructional methods of a class in which they are enrolled.

> *Problem case C:* A high school science teacher introduced a new commercially available course titled "Modern Astronomy" that was available in the form of (a) an instructional packet for each student (textbook, worksheets) and (b) an instructional packet for the teacher (teacher's manual, tests items, wall posters, and a compact disc for projecting—via a computer—still pictures, diagrams, and motion pictures of astronomical phenomena). The teacher offered the course as an elective for all high-school juniors and seniors. Twenty-seven students entered the class the first time it was offered.

As the semester progressed, it became obvious that nearly half of the class members sorely lacked the preparation needed to succeed with the textbook and workbook assignments or with the narratives that accompanied the compact disc presentations. The creators of the course had assumed that students would already be well versed in the dominant present-day atomic theory of matter, principles of scientific methodology, advanced algebra, and historical conceptions of the solar system (biblical, Ptolemaic, Copernican). Many class members lacked part or all of that preparation. Before mid-semester, eight students dropped the class, and five teetered on the borderline between a D and an F grade. Therefore, the inertia created by insufficient preparation rendered the commercial astronomy program's methodology inappropriate for a substantial number of students.

Remedy options: The following are among the alternatives available to the teacher for reducing inadequate preparation as a barrier to students succeeding with "Modern Astronomy."

Supplementary assignments. For students who lack knowledge of atomic theory, principles of scientific research, and earlier notions of the solar system, the teacher could assign readings that filled in the missing background knowledge. However, such a self-study approach would not likely make up for algebra deficiencies.

Tutoring. Students who had already mastered the needed foundational knowledge could be asked to tutor classmates who suffered knowledge gaps.

Entrance requirements. The next time the course was to be taught, the teacher could prepare an information sheet specifying for potential students the background of knowledge they would need to succeed in the class. Consequently, before students enrolled, they would understand how well they were prepared for this variety of "Modern Astronomy."

Pretesting. In the future, the first day or so of the class could be used for testing students' command of necessary background skills and knowledge. On the basis of the test results, the teacher could immediately arrange for ways to help individuals fill in their knowledge gaps before the class started the "Modern Astronomy" program itself.

Method Complexity

Proposition: The more complicated a new instructional method, the greater the inertia experienced in applying the method.

Problem case D: In a city that included four middle schools, the assistant superintendent in charge of instruction represented the school district at a one-week summer workshop titled "Social Studies in Action" at a nearby state college. The workshop emphasized ways to link schools more closely with their surrounding community by increasing

- Student excursions to socially significant sites (government offices, factories, business firms, museums, historic monuments, hospitals, courts, and more)
- Members of the community coming to class to speak to the students
- Students actively participating in community-action projects (aiding the infirm and elderly, cleaning up graffiti, helping with after-school activities for younger children, tutoring pupils who experienced difficulties with their studies, engaging in peer counseling, and the like)

Upon returning to his duties in the school district, the assistant superintendent felt that he knew the perfect place in which to locate the community outreach teaching methods that had been featured in the summer workshop. That place was the middle schools' social studies course for seventh graders, titled "Living in Communities." He believed that, rather than merely urging teachers to include more community-linked events in the seventh-grade course, his innovation would more likely be implemented if he set a specific goal for classes to achieve. Consequently, at the beginning of the school year he met with the seventh-grade social studies teachers from the four middle schools to describe his goal and to offer—in oral and written form—examples of suitable excursion sites, visiting speakers, and community action projects. In quantitative terms, the goal was for each class to participate in at least one excursion per month, to invite at least three speakers per month, and to engage in at least one action project per semester. At semester's end, teachers would send the assistant superintendent a summary of how well their classes had met the goal.

Following the close of the first semester, the assistant superintendent had received only two reports from teachers until he sent reminders to the rest of the teachers. When all reports were in, the results showed that in the case of only one class had the quantitative goal been completely reached. The remaining classes fell short in various degrees. Most reports included descriptions of difficulties encountered in carrying out the plan. Furthermore, the month-by-month accounts of class activities showed that, as the semester progressed, the plan had been increasingly abandoned. Problems that occurred during the initial months had discouraged teachers from continuing their efforts in later months. December, in particular, proved to be a bad month for the community outreach activities because the holidays altered community members' usual routines. A compilation of the teachers' written descriptions, along with teachers' oral complaints to their school principals, revealed the following difficulties that contributed to the resistance the program suffered.

Excursions. In planning an excursion, teachers often had problems finding parents who would join the excursion as teacher aides. Some students frequently failed to have their parents sign the permission form that enabled their daughter or son to join the trip, so those students had to stay behind at the school. And scheduling school buses for transporting a class to a site frequently proved difficult.

During an excursion, some students were unruly, wandered away from the group, made rude remarks to passersby, and failed to pay attention to the people, objects, and events they were supposed to be learning about. Consequently, teachers were obliged to spend too much time trying to keep the group under control and too little time directing the learning experience. It was difficult at some sites for the entire crowd of students to see objects of interest (such as an item in a museum exhibit case or a particular worker's activity in a factory) or to hear the explanation given by the person guiding their tour. In addition, when a class visited a store or factory, an employee's efforts to keep the students from interfering with the work routine resulted in class members not being able to see some of the most interesting sights. During a visit, some students asked questions about things they wanted to learn, so their guide needed to stop to answer their questions. This interruption slowed the progress of the visit, frequently preventing the group from seeing all that the teacher had intended they see; and the interruption irritated students who were not interested in what was being explained. Still other class members, who had questions about what they were seeing, failed to ask their questions because they feared they would appear stupid or be accused of wasting time. Students often failed to take the notes they needed for answering questions about the visit after they returned to school.

Finally, comments appended to teachers' semester-end reports frequently questioned the wisdom of using an entire morning, or sometimes an entire school day, to visit a site that yielded less profit—in terms of the quantity and quality of learning—than typically resulted from spending the same amount of time in class.

Similar to the excursion portion of the community outreach plan, the visiting speakers and action projects portions also posed difficulties. The kinds of visiting speakers that students would consider worthwhile were difficult to find and schedule. In addition, visiting speakers often proved boring and disorganized, or they spoke in platitudes, and wandered off the assigned topic. Some were embarrassingly bigoted and badly informed about social issues, yet teachers felt obliged to avoid confronting or correcting such visitors because they were the school's invited guests.

For several of the social studies classes, the action projects part of the plan turned out to be even more difficult to control than the excursion part.

In conclusion, it was clear that, in practice, the assistant superintendent's community excursions plan fell well short of his goal, chiefly because teachers had found that implementing his proposed innovation was unduly complicated.

Remedy options: The following are three ways that the complexity of the community resources proposal might be reduced.

Fewer excursions, fewer speakers. Perhaps the most obvious way to care for teachers' complaints would be to eliminate the set number of required excursions and speakers that the assistant superintendent had specified. In other words, each teacher would decide how often visits to the community and visitors from the community would be used.

Videotaped excursions. One way to furnish students with intimate knowledge of places and people in the community without their having to leave the classroom would be to create videotaped documentaries. For example, when an entire class took a field trip to a site, two or three students—or perhaps parents—could videotape events at the site. The resulting videotapes could then be edited to produce a coherent story of the excursion, along with an accompanying narrative, to be shown to classes in subsequent years. Furthermore, a videotape prepared by one class in one school could be duplicated for use by other classes in other schools. As the years advanced and more videotaped documentaries were produced, the community outreach program could thus expand significantly without the problems that multiple excursions by a single class would involve. Thus, by adopting the videotape plan, the number of actual excursions that a given group of seventh-graders took during the year could be reduced to one or two, while the number of videotapes viewed could be markedly increased.

Interviewing visitors. The problem of visiting speakers being poorly organized, boring, and wandering off the topic could be solved—at least partially—if the visitors are not invited to "give a talk" or "tell of your experiences." Instead, they could be invited to be interviewed by the students in the class they visited. In order to inform guests ahead of time about that the kinds of questions students would ask, the invitation to be interviewed could be accompanied by several of the sorts of questions that would be posed. In effect, casting the visit as an interview rather than as a speech would give the teacher and students greater control over what would occur, thereby helping ensure that visitors contributed constructively to the class's objectives.

Equipment/Supplies Availability

The word *equipment* in the present context refers to the settings (buildings, land areas, waterways) and permanent objects (machines, furnishings) needed for a particular instructional method. The word *supplies* means expendable objects (pens, paper, notebooks) that a teaching/learning procedure requires.

> *Proposition:* The more difficult it is to provide the equipment and supplies required by a new instructional method, the greater the resistance to employing that method.

In the realm of equipment and supplies, the personal computer is the prime present-day example of inertia serving to retard the adoption of a methodological innovation. And it is not just teachers' apprehension over the computer itself that produces inertia, but the inertia is exacerbated by the array of peripheral apparatuses that accompany computer technology—printers, scanners, copiers, fax-modems, digital cameras, videocameras (camcorders), and such data-storage devices as diskettes, compact discs, and external hard drives.

The term *computer revolution* certainly applies in the world of schooling. In the present era, which is often called *the information age*, computer skills are required in a growing variety of vocations and are becoming embedded in people's personal lives as necessities for communicating with others (e-mail, chat groups), acquiring knowledge about the world (via the World Wide Web), storing records, completing tax forms, pursuing recreation (movies, music, sporting events, hobbies), and far more. The educational advantages of personal computers have become so attractive over the past two decades that *computer literacy* has taken its place beside *reading literacy* and *math literacy* as a basic objective in the education systems of nearly all advanced industrial nations. That objective is also being included at an increasing rate among the goals held in affluent schools in developing nations.

Under these circumstances, schools are forced to contend with teaching/learning problems caused by computer technology's novelty, complexity, cost, and obsolescence.

First, consider novelty and complexity. For many veteran teachers—ones with years of classroom experience—the computer revolution came as an unwelcome shock. The task of incorporating computers into teachers' repertoire of teaching methods seemed daunting. To bring themselves up to date, they would need to develop sufficient command of an entirely new set of skills in order to guide students in using computers. These skills included mastering a new vocabulary—*bits, bytes, online, e-mail, user ID, links, inbox, HTML, Internet, World Wide Web, browser, search engine, chat group, digital imagery,* and more. In addition, teachers would need to master the ever-increasing ways that computers can enhance learning—typing letters and reports (aided by a thesaurus, word counter, spell checker, and grammar corrector), locating information on the Internet, illustrating reports with printed drawings and photographs through use of a scanner, producing computerized photos with a digital camera, projecting colored-slide and motion-picture presentations, creating websites, engaging in conversations with students in distant schools, and more. The problems encountered in adapting to these new expectations have been particularly acute for those teachers who were already intimidated by the difficulties they experienced with even simpler instructional equipment—motion-picture projectors, tape recorders, slide projectors, and the like.

Among teachers who traditionally viewed themselves as the authoritative source of knowledge in their classrooms, the complexity of computers could be especially distressing when it became clear that many students were far more adept at using computers than were their teachers. In such instances, a new interpretation of the roles of teacher and of student seemed in order—the two should now be seen as co-learners, each helping the other reach the educational goals.

Next is the matter of *cost.* Although the prices of personal computers and allied devices have dropped dramatically over the past two decades as the result of technological progress and competition within the industry, computers are still far more expensive then textbooks, teacher lectures, and class discussions. Added to the cost of purchasing computers is the expense of wiring a school so that individual computers become part of an extensive network of machines located in various classrooms and laboratories. In addition, computers and their attachments tend to be ailment prone, suffering breakdowns that require repair or replacement. Consequently, substantial and continuing funding is necessary to sustain teachers' extensive use of computers among their instructional methods. For example, a technology survey in California schools showed that

> Problems with Internet connections, networking, and hard drives often go unaddressed for a week. Almost all schools—91 percent—have no network specialist on site. . . . The problem stems from a state push to get computers into classrooms without providing the funds for ongoing technical support. The technology survey found that 80 percent of the time it took up to five days for a computer problem to get fixed. For a hardware repair, it took from two days to a month in 89 percent of the cases.
>
> "Schools and school districts are relying on teachers and students for the most part to upkeep and upgrade and maintain computers," said Mike Lansing, board member for the Los Angeles Unified School District. "Most districts haven't come to grips with the reality of dealing with technology to

keep it running at the level it should be. It's only going to get worse as more schools have more technology but still don't have the positions to support it." (Moilanen, 2001).

Now consider *obsolescence*. School systems that intend to keep up with the times are obliged to teach students how to take advantage of the latest computer technology, a technology whose development progresses at an astonishing rate. This year's computer hardware (personal computers, scanners, printers, storage devices, and more) and software (programs that tell computers how to perform various functions) will be obsolete within less than half a decade—and in some cases even by next year. The challenge to keep pace with the growth of computer technology is like a bowman shooting at moving target. Computer development refuses to hold still. Not only is the latest version of equipment different from its predecessor, but the latest version is often incompatible with equipment that the predecessor employed. For example, a music-composition software program titled "Concertware" worked nicely on a 1985 computer but would not function on ones from 1990 onward. A diskette (floppy disk) with a memory capacity of 800 kilobytes or of 1.4 megabytes could fit into a slot in the computer up until the mid-1990s. But the most popular computers by the late 1990s had no such slot, nor could the newest computers read diskettes even if a separate exterior disk drive was employed. A superdisc that could store 120 megabytes of information appeared on the market for only a short time in the latter 1990s, replaced by zip disks (250 megabytes) and compact discs with even greater capacity (700 megabytes). Consequently, by 2001, there was no way that a new computer could read a superdisc. The cables connecting external devices (printers, scanners, external disc drives) to computers also changed, so that a SCSI plug for connecting to an external device would be replaced by a USC (universal serial bus) or fire-wire connector. Sometimes an adapter cable would be available to render the new device compatible with the old, but this did not always happen. Equipment manufacturers contend that such problems are inevitable in an industry that so rapidly creates improvements. However, some critics have charged that at least part of the motivation behind developers' new products has been *planned obsolescence*, the intent to render existing equipment unusable so that it must be entirely replaced if customers are to enjoy the advantages of recent developments. In any event, the rapid rate at which a school's computer equipment becomes outdated contributes to the inertia teachers face in seeking to incorporate the most advanced computer technology into their teaching procedures.

Problem case E: During a typical week in a junior high general science classroom, the following conditions increased the inertia the instructional program suffered following the introduction of personal computers.

- Each day, five science classes, ranging in size from 27 to 33 students, used the science classroom, which was equipped with six computers. Whenever a class assignment called for searching the Internet, viewing material on a compact disc, or working problems on a computer, the teacher had difficulty scheduling every student to use a computer. And because some students worked faster and more efficiently than others, conflicts arose between students about how much time they spent on a computer.
- The scheduling problem was aggravated by two computers suffering operating problems during the week. The teacher was able to solve one of the difficulties himself, but he could not get around to fixing the problem until after school, which meant the computer was inoperative throughout most of the school day. The trouble with the other ailing machine was more serious and required a trained technician, who had to be summoned from the district office. That computer was out of commission for the entire week.
- The classroom's computers were connected together in the form of a network, which included two printers. Frequently, students were unable to print the results of their work immediately because others were using the printers at the time. In addition, one class member tripped over a wire in the network, pulling the wire loose and causing three of the computers to lose their Internet connections until the wire was repaired.
- At the close of one class period, a desperate fellow teacher begged the science instructor to come to her classroom to show her how to use the projector that cast the images from a computer onto a large television screen at the front of her classroom. Consequently, the science instructor was delayed in returning to his own classroom, where members of his next class of students were amusing themselves by engaging in horseplay until he appeared.

Remedy options: The following measures might help reduce the inertia generated by the foregoing problems.

Supplementary computers. The shortage of computers in the class could be relieved somewhat if students who had laptop computers at home were willing to bring their computers to the science class on days that the teacher's methods call for computer use. However, the disadvantage of this option is that the laptops wouldn't be connected to the classroom's computer network, and their operating systems might not be compatible with that of the type of computer on which a particular day's lessons depended.

Student technicians. The school could create a student-technician training program, either as a regular class or as an extracurricular club, so that some of the burden of keeping computers in working condition could be assumed by students. Students not only could be trained to diagnose and correct software and hardware problems but also could be prepared to help teachers who were still new to using computers as instructional aids.

More money. Teachers and school principals could urge the school district to invest in hiring additional computer technicians. Parents' help could be solicited to urge the school board and central administrative personnel to fund repair work more adequately.

Reasonable Expectations

Each time a reform is proposed, people develop expectations about the ways in which the reform will improve education. Once the reform is put into practice, people judge its success by how adequately its results meet their expectations. The greater the shortfall of results in comparison to the expectations, the greater the inertia generated against retaining the reform.

Proposition: The less adequately the expectations for a new instructional method are fulfilled, the less likely the method will be permanently retained.

Problem case F: A saleswoman from Our Expert Learners, Incorporated, met with the director of reading instruction in a school district that operated eight elementary schools, two junior highs, and one senior high. The saleswoman hoped to convince the district to adopt her company's *Our Expert Readers* series as the basic materials for teaching reading from kindergarten through grade six in all of the district's elementary schools. In support of her proposal, she presented a glowing description of the superiority of *Our Expert Readers* in comparison to other popular reading series, including the series currently adopted throughout the district. Her description included (a) highly enthusiastic testimonials from teachers in various parts of the country, (b) the results of "scientific studies" (ones perhaps sponsored by Our Expert Learners), (c) a list of the supplementary materials that accompanied the basic reading textbooks, and (d) the prediction that pupils' reading performance under *Our Expert Readers*, when compared to their current performance, would

- Be at least one grade-level higher on the average, and probably two or more grades higher

- Show a smaller gap between the best and the poorest readers. Not only would the best readers achieve at a higher level than previously, but the less apt readers would particularly profit from the new series, therefore reducing the variability in reading skill within a class
- Reflect pupils' greater enthusiasm for reading

In addition, the representative from Our Expert Learners confidently predicted that teachers would welcome the series for the detailed lesson plans in the teachers' manuals, the interesting content of the textbooks' stories and articles, the accompanying tests, and a variety of supplementary instructional aids. Those aids included (a) storybooks that paralleled the reading texts, (b) workbooks giving children practice in both reading and writing, and (c) compact discs containing reading exercises colorfully illustrated with cartoons, drawings, and photographs. The discs could be viewed either on a personal computer by an individual child or projected onto a screen to be seen by a small group or an entire class.

The district's director of reading instruction was sufficiently impressed by the saleswoman's presentation to say that she would be willing to try *Our Expert Readers* during a one-year period in a pilot study involving one or two primary-grade classes. The Our Expert Learners representative objected, saying that such a tryout would be insufficient. She said it would be far more desirable to adopt the series at all grade levels and in all eight elementary schools so as to "cancel out the influence of any peculiar characteristics that could affect results in the one or two pilot-study classes." However, the director of reading instruction was firm in her insistence that a pilot study would be necessary. She explained that the enormous expense of purchasing new reading texts and supplementary packets for the entire school system—along with disrupting the existing reading program—required that district personnel first determine for themselves that the change to *Our Expert Readers* would be wise. To somewhat accommodate the saleswoman's objections, the reading instruction director suggested that the pilot study be expanded to include two first-grade and two second-grade classrooms. The saleswoman was obliged to agree.

The district's assistant superintendent of instruction concurred with the reading director's plan, and enough books and supplementary packets were ordered to equip four classes with *Our Expert Readers* materials. The week before the new school year began, the four teachers who would take part in the study met with the director of reading to plan how they would conduct the pilot study. The teachers intended to follow the teachers' manuals closely, to keep records of each child's progress, and to administer a standardized reading test at four times during the school year.

The following June, the four classroom teachers and the director of reading instruction compiled the results of the study (test scores, teachers' records of individual children's performance, and anecdotal reports of significant observations and events throughout the year) and compared those results to similar evidence from the rest of the district's first and second grades. They concluded that the pupils in the pilot study, on the average, progressed no better and no worse than pupils using the traditional text materials and methods. The gap between the best and poorest readers was much the same across classes under both the new and older reading series. Teachers reported that children's enthusiasm for reading in the pilot classes appeared to represent the same range of interest as in other classes—no more and no less. The pilot-study teachers, however, did feel that the material on the compact discs made an additional contribution to the reading program.

In summary, the expectations set by the saleswoman from Our Expert Learners were unfulfilled in practice. Consequently, district officials abandoned any intention of adopting the *Our Expert Readers* series. They did, however, announce that they would order copies of the series' compact discs for teachers who would like to use them.

Remedy options: In light of the pilot-study results, there was little that the Our Expert Learners representative could do to persuade school officials to change reading programs. The most she could hope for was that the four classes that had used *Our Expert Readers* would continue to use the series so that her company could still supply materials for at least those classes. She could also hope that the compact discs would be widely adopted by other teachers in the district and that the discs might encourage teachers to urge the purchase of at least a few copies of *Our Expert Readers* textbooks as supplementary reading books in their classes.

Time Constraints

Teachers are typically pressed for time in their attempts to help students develop a host of skills and knowledge while, in the process, giving attention to the needs of individual learners.

Proposition: The more study time that a new instructional method
   requires, the greater the resistance to adopting that method.

Problem case G: A science consultant from the state department of education convinced the principal of an elementary school that an innovative *discovery method* of teaching science should be implemented in all classrooms. As the consultant explained, the intention behind the program was to give pupils the same experience as that of scientists who seek to make sense of the physical world. Therefore, rather than describing to children events in the physical universe and explaining why those events occur as they do, the discovery method encouraged children to observe happenings and to speculate about what caused things to occur in such a fashion. According to the consultant, the method was based on the theory of children's mental development proposed by Jean Piaget, the eminent Swiss child psychologist (Piaget & Inhelder, 1969). And she explained that

> The discovery approach properly fits the stages of children's intellectual growth rather than requiring children to rote memorize concepts whose actual meanings are beyond their level of understanding. Therefore, the method ensures that children truly comprehend the scientific principles they discover rather than merely mouthing a textbook's "facts" and explanations of events in the physical world.

The version of the method designed for use in elementary schools consisted of a graded series of problem situations presented to children whose task was that of (a) describing what they saw and heard and (b) estimating what caused such an event to happen as it did. The teacher guided the children's thinking by posing questions about the objects and episodes that were the focus of a particular lesson, such as a flag waving, clouds moving, ice forming in a refrigerator, objects falling off a table, an airplane taking off from the ground, cut flowers wilting, and far more. Rather than correcting children's faulty explanations, the teacher was expected to ask leading questions that would enable children to correct their own miscalculations.

To introduce the discovery method to the school's teachers, the consultant led a one-day inservice workshop at which teachers received instructional guidebooks that included descriptions of learning activities for different grade levels (adjusted to the Piagetian stages of mental development typically found at a given grade level). The consultant also showed a videotape of teachers demonstrating the method's *guided thinking techniques* in a kindergarten, a first grade, a fourth grade, and a sixth grade.

The school principal agreed to give the discovery method a one-semester trial, after which he would collect teachers' reports of their experiences with the approach. Reports would be in the form of a written evaluation by each teacher and of an open discussion during a faculty meeting.

Following the one-semester trial, the principal summarized the results of the evaluation in the following manner.

> Teachers generally agreed that the discovery method was a good idea, for it led children to think creatively and critically. And they agreed that the

guided-thinking technique was valuable. (Many teachers already used such an approach in various curriculum areas—language arts, social studies, personal-social relations, health, the arts, and physical education, as well as physical science.)

However, all of the teachers objected to basing the entire science program on the discovery method. Their chief objection was that the time consumed by the method in order to derive a single useful generalization about scientific phenomena was excessive. Children's attempted explanations of a phenomenon were often quite diverse, thereby requiring a class to analyze each proffered explanation by means of the teacher posing additional guide questions that could reveal whether faulty observation or illogical interpretation had led to a pupil's conclusion. Therefore, from the one-semester tryout of the discovery approach, teachers concluded that using discovery as the sole method of teaching science yielded too little knowledge and skill for the time the method consumed.

Furthermore, providing a scientifically accurate explanation of a phenomenon solely on the basis of children's own observations (such as why an extremely heavy metal airplane can fly through the air) was well beyond the children's ability. It was not uncommon for a persuasive pupil to convince classmates of the validity of a rationale for an observed event, even though that pupil's estimate of cause ("gases inside the plane floated the plane into the sky" or "invisible spirits caused it to go up") would be rejected in the scientific community.

A third objection was that most phenomena in the physical world cannot be observed directly by pupils. Therefore, if the whole science program centered on personal discovery, pupils would be deprived access to a great quantity of valuable scientific knowledge. Children are not able to directly observe orangutans living in a Sumatran jungle, penicillin killing germs in a sick child's body, or the path taken by the planet Jupiter as it circles around the sun.

In conclusion, all of our teachers tried out the discovery method as described in the state education department's literature, but none used the method as the exclusive approach to teaching science. The method was more widely practiced in the lower grades than in the upper grades whose pupils had greater ability to read descriptions of scientific events and to understand more complex scientific explanations than could younger pupils. Far more time was spent in the upper grades in studying science by means of textbooks and illustrated lectures than in discovery activities.

As a result of the principal's evaluation, the discovery method was abandoned as the exclusive—or even the dominant— method of teaching science, particularly in the upper elementary grades.

Remedy option: The most obvious solution to the inertia that the discovery approach encountered was to let each teacher incorporate the approach into his or her own repertoire of science teaching techniques in whatever way that each felt was most appropriate. This solution had already spontaneously been adopted during the one-semester tryout period. As the semester had advanced, the discovery technique had been increasingly less used, especially in the upper grades where teachers judged that quantity of science skills and knowledge students gained did not merit the amount of time the approach required.

Conclusion

The six vantage points from which reforms of teaching methods have been viewed in this chapter have been those of teachers' preparation, learners' preparation, method complexity, equipment/supplies availability, reasonable expectations, and time constraints. Other perspectives useful for analyzing the inertia that innovative methods encounter include:

- *Cost.* How expensive, in terms of money, is the new method compared with the practice it is to replace? If the cost of the reform is greater, are the benefits of the change worth the extra expense?
- *Conflict with tradition.* To what extent does the proposed innovation conflict with traditional teaching methods or materials that teachers, students, or parents value highly and believe should not be replaced?
- *Threat to self-confidence.* To what extent will a proposed new method threaten students' sense of worth either by exposing them to ridicule from classmates or by reducing their confidence in their ability to succeed with the class's learning tasks?

Discussion Topics

Whenever a teacher intends to introduce a learning activity that students find unfamiliar, it is useful for the teacher to foresee problems that might arise and thereby plan ways to prevent or minimize the inertia that the problems generate. For each of the following situations, identify difficulties the teacher might face when implementing the described learning activity and suggest methods of coping with each potential difficulty.

1. A third-grade class plans to paint a mural—4 feet tall, 9 feet wide—depicting the history of the founding of the town in which their school is located.
2. The teacher of a high school health education class intends to invite three former drug addicts to tell the class about their experiences. The teacher hopes this event will deter class members from using illicit drugs.

3. In a seventh-grade general science class, the teacher wants to take her 27 students on a field trip to a stone quarry where a geologist will explain the history of the layers of rock that have been exposed by the quarrying operation—layers representing successive eras in the life of the earth at that location.

4. A high school art teacher wishes to give students experience in sketching the human figure by having class members take turns serving as models that assume different poses.

5. To introduce fifth-graders to the writing of formal reports whose content is derived from published sources (books, magazines, journals, Internet websites), a teacher directs each pupil to select a topic to investigate. Each report is to include a title page, an opening summary, the body of the report, and a list of references used.

5

Evaluation Techniques

In the teaching/learning process, the aim of evaluation is to determine how well the students have mastered the learning objectives. This chapter focuses on six factors which can influence the inertia that confronts a newly introduced evaluation technique. The first four are functions that evaluation procedures can perform. The last two are characteristics of evaluation techniques that can influence the strength of inertia.

Evaluation Techniques

- Assessment function
- Diagnostic function
- Predictive function
- Motivational function
- Objectives suitability
- Learner suitability

Assessment Function

An evaluation technique is performing an assessment function when it answers the question: How well have the students mastered the learning objectives? Or, how closely have the learners come to the goal?

Proposition: The less accurately a newly introduced evaluation technique assesses students' progress, and the less informative the technique is for the people most concerned with the student's performance, the greater the inertia that technique will face.

Problem case A: The traditional device a junior high school used to inform students and their parents of the students' progress was a report card that listed each class in which a student was enrolled, along with a letter grade intended to reflect the quality of the student's work in that class. The letter grades ranged from *A* (superior) though *B* (good), *C* (average, acceptable), and *D* (below average, barely passing), to *F* (failing). The letter grades were supposed to show how closely students came to the standards the teacher set for the class. The teachers often used a percent-of-perfect as the measure of which letter a student's performance warranted. For example, getting between 90% and 100% of the items correct on a test earned a grade of *A*, between 80% and 89% a *B*, between 70% and 79% a *C*, from 60% to 69% a *D*, and anything lower an *F*. At the close of the semester, averaging the daily grades on tests, essays, student projects, and the like produced a final semester grade, with some assignments weighted more heavily than others.

The school's faculty members were obliged to consider the desirability of their traditional system when they attended an inservice workshop titled "Individualizing Instruction." Among the principles of individualized instruction that the workshop leader emphasized was that of adjusting reports of students' progress to the ability levels of the different students. This could be accomplished, the leader said, by reporting how well each student performed compared to that individual's own potential rather than compared to other class members' performance. Thus, students of limited ability, who worked hard and thus advanced as well as could reasonably be expected, deserved high commendation for their progress. In contrast, students of remarkable talent who "got by" with little or no effort, and thereby fell far short of their potential, did not deserve commendation, even though their test scores and essays were superior to those of their diligent classmates of lesser ability.

Following the workshop, the school principal appointed a committee of four teachers to consider revising the school's report card, with particular attention to suiting the reporting scheme to learner's abilities. In their deliberations, the committee members considered two alternatives—a written description and a report card employing symbols intended to reflect how well students worked up to their ability levels. The written description would enable teachers to explain a student's performance in the different types of class assignments in comparison to the student's apparent background of skills and knowledge. But if, instead of a written description, a report card was adopted with new symbols rather than the traditional letter grades (*A* through *F*), those symbols would compare each student's achievement to that individual's apparent potential.   To render the new symbols understandable to students and parents, the symbols would be defined as follows on the report card.

U = Student is working well up to potential ability level
N = Student is nearly up to ability level, but could do better
M = Student needs much improvement to reach potential ability level
F = Student's work is far below ability level, very unsatisfactory

The committee finally decided to recommend a combination of the two alternatives—a report card using the new symbols for each class in which a student was enrolled and a brief a written description from each of the student's teachers that appraised the student's work habits, class participation, strengths, and areas that needed improvement. The school principal approved the plan, and new report cards were printed for the upcoming semester. To help teachers adapt to the new scheme, the committee prepared a guide sheet that illustrated how individualized descriptions of student performance could be written.

When the new reporting scheme was first put into effect, a printed explanation of the system—its form and its purpose—was given to students and sent to their parents. This initial tryout drew immediate reactions from teachers, students, and parents alike. Some of the response from teachers and parents was favorable, but by far the largest amount was harsh. Teachers had several sorts of complaints. They had trouble with the symbol system, because they often felt unsure about the level of a student's "true ability" or "learning potential." In addition, they resented the time it required to write a description for each student. Some said they solved the problem of individualizing the descriptions by simply using a few stock phrases over and over with different students, such as "Jason is a cooperative class member" or "Chelsea is well liked" or "Leslie needs to be more consistent" or "Michael should be more attentive in class." Consequently, the descriptions of many students were much alike—not truly individualized.

Many students—particularly the high achievers—were upset by not receiving grades that showed how they compared either with the teacher's standards (*A, B, C,* etc.; or percents of test items correct) or with their classmates (percentile ranks). Many parents wanted those same kinds of comparisons. As one father complained, "Out in the real world, you get judged about how well you do compared to other people, and this new report card doesn't do that at all."

In view of the large amount of negative reaction to the new reporting system, the school principal recognized that his attempted reform faced heavy resistance.

Remedy options. The following are four potential measures the school might adopt to reduce the inertia the reporting plan faced.

Abandon the innovation. Perhaps the most obvious solution would be for the school to return to the traditional report card, which used familiar letters to show how closely students had approached the teachers' standards in the various subject matter areas. However, reverting to the old scheme failed to care for the principal's concern about the report card's not indicating differences among students in their ability to master the learning objectives.

Explain the plan more fully. The principal could send students and their parents a more detailed explanation of the logic behind the new system, hoping that they would accept the line of reasoning that had led to comparing each student against his or her own past record and apparent level of talent.

Alter the plan. The school might retain the new system but add another section similar to the traditional report card so that parents would have two sorts of assessment of their offspring's achievement—the teenager's performance compared with both (a) his or her apparent ability level and (b) the teacher's standards that are the same for all class members.

Provide supplementary information. The new scheme could remain intact. Then, if parents wanted to know how their daughter's or son's record compared with either the teacher's standards (*A, B, C,* etc.) or with the remainder of the class members (the teenager's rank), the parents could request that information, and it would be furnished by the teacher.

Diagnostic Function

Evaluation serves a diagnostic purpose whenever the assessment technique being used identifies (a) how well the student has mastered each specific skill and type of knowledge included among the learning objectives and (b) the precise nature of the skill and knowledge errors that need to be corrected if true mastery is to be achieved.

Proposition: The less accurately a new evaluation technique identifies the details of a student's inadequate performance, the greater the inertia the technique will encounter.

Problem case B: The supervisor of language arts instruction for a city school district wished to help teachers improve the quality of students' written English. Many of the students came from immigrant families who spoke a language other than English in their homes so that such students usually lacked accurate models of the standard English taught at school. As a result, flaws frequently appeared in students' oral and written English. The supervisor recognized that if teachers were to attack this problem of faulty usage, they could profit from adopting a method of assessment that would reveal the kinds and frequency of usage errors students committed. On the basis of the collected information, instructional strategies could be devised for helping learners correct their mistakes in an efficient manner.

The evaluation device the supervisor chose for identifying usage errors was a *Written English Diagnostic System* advertised in a test publisher's catalog. The system consisted of a four-panel cartoon depicting a series of events in the daily life of a boy and girl. Each student in a class would be provided a copy of the cartoon and asked to compose a letter to a friend, describing what was happening in the sequence of pictured events. Each student's letter would subsequently be analyzed to reveal the number and kinds of errors committed. The way that letters were to be analyzed was described in the diagnostic system's *Evaluation Guidebook*. The teacher—or a teacher's aide—who analyzed the students' compositions was to record the number of errors in each of seven diagnostic categories:

1. Style—how completely the events in the cartoon strip were described
2. Sentence structure—how accurately sentences were composed
3. Grammar—the accuracy of verbs, nouns, pronouns, adjectives, adverbs, prepositions, and conjunctions
4. Vocabulary—the aptness and precision of word usage
5. Punctuation—proper punctuation
6. Capitalization—to begin sentences and to indicate proper nouns
7. Handwriting—the legibility of the writing

To test the effectiveness of the *Written English Diagnostic System* before it would be adopted throughout the school district, the supervisor asked five teachers to try it out with their classes at grades 3, 5, 7, 9, and 11. The tryout produced mixed results. The four-panel cartoon proved to be a successful way to elicit samples of students' writing skills, since the same cartoon strip could be used at all grade levels, thereby providing the basis for comparing writing skills across grades. However, the diagnostic feature of the system was a disappointment, for it showed the number of errors committed in each diagnostic category but failed to show precisely what sorts of errors were being made. Learning that a student committed seven sentence-structure errors furnished a teacher no information about what sorts of errors needed correction. In effect, the ostensible diagnostic feature of the system was not sufficiently diagnostic. The teachers decided that the system, at least in its present form, was not worth the bother. The system (a) failed to provide the information teachers needed for deciding how best to improve students' writing skills, and (b) required considerable time for analyzing a given student's essay in detail.

Remedy options: The following two remedies could be adopted in an effort to correct the system's main shortcomings.

Providing detailed diagnosis. The language arts supervisor could set up a research-and-development project that involved the detailed analysis of the letters students wrote during the tryout at the five grade levels. Two or three analysts who had an excellent command of English usage would inspect the students' letters to identify the types of errors committed under each of the seven categories in the *Written English Diagnostic System.* The errors would be listed according to their frequency. Carrying out this activity would result in seven error lists organized as a *record form.* Furthermore, a *Diagnostic Guide* would be prepared, explaining the nature of each type of error and offering samples of each error from the students' papers. Here are examples of two diagnostic categories—sentence structure and grammar—that could be derived from the analysis and then listed on the *record form* (Thomas, 1976, pp. 32-33).

2. Sentences
  2.1 Subject missing
  2.2 Verb missing or incomplete
  2.3 Comma splice
  2.4 Begins with *and, but, then*
  2.5 Strung together with *and* or *then*
  2.6 Sentence meaning unclear
  2.7 Sentence-ending punctuation error or missing

3. Grammar
  3.1 Verb-noun agreement error
  3.2 Verb-tense shift
  3.3 Other verb errors
  3.4 Pronoun errors
  3.5 Distant pronoun referent
  3.6 Preposition missing

The other five major categories would be completed in a similar manner, featuring the sorts of errors found in the tryout letters.

The following are illustrative items that could form the *Diagnostic Guide*'s definitions of error types and examples of errors (Thomas, 1976, pp. 36-37).

  2.2 Comma splice. A *comma splice* or *comma fault* is a type of run-on sentence. A comma is used instead of a period, semicolon, or comma-plus-conjunction (*and* or *but*). Examples: "The girl fished, she caught a big one." "The horse kicked the bucket, the bucket landed on the boy's head."

  2.4 Strung together with *and* or *then*. Similar to the problem of the comma splice, the conjunction *and* is often used to string many sentences (inde-

pendent clauses) together. If only two independent clauses are connected with *and*, the construction is correct and should not be counted
as an error unless the two clauses are rather different in nature and thus
fail to join two closely connected ideas. However, it is an error when
(a) *and* connects more than two independent clauses or (b) *and* connects
two independent clauses which sound awkward when so connected
(and which would sound better if they were punctuated as separate
sentences).

Example: Correct use of *and*—"The boy jerked the fish, and it hit the
coconuts."

Example: Incorrect used of *and*—"The girl is fishing and the horse is
eating and the girl pulls out a big fish and the fish hits the coconuts and
the coconuts fall on the horse."

"The girl caught a fish, and the tree was behind her."

The *Record Form* and *Diagnostic Guide* might improve English-writing
instruction in two ways. First, the supervisor's research project, in which
students' errors at the five grade levels were compiled, would reveal
which types of errors were most common. Teachers could then prepare
lessons aimed at correcting those frequent errors and teach those lessons
to their entire class, because many students could profit from the experience. However, it would not be an economical use of time to teach an
entire class how to correct mistakes that are not committed by most students.

Second, a sample piece of writing—essay, letter, report—for each student could be analyzed by use of the *Diagnostic Guide* and the result
summarized on a *record form* for that particular student. The summary
would provide an "error profile" for that individual, indicating which
sorts of errors she or he should learn to correct. Then individualized
learning activities (worksheets, oral explanations) designed to remedy
those errors could be offered that student.

Providing diagnostic aid. Much of the inertia that would be encountered
by the *Record Form* approach to the diagnosis problem results from the
time required for a teacher to produce an error profile for each student.
The time burden is particularly heavy in junior and senior high schools
where one teacher may have 130 to 180 students during a semester. One
solution for this problem is to enlist the help of a teacher's aide or of a
knowledgeable high school student to prepare the record forms. The
classroom teacher, thus relieved of the task of analyzing each student's
writing sample, could (a) teach the entire class lessons focusing on frequently committed errors, and (b) recommend individual activities for
students whose errors are unusual.

Predictive Function

A variety of evaluation techniques have been used to predict how people will perform an activity in the future, such as how well high school students will fare in college and how well a job applicant will do the job if hired. Typical devices have been intelligence tests, more specific aptitude tests, achievement tests, testimonials from an applicant's acquaintances (former teachers or employers), autobiographical sketches, and interviews.

Proposition: The less accurately a new evaluation technique predicts students' future performance, the more resistance there will be to retaining that technique.

Problem case C: A faculty committee of a university's College of Creative Studies wished to improve its method of deciding which high school students to admit to the college's programs. In the past, the main criteria used for choosing applicants who would prove to be truly creative included (a) the overall grade point average from the high school record, (b) scores on the Scholastic Aptitude Test, and (c) letters of recommendation from applicants' high school teachers. Following the suggestion of an educational psychologist whom the committee consulted, the college substituted J. P. Guilford's series of creativity tests for the traditional Scholastic Aptitude Test (Guilford, 1967; Guilford & Hoepfner, 1971). The Guilford battery consisted of seven tests designed to measure students' *word fluency* (speed in producing word structures), *ideational fluency* (speed in producing many ideas that fit particular specifications), *associational fluency* (speed in creating alternatives for a given word), *expressional fluency* (speed in writing four-word sentences using words that begin with the letters given in the test), *adaptive flexibility* (speed in producing revised versions of graphic figures), *related personality factors* (students' expressed opinions that ostensibly would reveal such motivational factors as self-reliance and needs for attention, for freedom, for adventure, for diversion, and for precision).

To gain an initial impression of how well the creativity tests might identify applicants who would do well in the College of Creative Studies, the committee administered the tests to a sample of the college's current students as well as to a sample of students in university departments that did not stress creativity. The results showed in that the College's creativity specializations that depended heavily on verbal skills (programs focusing on literature and drama), students' test scores correlated fairly well with the quality of their actual productivity. However, in other specializations (music, graphic arts, dance) the tests did not distinguish well between the more inventive students (in terms of their performance in their specializations) and the less inventive. Therefore, the committee decided that the time, expense, and logistics required for administering the creativity tests to all high school applicants was not worth the information the tests provided. Thus, the creativity tests were dropped from the admissions program.

Remedy options: The committee's effort to improve predictions of student success might include the following pair of alternatives.

Partial testing. The Guilford battery might be retained for students who, when applying for admission, already know that they wish to specialize in one of the major fields in which verbal skills are prominent, such as literature or drama. However, students who intended to major in a markedly different field (graphic arts, dance, musical performance or composition) would be exempt from the creativity tests.

Samples of creative products. Perhaps the most often used measure of an individual's potential for success in a particular endeavor is the record of that person's performance in that same type of endeavor in the past. The high school student who did well in algebra and geometry in the past is likely to do well in calculus and trigonometry in the future. The student who had composed original music and performed it skillfully in the past is apt to do so in the future. The student who had acted convincingly in high school plays would probably do so in the university. Therefore, the college could require that applicants include samples of their creative products when they apply for admission—an audio-recording of songs, a video-recording of a scene in a play, a photo of a charcoal drawing or oil painting.

Motivational Function

The prospect of being evaluated is generally considered by teachers and students alike as having great motivational value. So, the closer students are to testing time, the harder they usually study.

> *Proposition:* The less that a new evaluation technique stimulates learners to study diligently, the more likely that technique will be abandoned as a motivational device.

Problem case D: For many years, the academic performance of seniors in a city high school fit a disappointing nationwide pattern. Students across the country traditionally worked harder at their studies during their sophomore and junior years than they did during their senior year. In an effort to combat the "senior-slump" phenomenon, the school principal suggested that the faculty adopt a "more serious testing program throughout the senior year, and particularly in the late spring. That should make clear to students that their senior year is not just playtime."

In keeping with this plan, throughout the next school year the faculty increased the frequency of tests for seniors, but by the end of the year it was apparent that the attempt had achieved little success. Even those seniors, who in their earlier high school years had always performed well, tended to slack off during their final year, despite the heightened testing. Consequently, the principal was obliged to admit that his proposal had failed to overcome senior year inertia.

Remedy options: To understand likely causes of the problem and to identify potential solutions, the faculty could turn to a study conducted in six states by Michael Kirst (2001). According to Kirst's analysis, the problem of seniors not addressing themselves to their studies seriously enough was increasingly affecting students' transition to college as the percentage of high school graduates going on to higher education grew from 50% in 1981 to 70% in 2001 (Alexander, 2001).

In Kirst's view, a main cause of the senior slump is a lack of proper coordination between secondary and tertiary educational institutions. High school students typically apply for college admission early in their senior year or during the previous summer. Therefore, the high school records on which colleges base their admission decisions contain no information about applicants' academic performance as seniors. Students are well aware of this and, as Kirst (2001) suggests, "view their final months prior to graduation as an opportunity to take less demanding courses and enjoy nonacademic pursuits."

> "The senior year has been left to high schools, but higher education bears responsibility," Kirst says. "Higher education must get much more involved in the transition points and the preparation."
>
> Colleges ought to cooperate with high schools, Kirst argues, to create policies on grade-point averages and class rankings that take senior-year performance into account in admissions, and they should be much more stringent about the grades seniors receive—even to the point of withdrawing admissions offers [if senior-year grades decline]. They should provide students with information about placement tests, and what preparation they need for them.
>
> High schools, too, need to rethink senior courses as a "gateway" to fulfilling college requirements, Kirst says. They should give all seniors the option of taking college-level courses and should make students aware of the importance of college placement exams. (Alexander, 2001)

Therefore, if Kirst's analysis is correct, it will take more than the efforts of one high school faculty to cure senior slump. There are, however, several steps they might adopt in addition to heightened testing. One would be to increase the amount of counseling students receive about what will be expected of them in higher education institutions, so that students are not unpleasantly surprised when they are assigned to remedial courses when they enter college. According to Kirst, some colleges place as many as 70% of entering freshmen in remedial classes (Alexander, 2001).

A second step could be to inform students that the high school intends to send a student's senior year, first semester grade report to the college or university to which the student has applied. Another step would be to restrict the number of "soft" courses that a student could take as a senior. However, both of these steps would generate awkward administrative problems so that the potential benefit might not seem worth the trouble.

Objectives Suitability

The term *objectives suitability* refers to how adequately an assessment technique reveals how well students have mastered what they have been taught.

Proposition: The less accurately a new evaluation technique assesses the objectives that it is intended to appraise, the greater the inertia the technique will face.

Problem case E: A small city school district was obligated to administer a state legislature-mandated battery of standardized achievement tests in grades 4, 7, 9, and 12. The battery included multiple-choice tests in the fields of reading, English language usage (grammar, syntax, punctuation, spelling), mathematics, social studies, and science. When the test results were compiled for the entire state, the success of students in different school districts were disseminated via newspapers, radio, and television. The published statistics showed that students in the city's public schools had scored above average in reading, language usage, and mathematics but had fallen somewhat below average in social studies and science. This announcement was followed by newspaper editorials and television interviews with prominent citizens demanding a "shake up" in the schools' social studies and science programs so that the glaring shortcomings of the present programs in those areas would be corrected.

In response to these charges that the schools were failing to provide satisfactory social studies and science instruction, the district superintendent claimed that the schools were doing a good job in both fields. The problem, he explained, was that the learning objectives the test makers had in mind when they created the social studies and science test items were in many cases different from those on which the district's social studies and science instruction focused. In other words, the tests were designed to measure skills and knowledge that the city's students had not been taught. At the same time, the tests neglected to assess students' command of skills and knowledge that were important elements of the local district's curricula, such as computer, art, and music skills. In accounting for the district's above-average results in some subjects (reading, language usage, math) but below-average results in others (social studies, science), the superintendent explained that

> There is far more agreement across the nation about what constitutes reading and language skill—and to a lesser extent, what math knowledge is most useful—than there is about what social studies and science knowledge is best taught at different grade levels. Social studies and science comprise vast domains of knowledge that are increasing daily at a rapid pace. Thus, there is much room for controversy about which parts of these domains are most important for pupils to study at different age levels. We are convinced that our choice of what to teach from these domains is a good choice. But the people who created the tests decided to measure different skills and knowledge than those we teach. That's why our test scores were below average. Because those social studies and science tests failed to measure what our students had learned, the tests were at fault, not our teachers and students. Therefore, we accept our test scores in reading, language, and math as fair reflections of our students' achievement in those areas. But the scores in social studies and science do not validly reflect our students' accomplishments in those fields.

Thus, according to the superintendent's analysis, the tests in reading, language usage, and mathematics were properly suited to the schools' learning objectives. However, the tests in social studies and science were not. Consequently, the superintendent refused to accept the social studies and science tests as appropriate instruments for judging students' achievement, for appraising the quality of instruction, or for assessing the adequacy of the curriculum's contents.

Remedy options: The following are three ways the school district might respond to the low test-scores problem.

Eliminate the social studies and science tests. In the future, the district could agree to participate in the reading, language usage, and mathematics portions of the state testing program but refuse to administer the social studies and science tests on the grounds that they lacked content validity. The term *content validity* refers to the extent to which the test items measure what students have had an opportunity to learn. However, such a refusal might invite sanctions imposed on the district by the state department of education.

Rescore the social studies and science tests. An item analysis could be conducted of the social studies and science tests to determine which, and how many, test items focused on the district's curriculum content at the grade level for which each test was intended. Then the students' test papers could be rescored for only those items considered appropriate to the district's learning objectives. (If the students' tests had originally been scored by means of a computer program, the rescoring task could easily be accomplished with a slightly revised program.) This would enable the district to report the outcomes in the form of the average percent of correct answers in social studies and in science for the district's students. Although those results could not be meaningfully compared with the test performance of students in other districts, the results would show the extent to which students within the district had mastered material they had been taught. These new results could then be disseminated to the public through the mass media and sent to the state education department.

Teach for the tests. The district could capitulate in its confrontation with state officials by abandoning the existing curriculum and developing new objectives and content for social studies and science as based entirely on the items in the state tests. In effect, the test items would become the focus of instruction. Teachers could collect copies of past years' tests and teach students how to answer the questions. However, there would be several objections to such a solution.

First, teaching the tests' contents assumes that the people who created the test items had made a wise choice of the sorts of social studies and science skills and knowledge most appropriate for children throughout the state at the different grade levels. Such an assumption would be difficult to support, given (a) the complex and extensive body of knowledge in both the social studies and science from which a curriculum can be composed, and (b) local conditions that might warrant different sorts of knowledge being more important for people living in some regions than for those living in others.

Second, students would not have a chance to study new discoveries (events, facts, theories) in the social and scientific worlds, because those discoveries were not in earlier tests.

Third, teachers would be discouraged from creating novel objectives, content, and instructional methods that could enhance students' learning.

Learner Suitability

A method of evaluation is considered appropriate for assessing a student's achievement whenever the student commands the skills and knowledge necessary to use that method satisfactorily. Therefore, from the viewpoint of learner suitability, it would be unreasonable (a) to expect a group of five-year-olds to answer printed true-false questions about how to take care of animals, or (b) to expect pairs of students during the early weeks of a beginning Spanish class to carry on extended dialogues with each other.

Proposition: The less adequately the demands of a new evaluation technique match the abilities of the learners to succeed with the technique, the greater the resistance the new technique will encounter.

Problem case F: The textbook for a high school auto-repair class was accompanied by a teacher's manual that included lesson plans and suggested methods for evaluating students' skills at diagnosing and correcting auto repair problems. One proposed evaluation technique was in the form of an essay-test item that (a) described a motorist's description of her car's malfunction and (b) required the auto-repair student to write the steps he or she would take in diagnosing the car's problem. When the instructor of the high school class used this type of item to learn how well the students understood the textbook chapter on auto fuel systems, he was surprised to see that three of his most diligent students had written very inadequate answers. Because each of them spoke English with a slight Spanish accent, the instructor suspected that all three came from homes in which Spanish was the dominant language. When he questioned the students, this suspicion was confirmed. The students' families had immigrated from Central America in recent years. Therefore, the boys' experience writing coherent narratives in English was very limited. As a result, the instructor concluded that an essay test was an unsuitable device for revealing how well the three students could diagnose fuel-system problems.

Remedy options: Here are three alternative approaches the instructor might substitute for the essay question in his effort to discover how well the students grasped the content of the textbook's fuel-systems chapter.

Multiple-choice test. The problem of diagnosing what was wrong with the motorist's car could be recast as a series of multiple-choice questions. The series could begin with the same description of the motorist's complaints that had been in the original essay question. Then a sequence of multiple-choice items could lead the student through a series of diagnostic steps, with the student required to choose which of the listed answers at each step represented the best decision at that point. The initial test item could ask the student which of five possible actions—five options—he would take first. Subsequent items could pose five options for decisions at other junctures of the diagnostic process. Those items could assume an "if-then" form, such as, "If you cleaned out the fuel line and the car still wouldn't start, what would you try next?" The five choices under that question would include one that would be the wisest thing to do at that point.

In summary, recasting the essay test as a multiple-choice or matching test would eliminate the need for a student to write a fluent narrative. It would, however, require that students be able to read English adequately. But if the teacher had doubts about their reading skills, he could read aloud each test item and its choices as the class members worked their way through the test.

Individual oral exam. In the case of a student whose reading or writing skills were inadequate, the essay test could be administered orally by the instructor or perhaps by a teacher's aide or by another class member who had already passed the test. In effect, the student who was being tested would listen to the customer's complaints about the car, then describe the steps he would plan to follow for diagnosing the problem.

Lifelike simulation. The evaluation method most closely resembling real-life conditions would consist of a lifelike simulation in which the instructor disabled an element in the fuel system of a car without the student knowing which element has been rendered inoperative. The instructor would then play the role of a distressed motorist who described to the student how the car malfunctioned. The student would then be expected to diagnose the problem by directly working on the car, then telling what needed to be done to fix it.

This lifelike simulation would remove the requirement that the student be able to read a customer's complaint and to write an essay describing how the auto's problem should be diagnosed. However, such an approach to evaluation takes far more time than a written test, especially if the technique is to be used with every student in the class.

Conclusion

Four assessment functions and two suitability factors have been the focus of attention in this chapter. The four functions are those of assessment, diagnosis, prediction, and motivation. The two factors concern how well a new evaluation technique suits both the learning objectives and the students' ability to cope with the technique. Other aspects of evaluation techniques that can influence the resistance a new evaluation procedure may suffer include:

- *Expense.* How costly—in terms of money, time, and effort—is the new evaluation technique compared with the practice it is to replace? If the cost of the reform is greater, are the benefits of the change worth the extra expense?
- *Emotional distress.* Compared with traditional evaluation practices, how much emotional distress might the new assessment method cause for students? Would that level of distress be worth the advantages the innovation offers?
- *Difficulty of use.* How difficult is it to administer the new technique? For example, how easily can a test be given and scored, and its out-

comes interpreted and reported? How much trouble do interviews involve? How readily can observations of a student's performance be recorded on a rating scale, as written notes, or on videotape?

Discussion Topics

From the viewpoint of accurate evaluation, a useful way to state a learning objective is in the form of the observable behavior students will exhibit when they have achieved that objective. The following three examples provide an opportunity for you to compare evaluation techniques in terms of (a) their advantages and disadvantages and (b) the amount of inertia they are likely to engender when first introduced to students. For each example, the nature of the classroom of learners is first described. Then the objective the students are pursuing is stated in terms of desired student behavior. Finally, two evaluation procedures are identified. As you inspect an example, your task is (a) to identify advantages and disadvantages of each of the two evaluation procedures for assessing the pursuit of the objective by that group of learners, and (b) to estimate which of the two techniques would face the greater inertia—that is, face more resistance or greater obstacles to its continued use as an efficient way to assess students' achievement.

- Example A:

  The class—Consists of 35 second-graders in a small, rural town where seasonal agricultural laborers move in and out during the school year.

  The learning objective—As a result of a three-week social studies unit titled "Workers in Our Community," the pupils (a) describe ten types of workers in the region, (b) tell what the workers do in their jobs, and (c) explain what contribution those workers make to community life.

  Two evaluation-technique options—

  (1) A class discussion in which the teacher asks different pupils to name a type of worker in the community, to tell what activities the worker's job involves, and to tell how that worker helps the community.

  (2) A printed test containing 30 true-false items focusing on types of jobs, the nature of different workers' jobs, and the contributions those workers make to the community.

- Example B:

  The class—Consists of 28 seventh-graders in an English language and literature class in a large inner-city junior high school that does not practice ability grouping. Therefore, students in the class represent a wide range of talent, of motivation, and of experience in reading, writing, and speaking English.

The learning objective—After reading O. Henry's short story *The Ransom of Red Chief*, students accurately describe (a) the sequential phases of the plot, (b) the surprise that awaits the would-be kidnappers, and (c) and how the author makes the story humorous.

Two evaluation-technique options—

(1) Each student writes a description of (a) the story's plot, (b) the surprise, and (c) how the author made the story humorous.

(2) A test consisting of 20 multiple-choice items (5 choices under each item) about the story's plot, the surprise, and the author's writing style.

- Example C:

The class—Consists of 37 eleventh-graders in a upper-middle-class suburban high-school's biology course.

The learning objective. After reading Chapter 9 in their textbooks and witnessing the teacher's illustrated lecture on DNA (deoxyribonucleic acid), the students (a) draw a diagram of the double helix structure of the DNA molecule, (b) label the components of the molecule, and (c) explain the importance of DNA for human development.

Two evaluation-technique options—

(1) As a homework assignment, each student prepares a poster display that (a) portrays the structure of a DNA molecule and (b) illustrates three practical uses of DNA discoveries in modern life.

(2) As a homework assignment, each student records on audiotape a lecture in which the student explains how the DNA double-helix form was discovered and what function DNA performs in human development.

Part III

The Internal Support System

The teaching and learning process, as found in modern-day schooling, is most efficient when supported by a variety of agencies and individuals inside the education system. The three interrelated types of support that are the focus of attention in Part III are those of policy-making, management, and services. *Policy-making* is the process of formulating the purposes and operating rules of the education system. *Management* is the process of organizing, coordinating, and controlling the activities of the system's units. *Services* are activities designed to enhance teaching and learning—such activities as inservice teacher training, the delivery of instructional supplies, and the maintenance of instructional equipment.

6

Policy-Making

The term *educational policies*, as used throughout this book, refers to statements of educational goals and of approved ways of pursuing those goals. To illustrate, here are three policy statements that range from the very general to the very specific.

- The purpose of basic education is to prepare the young as responsible, loyal citizens and as efficient, constructive workers who enjoy excellent physical and mental health.
- English will be the required language of instruction at all levels of the school system.
- Students are not to chew gum in class.

When judging the worth of an educational policy, I find it useful to test the policy against five criteria. Thus, a policy is judged desirable to the extent that it (a) is socially acceptable, (b) is an improvement over previous policies that bear on the same aspect of education, (c) does not generate undesirable side effects, (d) is well suited to the people to whom it applies, and (d) is readily translated into practice.

The expression *social acceptability* refers to how much the people who are affected by a policy approve of that policy. For example, a policy that specifies the kinds of punishment that students will suffer for misbehavior in school affects parents, students, and the school staff. A policy governing the property tax that provides funds for schools directly affects property owners. If a policy is not socially acceptable, it probably cannot be implemented satisfactorily.

Policies that fail to improve educational conditions, or that result in harmful side effects, are likely to be abandoned. Likewise, constant trouble can be expected if policies fail to fit the abilities and motivations of the people to whom those policies apply. For instance, a regulation

105

requiring kindergarten children to remain silent and stationary for long periods of time will be very difficult—if not impossible—to enforce.

Finally, policies that cannot readily be put into practice will remain mere verbiage—empty words exerting no influence on the conduct of education.

In summary, policies are guides to action. And the dual assignment of most personnel in the education system is to devise methods for reaching the goals and to put those methods into practice. The three aspects of policy-making on which this chapter focuses are preparation, consistency, and implementation.

> **Policy-Making**
>
> - Preparation
> - Consistency
> - Implementation

Preparation

The preparation aspect of policy-making is concerned with how adequately people are equipped to take part in setting educational policies. Answering the question "What sorts of participants produce the most effective policies?" can involve a variety of considerations. I would suggest that, if a policy is to be successfully transformed into practice, then policy-makers should have accurate knowledge about

- The intended mission or role of the particular educational institution in which the policy is applied (a public school, a private school, a preschool, a college, a nonformal training program, or the like)
- The present policy that the new policy replaces, including knowledge of what is unsatisfactory about present conditions
- The social acceptability of the proposed policy
- How the policy can be implemented

Accepting these four sorts of knowledge as important in policy formation can lead to the following proposition.

Proposition: The less accurate the knowledge that policy-makers have about their institution's intended mission, about the inadequacies of present policy, about the social-acceptability of a newly proposed policy, and about how that policy can be implemented, the greater the resistance their policy will face.

In some cases, one person will be well informed about all four of these matters. But in other instances, such knowledge will be held by different individuals. In those cases, a policy statement can profit from the participation of two or more individuals, each of whom has trustworthy knowledge about only one or two of the matters that can affect the policy.

Problem case A: In a small North American city, members of several church groups and social welfare agencies formed a committee to urge public school officials to insert into the elementary school curriculum a special class period dedicated to moral and citizenship education. The committee's expressed intent was to convince policy-makers that such a curriculum provision would help curb the rise in crime and drug use among the community's school-age children. In support of their recommendation, committee members cited a variety of nations whose schools included such a class period several days a week. Prior to meeting with the school board and school administrators, the committee publicized its campaign via church notices, newspaper articles, and radio interviews.

The school board and top-level administrators responded favorably to the moral education committee's proposal and drafted a policy statement that required the teaching of morals and citizenship three periods each week in all elementary schools, grades 1 through 6. To implement the policy, the school district's curriculum-planning office issued a set of aims and suggested topics to be studied at each grade level. The program was scheduled to take effect with the opening of the fall semester.

Early in the semester, a host of complaints from elementary school principals alerted central-office personnel to problems teachers experienced in their attempt to implement the moral education policy. First, many reported that they already had been teaching morality and ethical behavior in their social studies, social living, and literature programs. Thus, setting aside three periods a week seemed redundant. Second, numbers of teachers felt that the topics suggested for each grade in the central curriculum-office's directive were not the most important topics for the age levels of the children in those grades. Other teachers pointed out that every time something was added to the curriculum, something that was already in the curriculum had to be eliminated. Therefore, they asked what they should eliminate in order to open three periods a week for moral education. One teacher regretted that she would have to drop her three-times-a-week music class to make room for the new offering. According to the principals' reports, many teachers were simply ignoring the directive and teaching in their traditional fashion, contending that they were already carrying out the spirit of the policy if not its exact form. In view of so much objection to the new policy, central office administrators concluded that the confusion about implementing the plan was so pervasive that it became impossible to determine the extent to which the policy had altered classroom practice at all.

Remedy options: Efforts to reduce the inertia that the policy faced could include both revising the present policy and, for the future, revising the way participants in policy-setting were selected.

Revising the moral education policy: The school district's top administrators could retain the policy's intent but alter the policy statement in a way that would provide more flexibility at the classroom level. The change could consist of (a) specifying the moral and citizenship objectives of the plan but (b) allowing individual teachers to determine how the objectives would be pursued in their own classrooms. Therefore, one teacher might focus on the objectives during three specific class hours each week, whereas another might integrate the objectives into class periods dedicated to language arts (reading, writing, speaking), social studies, and physical education (fair play, sportsmanship).

Revising the selection of policy-making participants: The individuals who participated in formulating the moral education policy had included members of the community-groups committee (who motivated the school board to establish such a policy), members of the school board (who authorized the policy), and the central office administrators who had prepared the statement. As it turned out, the policy statement could have profited from the participation of teachers and elementary school principals. Therefore, in the future, it would appear wise for the school-district's top administrators to include in policy-planning all of the kinds of people who would be intimately affected by a policy. Some school systems obviously attempt to accomplish this by including a teacher or two and perhaps a parent in the decision making when a new policy is being contemplated. However, because teachers are not all of the same mind, and the conditions in one classroom often differ significantly from those in other classrooms, consulting only one or two teachers (or one or two parents) will often not suffice. Thus, when a policy is going to affect classroom practice (or family life), it is useful to include a variety of teachers (or parents) in the policy-making process. This can be accomplished by school authorities conducting an opinion survey among teachers (or parents) so that a range of viewpoints is available to the school board and to administrators when they cast the policy in words. Thus, it's not necessary to have all participants present at a committee meeting. It's only necessary to have different perspectives and likely consequences available to the people responsible for drafting the policy statement.

Consistency

The problem of consistency in policy-making has been described by Richard Elmore in the following fashion.

A [prominent] theme of American political discourse is the tendency to subject established public institutions to persistent, but constantly shifting, political demands. . . . For American policymakers, the long-term stability and integrity of public institutions is much less important than acting out various versions of prevailing political ideologies through policy making. . . . Public policy, under these circumstances, takes the form of various incomplete, underdeveloped policy ideas that arise, and are shaped into policies, and enacted in successive waves, rather than in the sustained, consistent direction or steering of public institutions. (Elmore, 1997, p. 297)

The following proposition is one that can be derived from Elmore's description.

Proposition: The greater the conflict among policies, the greater the inertia experienced in attempting to put the policies into practice.

Problem case B: An analysis of the rules relating to the control of student behavior in a city school system revealed a variety of mutually incompatible regulations that resulted from (a) policies being set by people at different levels of the schooling hierarchy (school board, superintendent's office, individual schools, individual classrooms) and (b) new policies being added to, rather than replacing, old policies that originally had been designed to govern the same sorts of behavior as those on which the new policies focused.

Inconsistency across levels of the educational system is illustrated by two examples.

- The state department of education provided funds to school systems on the basis of the number of students in school each day. The fewer the students attending on a given day, the less money the school district received. State regulations specified the conditions under which a student would be counted as "in school." Those conditions included certain forms of "excusable absence." However, in implementing the statewide policy, individual school districts as well as individual schools created their own regulations about what constituted "in school" (how many hours a day a student had to be present, what sorts of off-campus field trips or athletic events counted as "in attendance," and the like). In addition, individual teachers might apply their own standards of "in attendance" when reporting who was absent from class. As a result, each time a new level of the educational administration hierarchy introduced its policy, the implementation of that policy suffered "drag," in the sense of inertia resulting from the conflict with policies already in effect from other levels of the hierarchy.
- To encourage students to take responsibility for their own and their classmates' behavior, the dean of students in a high school set up a

student court in which certain types of student misconduct were heard and disciplinary actions were taken. The students who functioned as the court's judges set policies that guided their decisions. However, those policies sometimes conflicted with guidelines the school's faculty members had traditionally followed. Thus, difficulties often arose over how the student court handled discipline cases, because the application of the students' standards was constrained by the faculty's established policies.

The effect of the accumulation of divergent policies on the successful application of a new policy is demonstrated in the following example.

• The school district had a long-standing practice of assigning students demerits (infraction points) for violating school rules. More serious violations drew a greater number of demerits. When students accumulated a specified sum of demerits, they were prohibited from engaging in certain activities (leaving the campus at lunchtime, participating on a school team, attending a dance or party). With a specified larger total of demerits, students were temporarily suspended from school. With even a greater number, they were dismissed entirely. But at the urging of several influential parents and three of the city's social workers, the district announced a new policy that would become known as "the compassion rule."

> Because the conditions obtaining in cases of apparent student misconduct can differ from one case to another, each case should be judged on its own merits. This means that in no instance should consequences for apparent misconduct be meted out automatically. In other words, the nature of an apparent infraction should not dictate the penalty or treatment imposed. The treatment in each case should be formulated solely on the relevant features of that particular incident.

When the compassion rule was added to the school district's administrative handbook, the demerit regulation remained in the handbook along with a number of other policy statements bearing on the handling of student conduct infractions. As a consequence, some teachers and principals adopted the compassion rule, whereas others continued with the demerit system. And even those who sought to apply the new policy often used the demerit system as a guide to the sorts of consequences to impose for misconduct. In effect, retaining the demerit policy increased the inertia that confounded the application of the compassion policy.

Remedy options: Each of the two sources of inertia (hierarchy levels and accumulation of policies) in the foregoing examples calls for different remedial measures.

Hierarchy levels: I doubt that the policy discrepancies across strata of the schooling hierarchy can ever be eliminated because policies set on the upper levels (state, district) must be rather general so that they will apply to many situations, whereas policies at the applied level (classroom, principal's office) must contend with conditions particular to the context and people involved. Furthermore, the application of policies is always affected by the personalities of the individuals who implement the policies as well as those who are the subjects of that implementation. Therefore, new policies will always suffer some degree of inertia. The most that can be hoped for is that by monitoring the application of policies and by convincing personnel in the education system of the virtue of a new policy, school systems can achieve greater consistency across policy-setting levels.

Accumulation of policies: Perhaps the most obvious way to reduce the conflict among policies that results from periodically adding new ones without removing old ones is for policy-makers—during the process of putting a new regulation into practice—to review the school system's existing array of regulations and to eliminate or revise those that conflict with the contemplated new proposal. However useful such an exercise may prove to be, it cannot eliminate the inertia that the new policy will face, because it is essential that policies must change people's minds. It's obvious that unless the people who are affected by a regulation understand and accept it, that regulation is a policy in word only. This means that the task of reducing inconsistencies among policies involves explaining each new policy and convincing people that it should replace earlier ones.

Implementation

Policies frequently assume the form of plans, such as national development plans and educational reform plans. Often those plans never reach the stage of implementation, or else the plans are implemented in an incomplete, distorted manner. As a result, life in schools continues in its preplan pattern, with inertia carrying the day. A variety of causes can account for the gap between policy and practice. In some cases, announced plans are little more than political ploys—devices used to mollify critics and permit the group in power to retain its favored position. For example, Jalil and McGinn's analysis of educational planning in Pakistan led them to conclude that the nation's socioeconomic-development plans, along with those plans' educational provisions,

> were written as political promises, as if rhetoric and intention were valued as much or more than the actual capacity of the government to deliver. After their pronouncement, plans were used selectively to justify some [of the implemented programs], ignoring others equally featured in original documents. . . . [Successive] governments have persisted in the formulation of objectives that clearly are unreachable within the

plan's horizon. Planning has continued to serve immediate political objectives as much as national allocation of resources to achieve long-term growth objectives. (Jalil & McGinn, 1992, pp. 89, 91)

Furthermore, policy-makers' desire to believe that "the word is the deed" contributes to their assuming that they have completed their work as soon as their plans have been proclaimed.

> [In schools in the United States,] policies often do not make sense to those who are charged with implementing them because the political logic of policy making is based on agenda formation and enactment, rather than on implementation. Professional [teachers and administrators] are left to sort through the accumulated debris of successive periods of policy making in search of authority and resources to solve the problems they face. . . . Most reforms over the history of American public education . . . tinker around the edges of the core—fiddling with institutional arrangements and superficial structure features of the system—without ever influencing what kind of teaching and learning students are actually exposed to in classrooms and schools. (Elmore, 1997, pp. 297-298)

There are several additional reasons beyond "the word is the deed" that policies may not be reflected in practice. For example, the people who are expected to carry out the policies in daily life may lack the skills needed to translate plans into actions. Furthermore, conditions in the education system may render intended reforms impossible to achieve, including such conditions as a shortage of funds, too little time, strong resistance from opposing groups, and competing priorities.

These observations about putting policies into practice appear to support a pair of propositions.

Proposition 1: The weaker the motivation of policy-makers to put a new policy into practice, the less likely the changes required by that policy will occur.

Proposition 2: The weaker the requisite skills and knowledge of the personnel responsible for putting a new policy into practice, the less likely that policy will be implemented.

Problem case C: A North American school district—whose motto was "An appropriate education for each individual"—issued a policy statement committing the public schools to provide a multicultural curriculum in which "members of all represented ethnic groups can learn about their own and other groups' contributions to the American way of life in general and to our own community's history in particular."

Three years after this policy was publicly announced, activists representing Native-American political organizations inspected the schools' social studies, literature, art, and music curriculum guides, textbooks, supplementary books, posters, picture collections, films, and videos. The representatives also interviewed a sample of students from different grade levels to discover what opportunities the students had in school to learn about their ethnic groups. The Native-American activists issued their findings in a report which contended that, although some attention was being accorded their groups' contributions to American culture in general, virtually nothing was being done to portray the roles of Native Americans in the history of the community. According to the report, the inertia problem resulted from two principal causes. First, the district's administrators were not sufficiently motivated to make implementing the policy a high priority. Second, neither the district's curriculum supervisors nor the classroom teachers had the time or investigative skills necessary for locating information about contributions of Native Americans to the local community's history and culture.

Remedy options: Efforts to implement the local-history segment of the multicultural curriculum policy could involve two stages.

Stage one. Motivation enhancement: The Native-American activists could give widespread publicity to their reports so as to bring to public attention the failure of school officials to implement their policy. The intent would be to exert political pressure that would stiffen the resolve of the officials to take constructive action. In order not to appear to be merely launching a negative attack on the schools' administrators, the activists could also publicize their willingness to aid in the effort to translate the multicultural plan into classroom practice.

Stage two. Methods and materials development: To help the school district collect the information and materials needed for carrying out the local-history part of the policy, Native-American representatives could: (a) arrange opportunities for teachers and students to interview members of the American-Indian groups that had lived in the community from early times and (b) collect items of physical culture from the American-Indian communities (photos, art objects, cooking utensils, clothing, jewelry, weapons, musical instruments). The schools' social studies program could include units of study in which students would write accounts of local history, accounts that would become part of the district's store of information for implementing the local-culture portion of the policy. Furthermore, students majoring in history or anthropology in nearby colleges could be invited to write research papers and theses on topics relating to the community's history and culture.

Conclusion

Among the aspects of policy-making that can affect the inertia confronting an intended educational reform, three have been selected for attention in this chapter—who participates in setting policy, the extent of consistency among policies, and policy implementation. Additional aspects that may also influence inertia include:

- Power. What is the relative strength of influence of the different people who participate in establishing a policy?
- Values. What are the philosophical convictions on which policy-makers base the regulations they issue?
- Rationale. What line of reasoning do policy-makers offer in support of the rules and principles they advocate?
- Breadth. How widely are proposed policies expected to extend? That is, what range of people and activities will apparently be affected by an intended policy?

Discussion Topics

The inertia confronting the implementation of a policy may result from various characteristics of the people who will be affected by that policy. Such characteristics include individuals' (a) values (what they regard as worthwhile, proper, and fair), (b) self-perceived needs, (c) conceptions of their own and others' rights and privileges, and (d) skills and knowledge. The following activity offers practice in analyzing policies in terms of those four characteristics.

For a school district with which you are acquainted, answer the numbered questions as they relate to each of these three policies:

- English will be the required language of instruction at all levels of the school system.
- The school district will no longer furnish free textbooks to high school students. In other words, students will be responsible for purchasing textbooks and other supplies required in each class.
- Students are not to chew gum in class.

1. Who are the persons affected by the policy?
2. Which characteristics (values, needs, rights, skills/knowledge) of each type of person could serve as a barrier to the implementation of the policy, and how would such resistance be expressed?
3. What might the policy-makers do to reduce the inertia that confronts their policy?

7

Management

The words *management* and *administration* are often used as synonyms referring to a school system's scheme for organizing the relationships among the system's participants in terms (a) division of labor (who is responsible for performing which tasks), (b) control (who has what power over whom), and (c) communication (along what pathways are messages expected to flow). Five features of management that affect the success of proposed educational innovations are addressed in this chapter.

Management Functions

- Data collection
- Authority and control
- Leadership consistency
- Communication
- Participation

Data Collection

Clearly, if an educational reform is to succeed, any decision about introducing it should be founded on accurate information about (a) the present condition of the educational practice that the innovation is intended to replace, (b) changes required to effect the reform, and (c) the costs—in terms of funds, time, training of personnel, and disruption of people's lives—that the reform will entail. For example, if a school building construction plan is to be successful, accurate data are needed about likely future student enrollments, the types of facilities required by both the present curriculum and the likely future curriculum (classroom size and facilities, types of laboratories, physical education equipment, auditoriums), laws governing health and safety, and more. Or, if a school district hopes to alter its salary and promotion provisions in order to attract and retain more competent teachers, then the administration can profit from compiling accurate data about (a) the salaries being paid in similar school districts, (b) the apparent prospects for future increases in district income (property-tax growth or decline, funds from the state), (c) student enrollment trends (district's population increase, real estate prices, types of families composing the population), and (d) the likely availability of teachers in the near future.

Such observations as these about the importance of collecting trustworthy data when introducing management reforms lead to the following proposition about inertia.

Proposition: The less adequate the data on which a new management procedure is founded, the greater the resistance met in implementing that procedure.

Problem case A: A school district's business manager attended a conference entitled "Frontiers of Educational Business Management" at which the representative of a software company demonstrated a computer program called *Site-Based Business, Complete.* In the conference room in which the demonstration was presented, the representative projected images from the computer onto a large screen at the front of the room so the audience could witness the exact steps taken to solve a variety of problems faced in the conduct of business affairs in a typical school. The business manager was extremely impressed by the broad range of matters that *Site-Based Business, Complete* dealt with so efficiently. Therefore, following the presentation, he spoke with the company representative, who told him that for $850 the district could purchase the *Site-Based Business, Complete* basic package that "handles everything you can imagine that may come up in a school—budgeting, accounting, record keeping, class scheduling—the whole thing." The business manager saw this as a great bargain, as a way of upgrading management procedures in all nine of the district's schools for less than $1,000, so he purchased the program on the spot.

Later, when he had returned to his district and began to install the program on his office computer, he discovered that the license for using the program restricted its use to one school. In other words, if he wished to make the program available in all nine schools, he would need to purchase nine copies of the program. He first contemplated ignoring the licensing agreement and installing the program at all nine schools. But he rejected that option when he realized that the company that controlled the program could easily find out what he had done and might well sue the school district. So he rejected that choice and decided to install the program at only one school. Then, on the basis of that school's experience with the program, he would decide whether to purchase copies for the remaining eight schools.

As he worked through the program, he also discovered that the "basic package" he had purchased lacked many of the features of the program that the representative had demonstrated during the conference session. Whereas the basic package did, indeed, provide for budgeting and accounting, it did not include sections that the representative had shown for (a) class scheduling, (b) students' cumulative records, (c) transportation (bus schedules, bus maintenance, drivers' records), or (d) future financial planning. According to the "Help" file that appeared among the menus of the installed program, those four functions were separate add-ons that needed to be purchased in support of the basic package. Two of the four cost $400 each, and the other two were $600 apiece. Purchasing all four, in addition to the basic package, would raise the cost per school to $3,850.

Furthermore, as the business manager tried out some of the program's practice exercises relating to budgeting and accounting, he discovered that they required greater expertise than he possessed if he were to function efficiently rather than merely muddle through. Again, under the "Help" menu that accompanied the basic program, he learned that the Site-Based Business company offered a one-week training course in major cities around the country for preparing people to operate the entire system efficiently. The tuition fee for the training was $2,000. Therefore, if the school district wished to have one or two staff members from each school take the training course, the cost for the nine schools would run to between $18,000 and $36,000 for tuition, not counting the travel and living expenses that the training week entailed.

In summary, the business manager's failure to collect adequate data before purchasing the computer program seriously jeopardized his plan to reform the schools' management practices.

Remedy options: The following alternatives include suggestions about (a) how the district should operate in similar future situations to avoid committing the same mistake again and (b) what might be done to make the most of the present situation.

a-1—Interrogate the salesperson. It's apparent that the business manager should not have been so hasty in purchasing the program without acquiring more detailed information about it. First, he could have asked the salesman for a detailed, published description of the program, its cost, and any subsidiary features that were needed in order to make the program fully operative (information about the add-on programs, the training course, and the need to buy a separate package for each school rather than one for the entire district). The business manager could also have requested the names of school districts in which the program had been operating for some time. Then, upon returning home, he could have phoned or written to those other districts to determine how well they liked *Site-Based Business, Complete* and to discover problems they had encountered. In addition, he could ask how well the company that sold *Site-Based Business, Complete* supported their product after it was put into practice. The compiled information then could serve as the basis for a decision about whether, and to what extent, *Site-Based Business, Complete* should be adopted.

b-1—Limited-scope tryout. The district's attempt to salvage the plan could begin with installing the basic program at one school so it could be used during a tryout period to determine how it compared with present practices. On the basis of the tryout, the district could decide whether to abandon *Site-Based Business, Complete* or to purchase programs for other schools as well.

b-2—Tutoring plan. To take advantage of the one-week training workshop, yet not spend the amount needed to train individuals from all schools, one person could be sent to a workshop session. That individual would then be prepared to train others in the district.

Authority and Control

Every organization that includes more than one person has an authority structure that defines—or at least reflects—the intended relationships among the organization's personnel in terms of the division of labor (work assignments), power, and communication. That structure is often represented graphically as an organization diagram or flow chart. Typically, the higher a position's location on the chart, the greater that position's power and control over other positions. Furthermore, the lines connecting the chart's components typically define (a) who has control over whom and (b) the routes through which messages are expected to pass. The word *authority* refers to an organization's officially intended job assignments, power relationships, and communication pathways. Organization charts are designed to reflect this authority structure. The diagram in Figure 7-1 illustrates a simplified organization chart for a hypothetical small school district.

In contrast to the relationships displayed on a authority chart, organizations' day-to-day functioning often reflects an unofficial pattern. In other words, who does which jobs, who has power over whom, and the ways messages pass through the system differ from the pattern dictated by the official plan. These deviations often determine how well a proposed reform is realized in practice. For example, in the division of labor, if a person who officially should perform a particular job is either unable or unwilling to do the job properly, then someone not in that official position will have to do the work if the reform is to be realized. Or, if a person high in the authority structure has a weaker personality than an individual lower in the system, the one at the higher location may lack the interpersonal power necessary to control the behavior of the individual in the lower position.

Figure 7-1

School System's Organization Chart

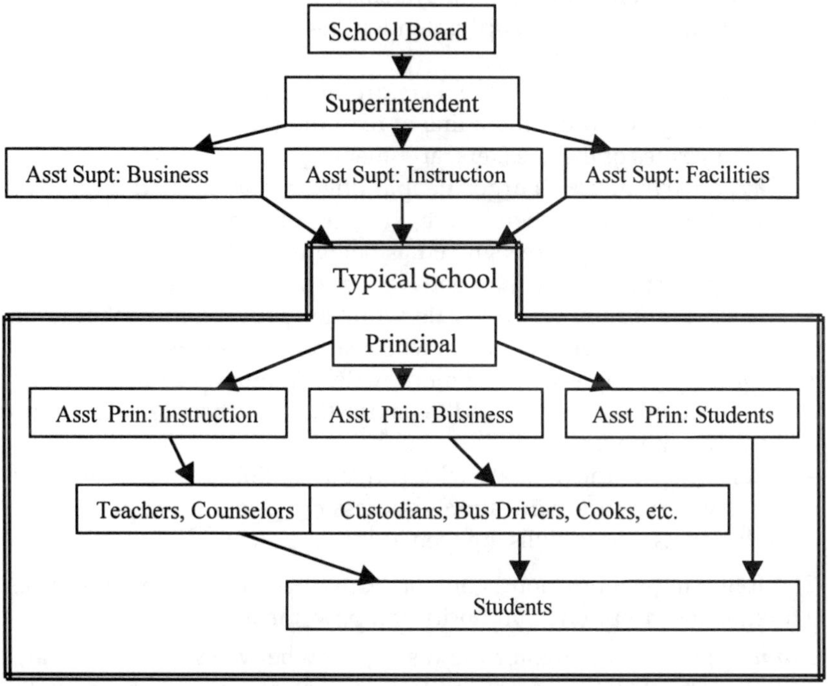

The following problem illustrates the influence on a proposed reform of the discrepancy between an organization's official and actual power relationships. *Power,* as the word is used here, refers to how much influence one person's presence has on the behavior of another person. If Person A acts differently when Person B is present (either physically or only in Person A's mind), then Person B has power over Person A in the situation at hand. Frequently, power is reciprocal, with each person exerting some influence over the others involved in a confrontation. If the power of two individuals is equal, a stalemate of action may result. However, one person's power is often greater than the other's, so that in a disagreement between the two, the one with the greater power prevails.

It is useful to recognize that individuals' power within an organization can derive from various sources. The following are a few of those sources.

- *Authority position.* Within an organization, people in a superior position in the official authority structure wield influence over ones in inferior positions by dint of the relative power defined for the different positions. In a school system, a principal is expected to follow the orders of the superintendent, and a teacher is expected to obey the principal.
- *Verbal cleverness.* Some speakers are more persuasive than others, more adept at producing a line of reasoning that convinces listeners of the virtues of the speakers' arguments.
- *Physical appearance.* Larger people often are able to triumph over smaller ones, even when a verbal rather than physical confrontation is involved. People recognized as being beautiful or handsome are often more persuasive than ones who are seen as plain or ugly.
- *Money and favors.* Individuals who can provide or withhold rewards have power over others who yearn for those rewards.
- *Popularity.* People who are more widely admired can more readily influence others' beliefs and behavior than can people who are not widely admired.
- *Valued skills.* Individuals who command skills which others consider vital to an organization's success can wield more power than individuals whose skills are seen as less important.

The following proposition is one of many that can be generated from the foregoing conception of authority and power in a school system.

Proposition 1: The greater the discrepancy between (a) the formal authority structure of an education system and (b) the actual power structure, the greater the inertia that can be suffered by reforms introduced by people holding positions in the upper reaches of the authority structure.

Problem case B: In early May, a high school's faculty members received in their mail boxes this notice, signed by the school principal.

On the basis of extensive consultation with the district's central administration and from the study of innovative school practices, Jefferson High next fall will change to a more productive class-schedule plan. Our traditional plan of having 45-minute class periods, with each type of class meeting five times a week, will be replaced by an alternating-block system. Under the block plan, most classes will meet alternate days for 90-minute block periods, so as to provide greater flexibility in the use of class time and greater continuity in the study of a given topic. Within a 90-minute period, a greater variety of activities can be pursued than is possible under the traditional system.

For example, during a 90-minute period, a teacher can begin with a demonstration or illustrated lecture, which is followed by students studying a textbook passage relating to the demonstration, and then students can engage in small-group discussions to propose solutions to questions raised by the demonstration and the textbook. All of this can be accomplished within a 90-minute period but it could not be accomplished in 45 minutes.

Furthermore, with a class meeting every other day rather than every day, students have more time between class periods to complete homework assignments. Therefore, more complex and demanding assignments can be given than is usually possible with the present daily 45-minute class schedule.

The details of the new plan are now being worked out and will be available for the guidance of Jefferson High's faculty and students by the close of the present school year. I am confident that faculty members, students, and parents will all be pleased with the new arrangement.

At the general faculty meeting held one week after the principal's announcement, the principal discovered that the optimism expressed in the closing sentence of his notice was not entirely warranted. Although the matter of the innovative class schedule was not on the faculty meeting's formal agenda, the matter was brought to the group's attention when the chairman of the school's science department raised his hand and forcefully objected to the imposition of the block-schedule plan. After he spoke in defense of the traditional 45-minute, 5-days-a-week system, he yielded the floor to the school's football coach, who supported the science teacher's objections and added several of his own. Many faculty members applauded when the coach finished speaking.

Thus, it became apparent that a power confrontation could affect the fate of the principal's class schedule reform. Although the principal held the upper hand in terms of the school's official authority structure, the science-department chairman and football coach commanded substantial informal sources of power. The chairman taught classes (chemistry and physics) for which well-prepared teachers were in short supply. Furthermore, he was well respected among educators outside the school, because he had published journal articles on science teaching and was a member of the regional science education association's board of supervisors. It was clear to everyone that, if he left Jefferson High, he would be welcomed in a variety of other school systems, and Jefferson's reputation as a high-quality academic institution would thereby suffer. The football coach also posed a power problem for the principal, because over the past five years his teams had compiled a record of 37 wins and 13 losses. Not only was his winning record much admired throughout the community, but he was an affable man, known for a ready smile and quaint sayings that were spread around the community by means of television interviews and newspaper articles. And the applause that had followed the coach's remarks at the faculty meeting suggested that the science teacher and coach were not without supporters among the rest of the faculty members.

In effect, the principal's suggested innovation was placed in jeopardy because of the discrepancy between the official authority structure and unofficial power sources among the school's personnel. It was quite possible that the principal's plan would fail, either outright by the faculty forcing the principal to yield or by the faculty's passive opposition during the upcoming school year when a host of "inadvertent" troubles with the new system could render it inoperable.

Remedy options: Two strategies the principal might adopt to salvage his plan could involve cooperative planning and/or ordering the change, with or without faculty concurrence.

Cooperative planning. The principal could attempt to reduce the threat to his plan by now doing what he would have been wise to have done when first developing his plan.

Originally, he could have involved the entire faculty—or a committee of faculty representatives—in creating a more effective class schedule by their cooperatively identifying alternatives to the school's traditional system. Thus, the advantages and disadvantages of different plans could be weighed by the group. Such a cooperative approach could also inform the principal of the kinds and strength of opposition to the block system. Thus warned, he could develop tactics for defending his proposal against people who opposed it. Furthermore, by including the faculty in the planning process, he would display his respect for their opinions and perhaps more readily enlist their support for his choice of a scheduling plan.

Although he had originally failed to include the faculty in evaluating the present system and in formulating a more suitable alternative, he might now attempt to repair some of the damage by appointing a committee—or by having the faculty chose committee members—to review the block plan and perhaps arrive at a solution that could be widely supported by the people whom the plan would most heavily effect—teachers, students, and parents. However, at this juncture such a procedure would be riskier than if the faculty had been involved in the initial planning, because now the battle lines had been publicly drawn during the faculty meeting; it thus would be more difficult for either side to yield concessions than if no public confrontation had occurred.

Mandate the change. The principal could impose the block plan, despite objections of faculty members. To minimize opposition, he could announce, or merely imply, negative sanctions that faculty members would suffer if they failed to cooperate fully with his proposal—such sanctions as unfavorable reports being placed in members' personnel files, reduced opportunities for promotion, undesirable extracurricular assignments, and the rejection of faculty members' requests for special equipment, supplies, and the reimbursement of expenses incurred in attending professional workshops and conferences.

Leadership Consistency

Whenever an administrator is replaced, it is not uncommon for the replacement to eliminate policies and practices identified with the former regime and then to institute new policies and practices intended to represent the new regime. Underlying such change is the desire of the new administration to establish its own identity by expunging symbols of the past.

Proposition: A change in management may increase the inertia faced by an innovation that is in the process of implementation.

Problem case C: An elementary school principal, Astra Dempster, had recently gained a reputation as a significant innovator by introducing a learning-partners program that involved (a) upper-grade pupils serving as tutors and "play buddies" for pupils in kindergarten and first-grade, (b) retired senior citizens helping pupils (of any grade level) who experienced difficulty with reading and mathematics, and (c) upper-grade pupils teaching older adults to use personal computers for sending e-mail and searching the Internet. Shortly after Ms. Dempster had established the program in her school, she described it to delegates at a countywide education conference. Later, a reporter from a local television station brought a camera crew to the elementary school to videotape scenes of the program in action. When the videotape was broadcast, the narrator identified the learning-partners program as the "Dempster Plan," a label that would be widely used in discussions of the innovation.

During the Dempster Plan's second year of operation, the program was still being refined when the principal was diagnosed as suffering rapidly advancing cancer that forced her to resign her position, much to the distress of the school staff, pupils, and members of the community. Jane Logan, an assistant principal in a nearby elementary school, was selected as Astra Dempster's replacement. Throughout the early months of Mrs. Logan's principalship, the previous principal's presence continued to hover about in the form of people often mentioning Astra Dempster's management style and, particularly, in their frequent references to the Dempster Plan. At the opening of the next school year, Principal Logan announced that the need to improve the achievement-test scores of pupils in the upper grades made it necessary for upper-grade pupils to concentrate on their own studies and no longer use school time to tutor younger children or teach older adults computer skills. Furthermore, funds that had been used in the past for transporting senior citizens to and from the school were now needed for other purposes. Although Principal Logan did not say that these changes were designed to destroy what her predecessor had built, it was clear that the Dempster Plan had now become a thing of the past.

Remedy options: People who wished to retain the learning-partner program (in fact, if not in name) might attempt several sorts of political action that would encourage the new principal to modify her decision. Such action could include the following.

A delegation. A committee of teachers and parents could be organized to meet with Principal Logan and express their desire to have the existing learning-partners plan continue.

Petition. The committee could collect signatures on a petition that urged the retention of the learning-partners program, with the petition sent to the principal and school board.

Another delegation. A delegation of teachers and parents, armed with a petition containing many signatures, could visit the superintendent of schools and his staff to urge them to save the learning-partners plan. The delegation would likely enjoy greater success if it included community members who were in positions of power and authority.

Letter writing. Teachers and parents could send letters to local newspapers and to school board members in support of the learning-partners plan.

Demonstrations. Supporters of the Dempster Plan could stage a mass rally in front of the school, with participants carrying signs endorsing the learning-partners program. Television and radio stations and newspapers could be informed ahead of time about when, where, and why the rally would be held.

Communication

A communication system most efficiently fosters the adoption and survival of a new management plan whenever messages essential for coordinating the parts of the plan (a) arrive at their intended destinations (b) at the right time, and (c) are clearly understood by the people who need the information the messages convey.

Proposition: The less efficient the method of communication used for instituting a new management procedure, the greater the inertia that method will face.

Problem case D: In a city school system that included 17 schools, what appeared to be an increase in threats to the health and safety of students and school personnel motivated the superintendent to create a new Office for Coordinating Health and Safety Services. In the past, health and safety problems occurring in a school had been handled by that school's staff in whatever way seemed best at the time. However, a host of evidence had accumulated to suggest that problems were not being solved in the most desirable fashion. In particular, there was no consistent plan for preparing a school's administrators, teachers, and support staff to cope with incidents of violence (fights, attacks by armed individuals), drug and alcohol abuse, teenage pregnancy, HIV infection, accidental injuries, and the like.

The four-fold assignment for the newly established Office for Coordinating Health and Safety Services was to

- Create a reporting system that would furnish immediate, appropriate help for health and safety emergencies in schools
- Educate school personnel in the use of the reporting system
- Inspect schools' health and safety provisions and arrange for correcting weaknesses in those provisions
- Coordinate the operation of all health and safety related elements of the school district and of relevant outside agencies (fire department, police department, juvenile court, city health bureau, county social-services office)

The success of the coordinating office obviously depended heavily on the efficiency of its communication system. The director of the office began by sending a printed announcement to all school district employees, informing them that, in the future, all health and safety emergencies should be reported by phone directly to the coordinating office. The office staff would then immediately assign an appropriate agency or individual to cope with the problem. The director likened this procedure to the 911 way of reporting emergencies in the general community. The centralized reporting system would replace what the director called "the present higgledy-piggledy method of people not knowing whom or where to call or whether to try solving the problem entirely by themselves."

Within three weeks of the date that the announcement was distributed, it became apparent that the coordinating office's communication plan was flawed. First, the office had only one phone line, so if the line was in use for any length of time, callers seeking to report an emergency were unable to do so. Second, what constituted an "emergency" was not at all clear. One teacher phoned to have "something done about an extremely rude 16-year-old in the lunchroom." Another complained that "a snake got loose from the zoology laboratory." A third one reported that a pair of teenagers were "fornicating in a car in the parking lot after school."

In addition, some people either neglected to read the coordinating office's announcement or else chose to ignore it, for they continued to treat issues of health and safety in their usual fashion—personally confiscating a switch blade that a sixth-grader carried; sending a pregnant, morning-sick 15-year-old to the school nurse; and reporting a faulty fire extinguisher to the school principal.

Furthermore, the office's staff members who answered the phone frequently failed to know what kind of help to seek and where to find it.

As a result of the numerous difficulties experienced during the early weeks of the director's emergency-reporting system, the number of incidents subsequently phoned to the office diminished as people in the schools reverted to their original methods of coping with health and safety threats. In effect, the inertia faced by the new system increased with the passing of time.

Remedy options: Several measures might be attempted to improve the efficiency of the coordinating office's operation.

Altered directions. The office could issue a new set of emergency directions for teachers, administrators, and support staff to follow. The directions could suggest that people phone the office only when they are unsure of what should be done in the apparent emergency. In other words, if they already felt that they knew how to solve a problem, they should act on their own best judgment rather than phoning the office. The office's new directions could usefully offer examples of problems that teachers or administrators should feel free to solve by themselves, such problems as routine cases of student discipline, common forms of temporary illness, and safety hazards around the school. It would be helpful if the directions also offered examples of emergencies that warranted phoning the office, such as emergencies requiring the services of specialists—police officers, paramedics, fire fighters, animal-control personnel, electricians, and the like.

Office facilities. The office could install more than one phone line for receiving emergency calls, and office staff members who would answer the phone could be trained more adequately to decide which kinds of services should be sought for treating which kinds of emergencies.

School visits. The director could arrange to attend a faculty meeting at each school in order to explain to teachers and members of the support staff (secretaries, custodians, bus drivers, counselors, lunchroom personnel) what to do in different emergencies. The director could also speak to the students during an assembly period, with his talk illustrated with colored slides or a videotape depicting how people should and should not respond to different kinds of emergencies.

Posters. Posters could be displayed at schools, suggesting to the faculty and students how to react to crises.

Participation

The word *participation* is used here in reference to the question: In the process of introducing and sustaining an educational reform, which assignments are best performed by an individual and which are best performed by a group?

As a guide to answering the question, I would suggest adopting a four-phase decision-making scheme in which each phase is defined as follows:

- The steps in an educational-innovation process are specified.
- For each step, the skills and knowledge needed for accomplishing that step's tasks are identified.
- The skills and knowledge of available personnel are analyzed.
- The requirements of a step's tasks are matched to the personnel who command the required skills and knowledge, and a decision is reached about which tasks can likely be performed more efficiently by an individual than by a group, or vice versa.

Two propositions about inertia can be derived from this conception of decision-making participation.

Proposition 1: The worse the match between (a) people's skills and knowledge and (b) the requirements of tasks in an educational development project, the greater the inertia met in attempting to carry out the project.

Proposition 2: The less attention paid to the conditions under which working alone rather than working together affects the efficiency of an activity, the greater the inertia faced in performing the activity.

Problem case E: A school district had received a government grant to explore ways that the Internet could enhance classroom teaching at different grade levels and in various subject matter fields. To carry out the program, teachers who were already enthusiastic computer buffs were selected to investigate the possibilities for improving instruction at their own grade level and in the subjects they taught. Throughout the school year, the participants in the venture met periodically to share their experiences under the guidance of the supervisor of the program. In keeping with the agreement under which the financial grant had been awarded, at the end of the year the district was responsible for submitting three products of their work:

- A report on how the project was organized, what problems had been encountered, how the problems had been addressed, and how well the goals of the project had been achieved.
- A guidebook for teachers, (a) describing ways to use the Internet to improve learning, (b) offering specific examples of classroom lessons that had incorporated information from the Internet, and (c) suggesting ways to solve problems that typically arose.
- A videotape that showed how the Internet had been helpful at different grade levels and in different subject fields. The videotape would be used for showing teachers in other school districts how they might employ the Internet to enhance learning.

A problem faced by the supervisor at year's end was that of deciding what method he should use to collect the teacher's experiences and their recommendations for the purpose of preparing the teacher's guidebook required by the conditions of the financial grant. He decided that the best approach would be to gather all of the participating teachers for a one-day meeting during which the entire group could cooperatively compose the guidebook. His three-fold purpose in adopting such a method was to

- Employ a democratic management approach that gave all project participants an equal chance to contribute to the guidebook
- Collect a great variety of ways the Internet could contribute to the improvement of instruction
- Compile the needed information while simultaneously writing a draft of the guidebook, thereby not only permitting everyone to contribute but also conserving writing time by establishing the structure and contents of the book during the meeting

To implement his plan, the supervisor set up the meeting room with computer equipment that enabled him to project onto a large screen the material he wrote on a computer as teachers offered their suggestions about (a) ways they had used the Internet, (b) how to organize the guidebook, and (c) how to phrase the guidebook's contents.

At the opening of the day-long meeting, the supervisor described the purposes of the meeting and the methods the group would use to compose the booklet. As the morning session advanced, the meeting became what one teacher (in a critical mood) later called "an exercise in chaos." For instance, a participant, when asked how she or he had used the Internet, would offer an example. Then the supervisor would type the example on the computer keyboard and ask, "How does that sound?" as the group read the passage that appeared on the large screen. Different group members would then often suggest improvements in the wording, and the discussion would continue until no one objected to the revised phrasing. The supervisor would next ask, "Where would it be best to locate this example in the guidebook?" That question elicited different opinions about the sections into which the guidebook could best be divided and about which section was most appropriate for the example currently being discussed. This laborious process resulted in what the same teacher/critic described as "a mishmash of segmented verbiage that was getting us nowhere." As the lunch hour approached, participants continued to offer examples but gradually ceased suggesting ways to rephrase the supervisor's writing or to propose where in the booklet an example should be located.

In summary, the innovative process that the supervisor had adopted to compile Internet-use examples and simultaneously write the booklet turned out to be a very inefficient way of organizing people's participation.

Remedy options: During the lunch hour, the supervisor could revise his plan so as to adapt one or more of the following approaches to the task of composing the guidebook. Each of these solutions could be based on the decision-making scheme proposed at the beginning of this section on participation.

First alternative. During the lunch hour, the supervisor—perhaps with one or two colleagues—would define the tasks necessary for producing a proper guidebook, such as (a) identify the guidebook's purpose and intended audience, (b) suggest the questions that the book should answer for such an audience, (c) collect ways of using the Internet to enhance teaching effectiveness, and (d) present those ways in a sequence that readers would find interesting and understandable. Then the supervisor would estimate which of the four tasks could most efficiently be performed by an individual working alone and which by a group. He would also suggest a process that defined a sequence of interactions between individuals and groups that would accomplish the job systematically and make the best use of time and participants' skills and knowledge. Consequently, the afternoon session of the guidebook committee might begin by the supervisor describing the group's revised approach in this fashion.

> I think that it's pretty clear to all of us that the way we operated this morning was very unproductive. It's apparent that gathering useful ideas can be done effectively in a group but that writing a well-organized presentation of those ideas is not accomplished effectively by a group. As a cynic once proposed—a camel is a horse put together by a committee. So this afternoon we will spend our time as a group for suggesting ideas that we'll collect by

means of this tape recorder. We won't try to organize those ideas. In other words, we won't try to write the guidebook together. Instead, we'll assign an experienced writer to do that job. Then, when a draft of the guidebook has been produced, we'll give each of you a copy to appraise; and we'll collect your suggestions for our author to use in rewriting the parts that you think need improvement.

With this revised plan in mind, I'll start by asking you to offer your suggestions about a series of matters that require our attention. First, I'll ask for your ideas about what questions our guidebook should answer for teachers or administrators who read it. After everyone has had a chance to suggest those questions, I'll ask for examples of how you have used the Internet with your students. Along with the examples, we'll need to know problems that arose and ways you tried to solve the problems.

So, now we begin our brainstorming session without worrying about how our ideas will be put together as a written document. That's the job of the person who will produce the written version.

In summary, the supervisor's proposal would involve alternating activities between individual and group participation. The work plan that the supervisor prepared for the afternoon session would be his creation—the product of his individual decision. His plan perhaps could be usefully reviewed by one or two colleagues in order to identify omissions or clarify confusing phrases before he presented the plan to the group of teachers. During the session, the teachers could profitably offer (a) questions the guidebook should answer for teachers, (b) specific examples of Internet uses, (c) problems that arose with the Internet, and (d) ways of solving those problems. In effect, by working together, a group of experienced Internet users should be able to produce a far broader array of questions, examples, problems, and solutions than would an individual working alone. As the next step, the tape-recording of the afternoon session could be given to an experienced writer to organize as a narrative that furnished answers in an understandable sequence and interesting style. The group could then contribute by reading the draft of the guidebook and suggesting what could usefully be added, corrected, or reorganized. Finally, the individual author could revise the document in light of those suggestions by teachers that the author found persuasive.

Alternative 2. In the afternoon session, rather than having the teachers engage in a general discussion of the four types of contributions that the supervisor wished to receive, he could ask them to use the time to write their individual suggestions about questions that the guidebook should answer and about examples of Internet use (with problems, and solutions). Compared with discussion, written contributions have the advantage of making economical use of the teachers' time—all of the participants would be contributing useful ideas during the entire session rather than everyone—other than the current speaker—spending the bulk of the time listening. Furthermore, the teachers' contributions would be in written form, rather than in the form of voices on a tape-recording—voices often difficult to understand when they come from different parts of the conference room.

In this second alternative, even though all participants function as individuals, not as part of a group, everyone still has an opportunity to contribute to the guidebook.

Alternative 3. A still different approach would not involve any group meetings at all. Rather, the person chosen to write the guidebook could visit classrooms throughout the school year at times when the Internet was being used, could videotape class activities, and could interview the teacher and students. Selected videotaped scenes could later be incorporated into the final tape that the financial grant required.

Conclusion

The five vantage points from which inertia in management processes has been viewed in this chapter have been those of (a) data collection, (b) authority and control, (c) leadership consistency, (d) communication efficiency, and (e) group versus individual participation in management activities. Additional vantage points to adopt include those of:

- *Budgeting.* What is the process by which the school system (a) estimates future costs and income and (b) determines how much money is to be allocated to the various segments of the system?
- *Personnel selection.* By what means are different types of educational personnel selected, and what criteria are used in choosing among candidates for positions?
- *Construction planning.* What procedures are followed in determining (a) the kinds of structures the school system needs and (b) how responsibility is assigned for designing those structures?
- *Public relations.* How is responsibility assigned for maintaining constructive connections with the public that the school system serves?

Discussion Topics

It's apparent that the problem cases throughout this book have been chosen to illustrate propositions about conditions that influence the kind and strength of the inertia that confronts educational reforms. The following activity offers you a chance to try creating such propositions.

As demonstrated in earlier chapters, each proposition is a statement about an estimated relationship between (a) a selected variable and (b) the amount of resistance that an innovative educational practice can be expected to experience. The typical proposition is an "if-then" statement. *If* a given condition of the selected variable obtains, *then* we can expect greater difficulty implementing the contemplated innovation. "If-then" statements are often worded in comparative "more/more" or "less/greater" terms, such as:

Proposition: The more that a proposed new public relations practice conflicts with traditional public relations methods, the more inertia the new practice will encounter.

Proposition: When an innovative employment policy is adopted by a school system, the less precise the definitions of jobs to be filled (tasks to be performed, skills required), the greater the difficulty experienced in selecting applicants who would perform the work satisfactorily.

You may find the task of creating propositions is easiest if you think of a problem case you've witnessed in the past or that you can imagine. You can then select a variable in the case that you believe contributed to the inertia the innovation faced. That variable becomes the subject of the first half of an "if-then" proposition. The second half will be the kind and degree of inertia the selected variable produces. In the above two examples, the selected variables were traditional public-relations practice and the precision of job definitions.

From the field of educational management, here are three selected variables you might wish to consider as you try creating propositions about causes of inertia. In each example, the management task is identified, followed by the innovation and a selected variable that may influence the inertia the task faces.

- *The management task*—promoting and dismissing personnel
  The innovation—a newly appointed high school principal
  The influential variable—the principal's emotional attachment to an employee who is a candidate for promotion or to an employee who is subject to dismissal because of budget cuts

- *The management task*—selecting a site for a school
  The innovation—a new school has been authorized
  The influential variable—the superintendent of schools' knowledge of residential growth trends and family demographics (family members of school age, stability of family's location) in the community

- *The management task*—establishing and enforcing a dress code that students are expected to adopt
  The innovation—introducing a new dress code
  The influential variable—parents' agreement with the code

8

Services

Services are activities designed to support the teaching/learning process. Typical services include those of

- Maintaining school buildings and equipment in efficient operating order
- Transporting students and supplies
- Fostering accurate, prompt communication among the school's staff members, students, parents, and the news media
- Keeping records of students' school performance, attendance, and family conditions
- Monitoring the receipt and expenditure of funds
- Providing help to students with special needs
- Assisting students in planning their educational and vocational careers, and more

The issues of inertia addressed in this chapter concern bureaucratic efficiency, critical mass, cost/benefit ratio, equipment maintenance, and record keeping.

Influences on Services

- Bureaucratic efficiency
- Critical mass
- Cost/benefit ratio
- Equipment maintenance
- Record keeping

Bureaucratic Efficiency

The word *bureaucracy*, as intended here, refers to the way people are organized in order to perform a specified kind of service.

Proposition: The less satisfactory the operation of the bureaucracy responsible for furnishing a particular service, the greater the inertia faced in attempting to reform that service.

Problem case A: A review of a school district's Exceptional Student Education Program revealed what auditors judged was "a confusing bureaucracy that has dragged its feet on upgrading facilities and doesn't deliver services as effectively as possible." The following problems were among the program's shortcomings that were exposed by the audit.

- There was no clear chain of command in the program, so confusion reigned about who had authority over which employees and over the services needed by the 28,000 children in the district who had been diagnosed as suffering from learning disabilities. Furthermore, there appeared to be little or no provision for the gifted students who were also supposed to be the concern of the Exceptional Student Education Program. The program had an executive director and about 25 staff members, who worked at the district's administrative center, and also had four area directors throughout the county, each with a staff of about 10. The area directors reported to the district's area superintendents, not to the program's executive director, who was therefore often unaware of what was being done in the schools. The auditors suggested that a uniform system could improve communication and save money because some staff could be consolidated.

- In the current system, when parents requested a hearing concerning their child's diagnosis, they might receive different information from different area offices. The resulting confusion would be less likely to occur if decision-making power were centralized with the executive director.

- The school district had spent only 4% of the $9 million designated over the past two years to make classrooms and bathrooms completely accessible to the disabled. In seeking to explain the delay, the executive director of contracts in the district's construction department said the district was trying to speed up the work of adding hands-free faucets, hand railings, and ramps for the disabled. But he said it was difficult to find contractors to do small repairs, and his facilities and construction department was trying to combine smaller renovation work with larger projects.

- Workloads among the specialists who treated the disabled were uneven. Some specialists were responsible for as few as 57 students, whereas one specialist had 575 high school students.
- Some students required bus aides to help them get to school, but the aides often charged for more time than they actually worked. The audit revealed that the district might have paid as much as $96,000 for hours not worked during the school year (Harrison, 2001).

Remedy options: The following are three approaches for improving bureaucratic efficiency.

Participants' efficiency suggestions. A summary of the Exceptional Student Education Program's shortcomings identified in the auditors' report could be furnished to the members of the bureaucracy who operated the program, and the members could be asked for suggestions as to how the system might operate more efficiently. An advantage of this approach is that the people closest to the daily operation of the program should be well aware of the bureaucracy's problems. A disadvantage is that the program's participants are not unbiased, objective judges. Thus, they may seek to maintain current conditions that provide them with advantages but do not contribute to bureaucratic efficiency. Or members of the bureaucracy may use this opportunity to place unwarranted blame on fellow members whom they dislike.

Internal restructuring. Using the contents of the auditors' report along with suggestions solicited from members of the bureaucracy, the school district's top administrator could alter (a) the bureaucracy's power structure, shifting the authority away from some positions to other positions, (b) the bureaucracy's communication routes, and (c) the persons occupying different positions in the system. An advantage of thus assigning the decisions about improving the system to administrators who are already in the school district is that the administrators are likely to understand the traits of program personnel better than outsiders would. A disadvantage is that personal feelings and commitments between the administrators and members of the program bureaucracy might result in decisions that do not contribute to the system's efficiency. The district superintendent might be unwilling to remove his daughter-in-law, his favorite golfing partner, or the mayor's nephew from positions of power in the bureaucracy.

Outside advice. Experts on organizational efficiency from outside the school district could be hired to suggest how the bureaucracy's structure and personnel might profitably be changed. Two strengths of this option are that it (a) takes advantage of the experience of experts who have studied and worked with many bureaucracies and (b) reduces the likelihood that decisions about improving the system's efficiency would be influenced by personal relationships between members of the bureaucracy and the planners. One disadvantage is that there might be conditions in the bureaucracy or the broader community that would influence what changes in the system could be made without producing undesired political consequences. Dismissing the mayor's ineffectual nephew might prompt the mayor to retaliate in ways harmful to the school system.

Critical Mass

The following are two ways an educational reform can be successfully introduced.

- The reform is mandated by a person ("the boss") or group that holds effective authority over the people who are responsible for implementing the reform. In other words, someone in a leadership position wields sufficient power over the implementers to ensure that the reform takes place.
- The reform is enthusiastically advocated by enough people (among those responsible for carrying out the reform) to ensure that the reform operates as planned. In effect, the social pressure needed to implement the innovation is not exerted by a superior authority but, rather, is exerted by the implementers themselves—that is, by peers. The term *critical mass* identifies the size of the group of enthusiasts necessary for ensuring that the proposed reform is actually put into practice.

Proposition: In cases of educational reforms that depend for their success on the willing cooperation of implementers, the smaller the proportion of implementers who favor a reform, the greater the resistance the reform will face.

Problem case B: The confluence of three events motivated a teacher to introduce a change in the way an innercity elementary school kept its building and grounds in good shape.

The first event was the school district's suffering a budgetary shortfall that required unusual austerities in order to lower operating expenses. One austerity consisted of reducing the number of custodians assigned to ensure that school buildings and grounds were neat and in good repair.

The second event—or more accurately, series of events—was a growing rash of vandalism and graffiti that damaged and disfigured school property.

The third event was a three-week summertime educational tour to Japan, where the tour participants visited schools and historical sites. A third-grade teacher from the innercity elementary school was a member of the tour group. One feature of the Japanese schools that particularly interested her was the tidy condition of Japanese school buildings and grounds and, particularly, in the system that kept the premises in such good shape. Rather than depending on a staff of custodians, each school depended on its staff and students to care for the property. Two times were set aside each day for cleaning and refurbishing classrooms, hallways, and grounds. Students, teachers, and administrators all joined in the effort, taking pride in completing housekeeping tasks as efficiently as possible.

During the first faculty meeting when the innercity school reopened after the summer vacation, the third-grade teacher proposed that the Japanese system be adopted. She described how the system operated and pictured for the faculty how their school's appearance—and the students' and staff members' morale—would improve. During the general discussion that followed her proposal, three teachers spoke in favor of the plan and two spoke against it, saying that the faculty had more than enough to do without becoming custodial supervisors as well. No other faculty members offered opinions. The principal said he would take the matter under advisement.

After the faculty meeting, the third-grade teacher met privately with the principal to solicit his support. The principal said that the decision was up to the teachers. He explained that it was not his administrative style to order faculty and staff members to carry out programs that they did not enthusiastically endorse. He believed it was futile to try forcing the majority to engage in activities against their will and desire. He said that unless there was a *critical mass* of participants who supported the reform, it would be futile to introduce the plan because it would be bound to fail.

But the principal did agree to send a ballot to all teachers and members of the support staff (secretaries, custodian, bus drivers, counselors, lunchroom personnel), asking them to vote either for or against the Japanese-style school maintenance proposal. Less than one-third of the respondents supported the plan. The principal declared that one-third did not, in his opinion, qualify as a critical mass, so the third-grade teacher's suggestion was rejected.

Remedy option: It would be possible for the third-grade teacher to institute her plan on a limited scale and, in the process, perhaps generate the critical mass needed for the plan's schoolwide adoption. She could set up the program for her own class. Twice each day, 15 or 20 minutes could be dedicated to refurbishing not only the classroom but also parts of the school building and grounds that needed attention. Pupils and teacher alike would pick up litter, clean graffiti from walls and walkways, replace broken slats in the fence, and the like. The teacher might draw other teachers into the program, such as those who had supported her proposal at the faculty meeting. Once the program was well under way, the education editors for the city's newspapers and television stations could be informed of the project, since the idea of a Japanese schooling practice being adopted in a local school would likely be seen as an attractive topic for a feature story. The publicity resulting from a newspaper article or television report might encourage the school principal and other teachers to join the program, thereby avoiding the public embarrassment that could result from their not participating in the project.

Cost/Benefit Ratio

As people consider the desirability of a proposed educational reform, their decision usually includes an estimate of how the costs will balance against the benefits to be gained. Sometimes this estimate is conscious and formal, with the estimated costs intentionally toted up and weighed against consciously considered benefits to determine if the rewards of adopting the innovation are going to be worth the trouble involved. In other instances, the estimate appears to be made intuitively, resulting in some such vague conclusions as "It sounds like it might be a good idea" or "That doesn't seem exactly safe; we might be taking too much of a risk."

The costs that an educational reform involves can be of various sorts—money spent, time used, energy expended, social relations damaged, reputation tarnished, goals not reached, worry, indecision, and more. Benefits are also of diverse kinds—money saved, time and energy conserved, social relations improved, reputation enhanced, goals attained, satisfaction gained from a task well done.

Because the factors that go into cost/benefit reckoning are of such different kinds, there is no common coin in which to make the calculations. Thus, reckoning an innovation's rewards in comparison to its costs involves an imprecise mental algebra in which each factor is weighted in terms of the reckoner's personal values regarding money, social relations, concern for one's reputation, and such. In people's cost/benefit calculations, the particular ratio of costs to benefits influences the amount of inertia the educational innovation will encounter.

Proposition: The higher the cost-to-benefit ratio that can be expected from an innovation, the greater the inertia that innovation will face.

Cost/benefit calculations are involved in all types of educational reforms—those concerning objectives, teaching methods, evaluation procedures, policies, management, and support services. Therefore, the following case illustrates only one out of many thousands of ways to apply cost/benefit analysis to proposed educational change.

Problem case C: In a small town high school, the supervisor of technology services recognized that many students had personal computers at home, enabling them to practice computer skills and search the Internet any time they chose. However, students who lacked home computers felt disadvantaged and therefore appealed to the supervisor for the opportunity to use the school's computer laboratory after school hours. The supervisor thought this was a good idea and suggested it to the principal, who agreed to a one-month trial period that would reveal how well the arrangement worked out. The principal suggested that the laboratory also be available to parents and other members of the community who did not have computers at home or who wished to learn how to operate personal computers. According to the principal, advertising this service in the town newspaper and over the radio station would also be a good political move, demonstrating to the public that the school's computer facilities were being put to maximum use.

Therefore, the computer laboratory, with its 30 personal computers and peripheral equipment (scanners, digital cameras, software programs), was made available each weekday from 3:30 to 5:30 p.m. and 7:00 p.m. to 10:00 p.m. as well as on Saturdays and Sundays from 1:00 p.m. to 5:00 p.m. Six high school students who were well versed in computer use were hired to take turns managing the laboratory under the guidance of the technology supervisor.

At the end of the one-month trial, the supervisor and principal reviewed the costs and benefits in order to decide if the temporary arrangement should become a permanent service and, if so, what changes might be needed.

To cast their cost/benefit considerations in a visible form, the principal and supervisor prepared two lists, one displaying perceived costs and the other displaying perceived benefits.

COSTS	BENEFITS
Student assistants' pay = $1,320	37 people had been served, some of them for only one session, and others for multiple sessions.
Lost equipment (6 compact discs and 1 digital camera missing) = $2,100	
Attendance declined during final two weeks, with few if any people coming Friday evenings and Saturdays.	14 students who had no computer at home were the most consistent users of the after-school plan; they expressed their appreciation for the program.
Members of the community who knew little or nothing about computers took up an inordinate amount of student assistants' time.	

<u>COSTS</u>	<u>BENEFITS</u>
During busy sessions, assistants had a difficult time helping everyone. Some participants' lack of experience using computers caused them to do things that made the machines malfunction, thereby putting the machines out of commission until the problems could be corrected some days later by a skilled technician. Some girls did not attend during the later evening hours because they feared for their safety as they walked home in the dark. The school district's assistant superintendent for business affairs questioned whether the district's liability insurance would be in force when only a student assistant, rather than a faculty member, was in charge of the laboratory.	Favorable articles appeared in the town newspaper.

When the principal and supervisor analyzed their two lists, they decided that the costs of the after-school computer-use plan so outweighed the benefits that the venture, at least in its present form, should be abandoned.

Remedy options: The following are three possible ways to decrease the cost-to-benefit ratio and thereby save the plan.

Limit hours. The expense for student assistants could be reduced by limiting the times the computer laboratory would be available. The past month's record of which days and hours had been most popular could suggest which times the laboratory might most economically be open. Reducing the hours would also conserve electricity.

Limit participants. Because nonstudent participants had taken up so much of the student assistants' time, restricting the privilege of using the laboratory to students would make the assistants' jobs easier and also warrant eliminating the hours when most members of the public had come to the laboratory during the tryout month.

Limit facilities. To prevent further losses of equipment (such as the six compact discs and digital camera that apparently had been stolen), the equipment made available in the after-school plan could be restricted to the computers themselves and to the programs already on the computers' hard disks (thereby eliminating the need for compact discs). Users could be required to provide their own diskettes or compact discs for storing reports, letters, or graphics they had composed.

Conclusion

The three inertia-related aspects of educational services illustrated in this chapter have been bureaucratic efficiency, critical mass, and cost/benefit ratios. Here are five additional viewpoints from which to analyze barriers to educational-service innovations.

- *Keeping records.* What kinds of records are kept, and what system is used for compiling records?
- *Furnishing curriculum materials.* By what method are curriculum materials (textbooks, periodicals, library holdings, music scores, art supplies, computer programs) supplied?
- *Maintaining equipment.* What system is used for monitoring the condition of equipment and buildings and for providing repairs and replacements when they are needed?
- *Transporting students.* What provisions are made for transporting students to and from school and to school-related events that are held away from the campus?
- *Offering personnel benefits.* What extra benefits does the school furnish its employees (wages, insurance, parking privileges, travel expenses, and the like)?

Discussion Topics

For practice in recognizing sources of inertia in different attempts at educational reform, consider the following cases. For each case, estimate what kinds of people or what conditions might obstruct the implementation of the intended reform.

Case 1: A school district that contained five elementary schools and one junior high had traditionally conducted its own food-service system that supplied the six schools with noontime meals for pupils and faculty members. However, the district's board of trustees decided that it would be more economical and would reduce the need to deal with difficult employees if food services were contracted out to a professional catering company. What sorts of problems do you foresee that might prevent a smooth transition from the old system to the new one, and what steps might be taken to diminish the inertia that such problems could cause?

Case 2: In a high school whose expenses rose faster than its income, the principal decided that the school could no longer furnish free uniforms for athletic teams, and particularly for the football team. In the future, student athletes would need to pay the cost of their uniforms. What forces do you imagine might frustrate the implementation of the principal's plan, and what might he do to minimize the damage to the proposal?

Case 3: To serve the needs of talented pupils, a school system introduced special elementary school classes for "the gifted." Which pupils would be admitted to the program would be determined by their scores on achievement tests in reading, writing, and mathematics. What problems might the schools' administrators expect as they put the plan into practice, and how might they attempt to cope with those problems?

Part IV

The External Support System

As described in Chapter 1, the model of education on which this book is based includes three sources outside of the education system that influence what and how students learn. Those three are the society's cultural traditions, political forces, and economic conditions.

The characteristics of a society that qualify as *cultural traditions* are those features that fall within the definition of culture as "a group's shared language, ideas, beliefs, customs, codes, institutions, tools, techniques, works of art, rituals, ceremonies, and so on" (White, 1994, p. 874).

As proposed in Chapter 2, *political power* refers to the effect that one entity—person, group, institution—has on the behavior of another entity. Power is measured by the extent to which one entity's behavior is influenced by the presence and actions of another entity. *Political forces*, as that term is intended in this book, refers to those persons, groups, and organizations outside the education system that seek to influence the system's goals, values, personnel, supplies, equipment, expenditures, methods of operation, and outcomes.

Economic conditions are characteristics of the society's ways of producing and distributing goods and services to the populace. Those conditions affect the education system by influencing the amount and sources of the financial support the system receives and by helping determine the types of skills and knowledge students will be taught to fit them for the labor market.

9

Cultural Traditions

Among the dozens of definitions of *culture* proposed by scholars, one that suits the nature of this chapter is Hofstede's proposal (1980, p. 25), which asserts that culture is "the collective programming of the mind which distinguishes the members of one human group from another." Whereas Hofstede's definition focuses on the beliefs and operations of the mind that are shared by a cultural group, other authors include in their conceptions of *culture* the objects and patterns of interpersonal relations that such a common view of life produces. Thus, people's shared modes of dress, of bodily adornment, of housing, of diet, and of forms of entertainment are all reflections of a "collective programming of the mind." Likewise, people's habits of social interaction—particularly as displayed in spoken, signed, coded, and written language—also reflect a group's shared psychic contents.

Cultural differences among groups and individuals can significantly influence the inertia faced by an educational reform. In this chapter, the five aspects of culture used to illustrate such influence are those of language, religious convictions, moral values, role suitability, and styles of thought.

Cultural Traditions

- Language usage
- Religious convictions
- Moral values
- Role suitability
- Styles of thought

Language Usage

Probably no part of culture is more important for students' school success than the language skills they bring to their learning tasks. It seems apparent that the greater the mismatch between students' language competence and the educational fare they are supposed to master, the poorer their learning progress will be. This observation, when applied to educational reform efforts, suggests the following proposition.

Proposition: The less compatible an instructional innovation is with the dominant language of each student, the more difficult the implementation of the innovation.

Problem case A: In a large city high school, a history teacher joined an English teacher in offering a one-semester, two-period-per-day elective class titled "English History and Literature." The intention of the course was to show how (a) the literature of an era was embedded in, and grew out of, events of the time and (b) history was often influenced by literary works that affected people's beliefs and inspired them to act—to perform such acts as waging war, changing laws, distrusting members of certain ethnic or religious backgrounds, and the like.

In the class's initial semester, the 35 openings for students were easily filled. Culturally, the students represented diverse social-class levels and ethnic/national backgrounds. Differences in social-class levels were reflected in the formal education status of class members' parents (university, high school, elementary school, illiterate) and in parents' employment status (professional, skilled craft, low-skilled labor, unemployed). There were a few students from each of the social-class levels. As for ethnic/national backgrounds, two-thirds of the students were from ancestors who had lived in the United States for two or more generations. One-third of the class members were from more recent immigrant stock. Frequently, a foreign language was spoken in their homes. Foreign-language backgrounds represented in the class included Spanish, Chinese, Vietnamese, and Korean.

The textbook selected as the basic literary material to be studied in the class included examples of English literature from the 14th century to the 20th century. To show students how literary subject matter and language changed over the centuries, the course's two instructors choose a literature text that offered poetry and prose in the original language in which the book's selections had been composed. To illustrate this, here are four segments of works included in the collection.

From the Miller's Tale in *The Canterbury Tales* by Geoffrey Chaucer (1342-1400):

> The Millere was a stout carl for the nones;
> Ful byg he was of brawn, and eek of bones.

> That proved wel, for over al ther he cam,
> At wrastlynge he woulde have alwey the ram.
>   (Aldington, 1941, vol. 1, p. 11)

The opening lines of *Romeo and Juliet* by William Shakespeare (1564-1616):

> *Enter Sampson and Gregory, armed with Swords and Bucklers:*
> *Sam.* Gregory, o' my word, we'll not carry coals.
> *Gre.* No, for then we should be colliers.
> *Sam.* I mean, as we be in choler, we'll draw.
> *Gre.* Ay, while you live, draw your neck out of the collar.
> *Sam.* I strike quickly, being moved.
> *Gre.* But thou art not quickly moved to strike.
>   (Shakespeare, 1987, p. 1241)

From *An Essay on Criticism* by Alexander Pope (1688-1744):

> 'Tis with our judgments as our watches, none
> Go just alike, yet each believes his own.
> In poets as true genius is but rare,
> True taste as seldom is the critic's share.
>   (Aldington, 1941, vol. 1, p. 530)

From the *The Rime of the Ancient Mariner* by Samuel Taylor Coleridge (1772-1834):

> The Wedding-Guest here beat his breast,
> For he heard the loud bassoon.
> The bride hath paced into the hall,
> Red as a rose is she;
> Nodding their heads before her goes
> The merry mistrelsy.
>   (Aldington, 1941, vol. 2, p. 680)

According to the instructors' plan, the historical period encompassed by the class would extend from the Norman conquest of England in 1066 through World War II in 1945. The first literary passages that students would read were two of Chaucer's Canterbury tales—the stories told by the Miller and the Wife of Bath. From the first week of the class, it was apparent that the students were having a very difficult time with the literature reading assignments. By the third week, four students had dropped the class. Many others were very discouraged with the literature portion of the course, and their despair was reflected in their obvious lack of enthusiasm.

It was clear to both of the instructors that culturally based language difficulties were the cause of the students' inadequate understanding and grumpy attitudes. For all class members—those from foreign-language backgrounds as well as the ones whose home language was

American English—the language culture of Chaucer's, Shakespeare's, and Coleridge's times was strange and to a great degree incomprehensible. The students who had the least difficulty with the literary passages were ones from homes where parents held university degrees. Such parents had often studied the same English authors in university classes and could therefore help their teenage offspring understand the reading assignments. Furthermore, the vocabulary and grammar of those parents' everyday language was closer to the speech of such characters as Coleridge's ancient mariner than was the daily language in homes where parents were high school dropouts or only semiliterate.

The students from homes in which a foreign language was spoken faced even a greater challenge, since the vocabulary and grammar they heard at home had little if anything in common with the textbook's language. Only by the most diligent, time-consuming effort could the students from Spanish, Chinese, Vietnamese, and Korean language backgrounds grasp what the English authors of the past were talking about. Consequently, the study of the literature passages—which the instructors had hoped would parallel the historical eras—lagged farther and farther behind as the semester progressed. The instructors were forced to admit that their experiment was something of a failure because of the cultural discrepancy between students' command of English and the language in which the literary passages were cast.

Remedy options: The following alternatives could be used singly or in combination to reduce the inertia caused by the language problems that the new history-literature course faced.

Simplified versions of literature. As explained earlier, the dual purpose of the literary selections was to help students (a) understand the writings in historical context and (b) recognize characteristics of the language in which those writings were cast and compare them to the characteristics of present-day American English. Those two goals could still be achieved if students studied modernized versions of past literary works, then analyzed only brief, illustrative passages of the original works. For example, Chaucers' tales are available in present-day English, as are summaries of Shakespeare's most popular plays. Therefore, in order to grasp the plots of such works and recognize the historical settings in which they were created, students could read these updated renditions. Then, to appreciate how the English language has evolved over the ages, students could study short passages of those works. Consequently, class members would achieve both of the instructors' aims without needing to struggle through an entire tale or drama in its original form.

Parallel passages. For such selections as those from Pope and Coleridge, the instructors could recast the passages into modern prose, then provide students with both versions, thereby enabling class members to understand the content of the passages, their historical settings, and how English in past eras is similar to, and different from, current American English.

Reading in a group. As students followed silently in their textbooks, the teacher could read aloud the works from the past, periodically interrupting the reading with an explanation of terms and historical allusions that would be difficult or impossible for class members to comprehend on their own. Students could also take turns reading aloud portions of a work in order to practice pronouncing phrases in what they imagined might be the style of the original author's time.

Recordings. Audiotapes or videotapes are available for some of the literary works of the past that the class studied, such as Shakespeare's plays and portions of *The Canterbury Tales.* The tapes could be played for the class as students followed the printed words in their textbooks so that students could experience how passages might have sounded at the time they were composed.

Religious Convictions

Over the centuries in virtually every society, a key aim of schooling has been to teach learners the beliefs and practices of the society's dominant religion. Such was the case in colonial America, where priests taught Catholic doctrine and Protestant pastors and schoolmasters taught young and old alike to read the Bible. The most widely used beginning-reading text in English-speaking North America from the 17th to 19th century taught the letters of the alphabet with such illustrative verses as "A = In Adam's fall we sinned all" and "U= Upon the wicked, God will rain a horrible tempest" (*New England Primer,* 1836, p. 11, 14).

However, when leaders of the newly formed United States composed the U.S. Constitution's First Amendment (1789), they committed the government to a doctrine of religious freedom: "Congress shall make no law respecting the establishment of religion." This passage was subsequently interpreted to mean that church and government should be kept separate. But over the following decades, Christian religious doctrine and practices continued to be taught in schools supported by government funds. However, as Americans' ties to the church increasingly loosened over the decades and more immigrants brought non-Christian religious convictions to the country, critics charged that continuing to teach Christian beliefs in tax-supported schools was a violation of the Constitution's first amendment. This issue became a subject of particularly heated legal contention in the final decades of the 20th century and into the 21st century. As a result, we can suggest a proposition about how such a controversy can affect attempts at educational innovation.

Proposition: The more an educational reform conflicts with the religious beliefs and practices of a society, the stronger the efforts to block that reform.

Problem case B: In a small city, political activists representing Americans United for the Separation of Church and State (AUSCS) joined with the local American Civil Liberties Union (ACLU) to file a lawsuit aimed at forcing the public school system to eliminate several practices that might be interpreted as violating the Constitution's freedom-of-religion principle. The practices to which the plaintiffs objected would include (a) prayers offered at school events (classroom meetings, student assemblies, graduation exercises, athletic contests), (b) mentioning God in the traditional pledge of allegiance to the United States, (c) posting the Ten Commandments, (d) teaching a biblical version of the creation of the universe and of humankind, and (e) celebrating such Christian holidays as Christmas and Easter.

When the lawsuit was announced in newspapers and on television and radio, a cascade of protests came to the superintendent of schools in the form of phone calls, e-mail messages, and letters. Nearly one hundred people joined a rally in front of the public school headquarters, with participants carrying signs declaring "Godless schools make for bad education" and "Say no to atheism!"

The school board, fearing the high cost and unfavorable publicity of a court case, voted 5 to 4 to abolish the practices that the plaintiffs found objectional. As a result, the AUSCS and ACLU withdrew the suit.

Remedy options: Two sets of remedies are suggested for this case. The first set is designed to ensure that the school board's reform is faithfully carried out in practice and does not succumb to resistance from opponents of the board's directive. The second set consists of measures that defenders of the traditional religious practices might adopt to salvage those practices, at least partially.

Set 1—Monitoring. Supporters of the board's directive could enlist the aid of students and teachers, sympathetic to the supporters' cause, to report school personnel (administrators, teachers, coaches, counselors) who continued to follow the banned practices.

Set 1—Substituting. Proponents of the complete separation of church and state could suggest activities to replace the banned practices and still accomplish desirable aims. For example, students could subscribe to a pledge of allegiance to the nation that omitted the phrase "under God." Or, rather than endorsing the biblical Ten Commandments, virtues that did not allude to theology but were commonly held guides to fair and amicable social relations could be taught. The last five of the Ten Commandments might thus be included among the revised list of virtues (don't—kill, steal, lie about other people, commit adultery, or yearn for others' possessions) but commandments with a theological focus would not (don't—worship gods other than Jehovah, carve idols of gods, use Jehovah's name lightly, or work on the Sabbath).

Set 2—Comparative religion. As suggested in the Ten Commandments case in Chapter 3, a study unit or full course titled "Comparative Religion" could be taught without violating the principle that has traditionally been applied in decisions about the separation of church and state. The principle asserts that public schools cannot promote one religion over another nor can they promote a religious lifestyle over a secular lifestyle, or vice versa.

Comparative religion qualifies as a proper focus of attention in public schools by virtue of its being a highly significant field of investigation in the social sciences. Such a course includes the study of a variety of religious persuasions, giving equal time to each and not advocating the adoption of one religion in preference to any other. Thus, Christian beliefs and ceremonies could be studied along with the beliefs and rituals of other religions—Judaism, Islam, Buddhism, Taoism, Voodoo, and the like.

Set 2—Christmas and Easter. In the spirit of a comparative-religion approach, the Christmas and Easter seasons might continue to be celebrated in schools if other religions' key holidays were given equal attention, such as Hanukkah and Passover for Judaism, Ramadan and Idul Fitri for Islam, and traditional American-Indian celebrations.

Set 2—Origins of the universe and humankind. The teaching of a biblical account of human beginnings, as found in the book of Genesis (in Judaism's Torah and Christianity's Bible), could be included in a science or social studies class so long as it was within a comparative approach to the question of human origins—an approach that included other accounts as well, such as Darwin's theory of evolution, the Japanese Shinto story of the two original human spirits (Izanami and Izanagi), and a Hindu belief that humans were created when a celestial

> *Self* appeared in the shape of a person, born of the Cosmic Egg. But when this person reflected on his condition, he realized that he was alone and afraid, and thus he was unhappy. So he became the size of a man and wife in close embrace. He divided this body in two. From that division arose husband and wife. . . . From that union humans were born. (Nikhilananda in Thomas, 1988, p. 34).

Moral Values

In discussions of values, a useful distinction can be drawn between facts and values. *Facts* can be defined as objective information—observations or measurements that are publicly verifiable. In contrast, *values* are opinions about the desirability or propriety or goodness of something.

That "something" may be a person, an object, a place, an event, an idea, a kind of behavior, or the like. Statements of fact tell what exists, in what amount, and perhaps in what relation to other facts. Statements of value tell whether something is good or bad, well done or poorly done, suitable or unsuitable, pretty or ugly.

Values come in different types. *Aesthetic values* involve judgments from an artistic viewpoint—a beautiful flower, a nicely turned metaphor, a delightfully melodic song. *Functional values* focus on how efficiently something operates or how well its parts coordinate—a leaky faucet, a speedy auto, an efficient committee. *Economic values* concern how much profit or loss an investment yields—a great bargain, a questionable stock, a disastrous loan.

Moral values concern proper and improper ways that people behave toward each other or how faithfully people abide by the dictates of such an authority as a chieftain, god, or respected document (criminal law code, Bible, Koran). Moral values are important concerns for people involved with schooling, including those people who introduce educational reforms.

Proposition: The more that an innovative practice conflicts with deep-seated moral convictions held within the society, the greater the inertia that the practice must overcome.

Problem case C: In a large city high school, the teacher in charge of an elective course titled "Modern Social Problems" attempted to infuse new life into his instruction by introducing each week's social problem with of a videotape or compact disc presentation. The series of presentations consisted of documentaries or fictional dramas about street crime, poverty, teenage sexual relations, AIDS (acquired immune deficiency syndrome), pornography, marriage and divorce, mental illness, spousal and child abuse, drug and alcohol abuse, political corruption, and war.

On Monday each week, the teacher handed a list of guide questions to the class before showing the week's documented or dramatized social issue. The questions directed students' attention to events in the movie that warranted particular attention. Their homework task would be to write answers to the questions and bring their answers to class on Tuesday when a discussion—involving either the entire class or small groups—would focus on the questions. The remaining three days of the week would be dedicated to in-depth study of the week's topic by means of textbooks, newspapers, news magazines, visiting speakers, excursions (to a jail, to a court, to a medical clinic), and the Internet.

By the fourth week of the semester, the high school principal and the teacher of Modern Social Problems were receiving daily complaints about the class from parents. Three students dropped the class because they had found it offensive. Disapproving letters-to-the-editor appeared in the city's leading newspaper, and the class was criticized on a local television talk show. The complaints were all directed at what the critics considered unacceptable moral values in the Monday video dramas—unmarried teenagers in bed together, nudity, youths reveling in the use of illicit drugs and alcohol, violent treatment of children and women, mental and physical torture, love scenes involving couples of the same sex, ethnic slurs, and language referred to as "foul" and "blasphemous." Samples of language that a girl in the class had copied were submitted by her mother in support of the foul-language charge—"I don't give a fuckin' goddamn what you think" and "I ain't taking no more of that shit."

The teacher defended the films on the grounds that they revealed "real social problems and behavior rather than the usual sanitized version of reality offered up by the schools." The principal replied that, however true the teacher's claim about reality might be, the superintendent of schools, the Parent Teachers Association, and a group of local ministers were putting pressure on him to "clean things up over there." In response, the teacher contended that some parents supported his use of the films by saying they would rather have controversial social issues discussed openly and under the guidance of a responsible educator than have teenagers build their attitudes on the misinformation and immature hedonism that their peers so often fostered. To end their conversation, the principal ordered the teacher to submit each video to him before using it with the class so that the principal could decide if it should be shown. The teacher called this censorship, but agreed to drop the use of films in the future after the principal threatened to abolish the class immediately if the teacher insisted on using the films without submitting them for review beforehand. The teacher concluded that his innovation had failed.

Remedy options: The following are ways the teacher might attempt to rescue his methodological reform.

Yield to the principal's order. As the principal had suggested, the teacher could submit the videos ahead of time to have the moral content approved before the videos were shown to the class. It would probably be wise for the teacher to have more than one video reviewed for each class session so that if one was rejected as morally unacceptable, there would be another that the principal might approve.

Obtain parents' approval. A printed summary of the content of each upcoming video—including any of the video's morally controversial features—could be sent class members' parents, who would need to give their written permission in order for their son or daughter to witness the presentation. One problem with this solution would be that students who were not permitted to see a video would not be prepared to answer the guide questions or participate in the Tuesday class discussion.

Set entrance requirements for the class. In the future, before students signed up for the class, the teacher could prepare a description of the weekly class topics and the videos that would be used in the Monday sessions. The description would be provided to parents of students who wished to enroll in the class. In order to join the class, students would be required to receive their parents' written permission.

Role Suitability

Every culture maintains *social roles,* which are defined in terms of the behavior expected of people because of their age, gender, occupation, religion, ethnic background, socioeconomic status, titles, and more. Expected role behaviors often differ from one culture to another. An outspoken 20-year-old man may be admired in one society as "up-and-coming and full of initiative" but, in another as society, as "ill-mannered and disrespectful." A 15-year-old girl dressed in shorts and a halter is judged "cute and in style" in one society but in another is deemed "uncouth and wickedly seductive." In one culture a store clerk who calls a customer by her first name may be viewed as "nice and friendly" but in another culture as "rude and intrusive." The success of educational innovations can be influenced by such contrasting conceptions of social roles.

Proposition: The more an educational reform conflicts with traditional beliefs about the proper roles people should assume, the greater the inertia the reform will face.

Problem case D: A county school system's director of business affairs resigned his position to become the superintendent of schools in a nearby city. One of the five applicants for his vacated position was a man in the business affairs office who had been the chief accountant under the now departed director. The accountant, age 37, had held his present position for the past six years. Originally he had immigrated to the United States at age 24 to take a graduate degree in business administration. Upon finishing his degree, he had stayed in the country to become an American citizen.

When the director resigned, the accountant informed the other five business office employees that he expected to be appointed to be the new director. Therefore, he was greatly distressed and disheartened when another candidate was selected for the post. What the accountant found particularly galling was that the appointee was a 30-year-old woman who had been the head of business affairs in a smaller school district. In the culture in which the accountant had been raised prior to coming to

America, men were regarded as more intelligent and more logical than women. Women were thought to act more on emotion than on reason. Men were expected to give orders that women were expected to obey. Furthermore, wisdom was thought to increase with age, so older people were believed to be better qualified than younger ones for leadership positions and decision making. Although the accountant recognized that such role expectations were not identical to those in present-day North America, he still felt that his homeland's traditions were correct. Therefore, he greeted the arrival of his new boss with strong feelings of resentment.

Whenever a leader resigns or is replaced, the new leader often introduces reforms designed to improve the organization's efficiency. The present case was no exception. One of the young woman's first acts was to change the accounting method the office had traditionally used. The new method was a computerized system she had adopted in her previous position. She also instituted a communication and reporting plan that was intended to exert tighter central control over school expenditures and to speed the exchange of messages between her office and school principals. Furthermore, she expected weekly written reports from each of her six employees, a duty the previous director had never required.

It soon became clear to the new director that the transition from the old practices to the new ones left much to be desired. Her office staff and the school principals often continued to use their long-established methods of communicating. Reports arrived late and frequently failed to include all of the required material, so it became necessary for her to request revisions. But the greatest difficulties were experienced with the new accounting system and with the weekly reports from the accountant. The process of eliminating the old system and installing the new was fraught with continual problems, and the accountant failed to submit weekly reports until the director went to him and demanded them. Furthermore, instead of describing what the accountant had accomplished over the past week, his reports were filled with criticisms of how the newly required management procedures were reducing the efficiency of the business affairs office. When the director brought these matters to the attention of the accountant, his responses implied that the problems resulted from the director's failure to understand the nature of the school district and of proper accounting procedures. The final evidence that convinced the new director that her accounting and weekly report innovations were failing came when the district superintendent called her to his office to ask about a variety of problems that had been reported to him. As he described the problems, the director recognized that the superintendent's information must have come from the accountant. This suspicion was later confirmed when she spoke at some length with another of the employees in her office—a woman who was sympathetic with the new director's plight and told her of the beliefs that the accountant had expressed over the years about proper gender roles and age roles.

Remedy options: Attempts to reduce the inertia that the accountant's actions had produced might include the following alternatives.

Dismiss. The director could speak again with the superintendent of schools and request that the accountant be either dismissed or transferred to a different office. In support of such a request, the director could describe what she had heard about the accountant's (a) conception of proper gender and age roles and (b) strong desire to be the county schools' director of business affairs.

Reassign. If there is another member of the business office staff capable of assuming the position of accountant, the director could remove the accounting duties from the present accountant, place the other staff member in that post, and assign the present accountant other tasks. By adopting the reassignment strategy, the director might achieve several goals: (a) gain control over the accounting functions by assigning a cooperative worker to the job, (b) demonstrate that she is not afraid of the accountant and is willing to wield her authority over him, and (b) punish him by removing his traditional responsibilities and thereby shaming him in the eyes of coworkers.

Confer. The director could ask the accountant to meet with her so that together they might solve the problems that had arisen since her arrival. She could ask how he thought his job could best be accomplished and what help she could provide. Then she could weigh his proposals and decide which, if any of them, she could profitably adopt. She could also explain her reasons for changing the accounting system and for requiring weekly reports. The dual purpose of this approach would be (a) to work out a compromise which both the director and the accountant could live with and (b) render their personal relationship more amicable.

Confront. The director could confront the accountant directly, telling him that she knows what he is trying to do and why he is doing it. She could then warn him of the consequences he can expect if he fails to "shape up and do the job right." Those consequences might include the director (a) detailing the accountant's incompetent performance in a report to the superintendent of schools, (b) removing the accountant from his post and assigning him other duties, and (c) in a meeting of the district headquarters' staff members, openly accusing the accountant of trying to sabotage the business office.

Instruct. The director could apologetically explain to the accountant that she apparently had underestimated the difficulty he would experience with the new accounting system and the weekly report requirement. Therefore, she planned to work closely with him, instructing him in the specific steps to take to make the system work and illustrating the way weekly reports should be written. In effect, the director would become the accountant's mentor, daily demonstrating how each problem he faced might be solved.

Styles of Thought

There is a substantial body of psychological and anthropological evidence supporting the observation that dominant ways of thinking can vary from one culture to another. Such evidence suggests that people's modes of thought are not entirely determined by genetic endowment, that is, by the structure of the human brain as inherited from parents. While the inherited structure obviously does influence how people think as they develop from infancy into adulthood, it is also true that people learn ways of thinking from both their informal experiences (watching how others speak, write, and act) and formal instruction (parents' advice, schooling). Such learned styles of thought are often shared throughout a cultural group, so that the typical ways of thinking of one group can differ from the typical ways of another group (Thomas, 2001b). This observation leads to the following proposition.

> *Proposition:* The more that the mode of thought required by an educational reform deviates from the traditional way of thinking of the people who are subject to the reform, the greater the inertia the reform will face.

Problem case E: One neighborhood in a small city was populated by a tightly knit ethnic group whose members were bound together by their strong commitment to a religious and linguistic tradition that their ancestors had brought to North America from their homeland. Among the group's cooperative ventures was a parochial elementary school—grades 1 through 6—that most of the neighborhood children attended. When pupils finished grade 6, they enrolled in a public junior high school.

The junior high's required seventh-grade social studies course focused on state and regional history. The man who taught the five sections of the course wanted students not only to understand events of the past but also to consider how history—and their own lives—could have turned out differently if certain events had taken a different turn. The teacher recognized that by asking students to engage in such speculation, he was expecting them to adopt a style of thought which, for many of them, might be quite unusual. He estimated that much—likely most—of the thinking the pupils had been expected to do in elementary school involved convergent thought. He was now asking them to engage in divergent thought (Guilford,1967).

Convergent thinking can be defined as the process of discovering, or recalling, the correct solution for a problem—of furnishing the right answer. *Divergent thinking*, in contrast, can be defined as the process of generating as many different potential answers as possible. Thus, divergent thinking requires departing from usual, routine solutions in order to link together ideas that have not, in a person's past experience, appeared to belong together. The contrast between the mental processes that these two styles of thought involve is illustrated by the following pair of test items.

> *Convergent thinking.* Carl first drove 23 miles to Ralph's house, returned home, drove 18 miles to Mike's house, and again returned home. How far did Carl drive all together?

> *Divergent thinking.* I'm holding a common brick, the kind typically used in building houses. Within the space of two minutes, tell me how many different ways you can think of that my brick could be used.

The first test item calls for discovering the single correct answer. The second item calls for producing an unlimited number of possibilities, with greater credit for divergent thinking awarded to students whose responses represent a collection of alternatives that are least alike. For instance, one student may say the brick could be used in (a) building a garage, (b) building a doghouse, (c) building a wall, and (d) building a chimney. That student would receive less credit for divergent thought than would a student who says the brick could be (a) ground into powder and mixed with oil to make paint, (b) used to pound a nail, (c) tossed in a shot-put contest, and (d) stood on by a person who is trying to reach a book on an upper shelf.

During the study of state and regional history, when the teacher asked class members to propose how history might have been changed if certain events had occurred differently, he found much variability among the students in how readily they could adopt divergent thinking. In particular, he found that the ones who had attended the ethnic group's private school were reluctant to try his creative-thought task. They said such things as "I just want to learn what really happened" and "I don't see why we're doing this, because it's not the truth." Therefore, he estimated that their earlier schooling, and perhaps their family lives, had emphasized the conviction that there was a single correct answer to any question, and that single answer was what students were supposed to learn in school. Thus, the teacher concluded that his effort to encourage divergent thinking about history was something of a failure, at least with certain class members, and especially with ones from that particular private school.

Remedy options: Approaches the teacher might attempt for helping students develop divergent-thinking skills could include peer modeling and group brainstorming.

Peer modeling. In a class discussion, students can be assigned to speculate about how history could have been altered if, at a crucial time, a certain event had taken a curious turn, such as there was a different victor in a war, a different winning candidate in an election, a leader had not died, a forest had not been destroyed by fire, a town had not been flooded. Each time a student suggested such a turn of events and then described a series of subsequent outcomes that might have resulted, the teacher could ask, "Can you tell us how you thought of such a thing? Can you explain what went through your mind?" When various students thus try analyzing their thought processes, other class members who have appeared less adept at divergent thinking may be able to improve their creative skill by trying to adopt modes of thought their classmates have described.

Group brainstorming. The process of brainstorming, when used as either a game or a serious creativity exercise, can assume various forms. One popular form involves the following steps.

(a) The group leader selects a problem or question and asks the group members to come up with as many different solutions or answers as possible, without considering how practical those solutions might be.

(b) Before the members suggest solutions, the leader warns them that no one is to criticize or scoff at anyone else's suggestions. The purpose at this stage of the exercise is to generate as many diverse solutions or answers as possible.

(c) When all proposals have been expressed, the group selects criteria to be used in deciding which of the solutions are most practical or viable—that is, which ones could actually be used to solve the problem.

(d) Next, the viability of each solution is tested against the criteria and a decision is reached about which one or more should be put into practice.

The purpose of such an approach is to encourage divergent thinking by praising the expression of novel—and what may appear at first glance to be fantastic and unreasonable—solutions to problems without judging their practicality. Only after these brainstormed possibilities are at hand does the group develop criteria to use in judging which of the alternatives can profitably be adopted.

By having the seventh-grade social studies class play the brainstorming game, the teacher might be able to stimulate the more hesitant students to think in a more divergent fashion.

Conclusion

This chapter's five perspectives from which to view cultural influences on inertia have been those of language usage, religious convictions, moral values, role suitability, and styles of thought. Other useful perspectives concern:

- *Etiquette.* In social situations, which ways of acting are considered polite, respectful, and constructive; and which are considered impolite, disrespectful, and damaging?
- *Child-rearing practices.* What ways of treating children and youths will result in their growing up as productive, socially acceptable, and happy individuals; and what ways will result in their wasting their potential talents, becoming socially destructive, and being discontented?
- *Humor.* What kinds of events—or ways of describing people and events—are thought to be laughable?
- *Emotional expression.* What sorts of emotional expression are regarded as appropriate on different occasions?
- *Explanations of cause.* What are the reasons that the events of the world happen as they do?

Discussion Topics

1. In this chapter's case D, the five remedy options suggested for use by the new director of business affairs would involve her dismissing the accountant, reassigning him to other duties, conferring with him, confronting him, or instructing him. But in the earlier description of the options, no judgment was offered about which of the five choices would likely lead to the most desirable outcome. You now have the opportunity to offer your judgment of that matter by ranking the five options in the order of their likely effectiveness. The most appropriate option, in your opinion, should be ranked number 1, the next most appropriate ranked number 2, and so on. Then defend you decision by explaining why you have arranged the five in that order.

2. In case C, the principal insisted on viewing each video before he would allow the teacher to show the video in class. Do you think there were better ways for the principal to deal with the problem?

10

Political Forces

The word *political* is used in this chapter to mean the influence that one entity exerts over another entity. An entity can be an individual person, a group, or an organization. The extent to which a political relationship exists between two entities is shown by how much the behavior of one affects the behavior of the other. For example, if a school board ignores a petition—signed by 165 members of the community—demanding that students sing *God Bless America* at the beginning of each school day, then that group of residents has no political influence over the school board, at least in regard to that particular song. However, if a group of environmentalists succeeds in convincing a state textbook advisory committee that a general science textbook used in junior high schools advocates practices harmful to forests and grasslands, and the committee thereby recommends that the book be dropped, then the environmentalists have demonstrated political power over the committee. Political power is usually not exerted solely in one direction, but is reciprocal. Each entity influences the other to some extent. The resulting confrontation of power results in a stalemate when the amount of power on both sides is equal. Or the confrontation can result in one side besting the other, either entirely or with some measure of compromise.

The two perspectives from which political power is viewed in this chapter are those of tradition and legality.

```
Political Forces
• Tradition
• Legality
```

Tradition

In the present context, the word *tradition* refers to an educational policy or practice that has been the customary way of doing things for an extended period of time, that is, for at least five or six decades, and usually much longer.

Proposition: The more firmly an educational tradition is established in a society, the greater the inertia faced in attempting to effect an educational reform that conflicts with that tradition.

Problem case A: Attempts to improve education often consist of activists from the community seeking either to eliminate a current educational practice or to introduce a practice that promotes the activists' philosophical stance or welfare. One of the most common forms of such political action focuses on a school's learning materials—textbooks, reading books, reference books, magazines, films, videos, posters, charts, compact discs, and the like. The following case illustrates such action in the realm of sex education.

In traditional American society, the responsibility to provide sex education for children and youths has not been assigned to public schools. Rather, it has been confined to the home and church. However, at a growing pace during the 20th century and into the 21st, teaching about sexual matters has become part of the curriculum, usually in the form of information about biological reproduction—the physical facts of ovaries, testes, the combining of sex cells, and the differentiation of cell structures over the months following insemination. Less frequently, and with greater opposition from parents and community groups, sex education programs have addressed such personal and social issues as venereal disease, premarital sex, extramarital sex, birth control, homosexuality, and bisexuality.

For instance, in response to two parents' objecting to the contents of a sex education book titled *It's Perfectly Normal,* the 17 members of a school district's Controversial Issues Review Committee inspected the book, then scheduled an open meeting to hear testimony from the parents who had contended that the book's explicit content was inappropriate for young children.

It's Perfectly Normal not only offered information about the physical characteristics of the two sexes, but also addressed such topics as masturbation, homosexuality, and AIDS. Both the author and the illustrator of the book defended it as an important and honest resource that had won scores of literary awards. *It's Perfectly Normal* had also gained distinction in 1998 by topping the American Library Association's list of books that people most often tried to get banned from or restricted in school libraries.

The reason that the Controversial Issues Review Committee included so many members was that school officials wished to have the group represent many segments of the community—parents, retirees, teenagers, librarians, principals, housewives, professional and business people, the clergy, and more.

As members of the committee investigated the matter, they learned that there were 25 copies of the book in 16 of the city's middle and elementary school libraries. They then informally solicited opinions of various community groups about what sex education information pupils should be able to find at school and at what age. Some parents believed the young should learn about such matters at home, if at all. Others complained that the book contained the "smut" that seeped into classrooms when religion was not included in the curriculum. Another faction condemned censorship and wanted children to have access to a book that provided "a solid, unembarrassed look at the human body" (Pesznecker, 2001).

Remedy options for the committee. In attempting to adjudicate the conflict between the contending factions, the committee had at least five options from which to choose. By majority vote, the committee members could (a) postpone a decision, (b) leave the decision up to the superintendent of schools and his staff, (c) require that the book be removed from the schools, (d) permit the book to remain in the schools with no restrictions placed on pupils' access to it, or (e) permit the book to remain available but to be checked out only by those pupils who brought a signed permission slip from their parents.

Problem case B: In North America prior to the early decades of the 20th century, the traditional interpretation of the origins of the human species was the biblical account in which the two progenitors of all humanity were a pair of individuals, Adam and Eve, whom God had created in their mature adult form. However, Charles Darwin's theory (proposing that all animal species—including humans—evolved from very simple organisms over eons of time) gradually became the innovative version of human origins taught in schools. But Darwinism did not go unchallenged. It met with stiff opposition from biblical creationists, most dramatically demonstrated in the widely publicized 1925 court trial of a biology teacher, John T Scopes, who was accused of teaching Darwin's theory in violation of a Tennessee state law that banned Darwinism from the schools. Scopes was convicted and fined $100, but the verdict was later reversed on a technicality. The law was ultimately repealed in 1967.

By the 1980s and 1990s, the theory that had been an innovation in the early part of the century had become a firm tradition. However, advocates of biblical creationism did not give up. Creationists in several states attempted to pass laws that either would eliminate the teaching of Darwinian theory or else would require that the Bible version also be taught as a reasonable alternative theory. Although most such proposals were rejected by legislators or struck down in the courts, in 1999 the 10-member Kansas state board of education ruled, in a 7-3 decision, that nothing about the theory of evolution could be included on state achievement tests. Observers interpreted this as a way to reform the teaching of biology by eliminating Darwinism from the curriculum (Kansas rejects theory of evolution, 1999).

Remedy options for advocates of the reform: Actions available to the anti-Darwinism forces included:

Testimonials. Spokespersons for the creationist position stated in the public press that the theory of evolution was not proven and that to tell students it was a trustworthy scientific discovery was a deception (Kansas rejects theory of evolution, 1999).

Electioneering. In looking forward to the November 2000 election in which voters would decide which candidate should be elected to the Kansas board of education, proponents of eliminating Darwinism from school curricula cited public opinion polls in support of their position. Pollsters employed by the Rasmusson Research firm reported that 62% of Kansans believed biblical creationism should be taught in the schools. And if Darwinism were included in science courses, 59% said a disclaimer should be issued to students, noting that the proposal about evolution was a *theory*, not established *fact*. Nearly 54% of those who rarely or never attended church also thought the Bible's version should be taught in school (Bible and Darwin supported, 2000).

Established law. Proponents of the reform also counted on the inertia that their recent official ruling provided against attempts to include Darwinian theory in science curricula. That is, they appreciated the fact that it is easier to let present regulations continue in effect than to try changing them.

Remedy options for opponents of the reform: Actions that pro-Darwinism forces could attempt included the following.

Disregarding the reform. Because the Kansas board's ruling did not directly proscribe the teaching of Darwinian theory, schools throughout the public education system continued to teach the theory as the preferred interpretation of how human life on earth began.

Testimonials. Following the board's vote, the news media publicized statements by a variety of opponents of the ruling. A man who had taught biology at Hutchinson High School for 18 years was quoted as saying, "We're going back to the 1880s. It does make us look to the people in the rest of the country that we're a bunch of hicks" (Kansas rejects theory of evolution, 1999). Kansas Governor Bill Graves publicly condemned the 1999 vote as an "embarrassment" to the state (Kansas restores evolution, 2001).

Precedents. To support their challenge of the board ruling, Darwinism advocates cited the examples of Arizona, Alabama, Illinois, New Mexico, Texas, and Nebraska, where similar attempts to eliminate the evolution version of human creation had been defeated either in legislatures or in the courts.

Electioneering. Widespread publicity was given in the public press about the attitudes different candidates for the board of education held toward the creationism/Darwinism issue. Furthermore, opponents of the board's 1999 decision cited selected results from the Rasmussen poll in support of their position, such as, 55% of respondents said that a board member's position in the biblical/Darwinian debate was important, and 59% approved of teaching evolution without requiring a disclaimer that cited the competing creationist theory. A reported 52% of Protestants and 65% of Catholics supported teaching evolution, whereas only 39% of Evangelical Christians were in favor of including evolution in the curriculum (Bible and Darwin, 2000).

Legal action. Three of the board of education members who had voted in 1999 to eliminate evolution items from state tests were defeated in the November 2000 election, replaced by pro-Darwin candidates. On February 14, 2001, the board reinstated the teaching of evolution in the state's science curricula and tests by a 7-3 vote (Kansas restores evolution, 2001). Thus, the 1999 reform was rescinded.

Problem case C: From the 18th century well into the 20th century, the United States evolved a strong tradition of *Americanization.* The nature of Americanization was foreseen shortly after the American Revolution of 1776, by a French immigrant, Crévecoeur, who wrote in 1782 that each person who fled from Europe to settle in America was being transformed into a new breed of individual

> who, leaving behind all his ancient prejudices and manners, receives new ones from the new mode of life he has embraced, the new government he obeys, and the new rank he holds. The American is a new man, who acts upon new principles. . . . Here, individuals of all nations are melted into a new race of men. (Crévecoeur, 1957).

The term *melting pot* was thereafter the byword signifying the goal of integrating the best qualities of all immigrants to form a new American identity. Because the region had been a British colony before American independence was won, and so many leaders of the new nation were of Anglo-Saxon ancestry, British culture heavily influenced the emerging American culture that inhabitants of the melting pot would acquire. English would be the language of government and of daily communication as well as the medium of instruction in schools. Producing this type of American became the tradition that dominated American society and school practice up to the middle of the 20ᵗʰ century. However, events over the decades following World War II cast into question the goal of producing a single, common variety of American. More immigrants from a greater variety of national backgrounds came to the United States. At the same time, members of ethnic minorities developed greater skills of political organization and more effective strategies to make their voices heard. Consequently, in recent decades, the melting pot analogy has increasingly been replaced by other images—*mixed salad* and *human aggregation*—that signify a plural, multicultural society comprised of distinguishably different peoples whose differences are to be respected. This change was forced chiefly by political pressure from ethnic groups (Native Americans, Blacks, Hispanics, Asians, and others) and from those members of the traditional White majority who subscribed to a pluralistic conception of nationalism (Thomas, 1993).

Schools' curricula have been one of the most important aspects of North American education systems influenced by the multiculturalism movement, with textbook reform a frequent target of cultural groups' activities. The usual purpose of activists' attempts to reform textbooks (particularly history, literature, and social studies publications) has been to render schools' curricula favorable to the characteristics that the group's members believe exemplify their particular history and culture. The word *favorable* refers to curriculum content that accords (a) more frequent reference to the particular group's culture, (b) greater appreciation of the culture's admirable qualities, (c) greater recognition of contributions the culture has made to society, and (d) greater acknowledgement of ill treatment the group has suffered at the hands of competing cultural entities (Thomas, 1997).

Native-American groups' campaigns to revise school textbooks is an example of an ethnic minority seeking to repair its image as traditionally presented in curriculum materials. The groups intend to revise the portrayal of American Indians in history and literature texts by

- Not lumping American Indians together with other ethnic minorities in descriptions of non-White-European immigrants to America. Instead, Native Americans should be described as a complex, separate category of citizens
- Not depicting Native-American groups as being all alike, because the ways of life of the many dozens of American Indian nations were, and continue to be, quite different from each other
- Describing Native-American nations' histories prior to the 16ᵗʰ century, rather than focusing exclusively on the American-Indian societies since the arrival of Columbus in the Western Hemisphere.

Textbooks should "portray the Indian as the first explorer, the first colonist, the first conqueror of the North American continent—the first American" (Lincoln, 1998, p. 95)

- Dedicating more space in textbooks to the histories and cultures of Native Americans, in keeping with the important roles they have played over the centuries
- Representing the many facets of American-Indian nations' ways of life, rather than picturing Indians solely as warring savages attacking peaceful European immigrants. This requires correcting the stereotypical image of "the cowboy to the rescue and the Indian doing the scalping" (Lincoln, 1998, p. 95)
- Showing the unique legal and political status of Native Americans in North America as the result of treaties and laws created over the decades (Ashley & Jarratt-Ziemski, 1999)

Remedy options for advocates of the reform: Native Americans and their supporters can avail themselves of the following political devices:

Publicizing. Distorted portrayals of American Indians, and corrected versions, can be described in articles sent to newspapers, magazines, newsletters, academic journals, and radio stations. Television, newspaper, and magazine journalists can be invited to report conferences, festivals, and school activities that depict Native-American life in an accurate way.

Appealing. The inaccuracies in curriculum materials' descriptions of Indians, along with corrected accounts, can be presented to political party activists, community organizations, and political office holders who are then asked to help in the campaign to reform those descriptions.

Withdrawing support. Native Americans can give widespread publicity to their withdrawing their support of organizations (political parties, fraternal clubs, business firms) and individuals (candidates for public office) that oppose the proposed textbook reforms.

Electioneering. In elections, Native-American groups can actively support candidates and laws that favor the proposed textbook revisions.

Litigating. Lawsuits can be aimed at correcting distorted portrayals of American Indians in curriculum materials.

Demonstrating. Public demonstrations for airing Native Americans' grievances can be conducted at schools, school-district administrative offices, state departments of education, textbook selection committees' sessions, school board meetings, and state legislatures.

Appointing, employing. American-Indian groups can urge the appointment of their representatives on curriculum-planning and textbook-adoption committees.

Remedy options for opponents of the reform: Critics of the changes that Native Americans recommend in learning materials often contend that (a) the existing portrayal of American Indians in textbooks is fair and balanced and (b) the proposed changes unduly emphasize the role of American Indians in the nation's history by inaccurately aggrandizing and romanticizing Native Americans, past and present. In opposing the suggested textbook reforms, critics can adopt some of the same techniques as those available to supporters of the reforms—publicizing, appealing, withdrawing support, and demonstrating. Further options include stonewalling, threatening, and co-opting.

Stonewalling. Because the opponents of a reform are often in positions of power (legislators, school board members, school administrators, curriculum planners, Parent Teacher Association officers, teachers), they can effectively block a proposed innovation by ignoring the pleas, arguments, and threats of the reformers or by indefinitely postponing a decision about the issue. Tactics for stonewalling include (a) appointing a committee to consider the issue, but the committee never issues a report of its deliberations, (b) setting up a research project to determine the truth about the content of textbooks, thereby delaying the need to effect changes until the study has been completed some time in the distant future, (c) holding hearings about the issue, thereby providing advocates of the reform an opportunity to voice their complaints but without requiring that a decision be reached by any foreseeable date.

Threatening, intimidating. People in positions of power in relation to the advocates of reform (employers, supervisors, legislators, lawyers, customers, clients, friends) can threaten—either openly or by implication—proponents of the reform with sanctions if they persist in pressing their cause. Reform advocates may be vulnerable to a variety of unwelcome punishments—demotion, loss of friendship, loss of opportunities, a reputation as a troublemaker, and more.

Co-opting. An additional way that opponents may cope with dissidents who are proposing a reform is to entice them into the group that wishes to maintain an existing tradition. Opponents may be induced by the promise of a prestigious, lucrative role in the group's organization—such as the school system, an academic society, or a political party.

Legality

The word *legal*, as used here, refers to formally stated policies or practices that people are expected to adopt. Legal declarations can be in the form of either written documents or time-honored customs that are designed to guide or control individuals' and groups' behavior. Not only do legal statements prescribe and proscribe behavior, but they also often include descriptions of sanctions that are to be suffered by people who fail to abide by the statements.

In the educational world, legal declarations can be issued at different levels of authority. Typically, the higher in the authority structure that a statement appears, the greater the number of people or groups to which the statement applies. Furthermore, the higher that a statement is located, the greater the difficulty met in changing it. The following is an illustration of a hierarchy of legal documents and customs in the field of education. The 12-level hierarchy advances from the most widely applied legal commitment (international) to the narrowest (individual classroom).

- *International.* An example of a legal statement of international scope is the 1948 United Nations' *Universal Declaration of Human Rights* in which Article 26 commits the signatory nations to support the principle that

  > Everyone has a right to education. Education shall be free, at least in the elementary and fundamental stages. Elementary education shall be compulsory. Technical and professional education shall be made generally available and higher education shall be equally accessible to all on the basis of merit. (Tarrow, 1987, p. 237)

- *National constitutions.* Some nations include a commitment to education in their basic constitution. For example, the Republic of Indonesia's constitution states that each citizen is entitled to receive an education, and the government is obligated to conduct a national system of education regulated by law (*Undang-Undang Dasar*, 1945).

  However, the U. S. Constitution does not address matters of education, but leaves to the states the responsibility for providing educational opportunities.

- *National laws.* National legislatures in virtually all countries pass laws bearing on education. For instance, in 1950, as the Republic of Indonesia gained political independence from the Netherlands, the national legislature issued a basic education law that specified the types of schools and the rights to schooling to which the country was committed. In 1989, that basic law was revised in order to expand and render more precise the government's commitment to education and to set the basic rules under which schools would operate (*Undang-Undang No. 12*, 1950/1954; *Undang-Undang No. 2*, 1989).

  Although designing educational provisions has continued as a state and local function in the United States, over the 20th century and into the 21st century, the federal government has increasingly issued laws intended to improve the distribution and quality of education throughout the country. A noteworthy example is the Elementary and Secondary School Act of 1965—a heavily financed, broadly encompassing law that sought to furnish the populace greater educational opportunities, particularly opportunities for learners who were physically, mentally, financially, or culturally disadvantaged. Since 1965 that act has been periodically revised as a result of experience with the act's implementation and in light of more recent lawmakers' beliefs about what the schools should emphasize. Descriptions of those revisions typically follow a statement of the aims the legislators' hope to achieve. For instance, a 2000 updated version of the 1965 act opened with this policy commitment.

> The Congress declares it to be the policy of the United States that a high-quality education for all individuals and a fair and equal opportunity to obtain that education are a societal good, are a moral imperative, and improve the life of every individual, because the quality of our individual lives ultimately depends on the quality of the lives of others. (Title I Amendments, 2000)

* *State constitutions.* State constitutions typically include descriptions of the state's objectives and responsibilities in the realm of education. By way of illustration, Article VII of the Alaska state constitution decrees that

> The legislature shall by general law establish and maintain a system of public schools open to all children of the State, and may provide for other public educational institutions. Schools and institutions so established shall be free from sectarian control. No money shall be paid from public funds for the direct benefit of any religious or other private educational institution.
>
> The University of Alaska is hereby established as the state university and constituted a body corporate. It shall have title to all real and personal property now or hereafter set aside for or conveyed to it. Its property shall be administered and disposed of according to law.
>
> The University of Alaska shall be governed by a board of regents. The regents shall be appointed by the governor, subject to confirmation by a majority of the members of the legislature in joint session. The board shall, in accordance with law, formulate policy and appoint the president of the university. He shall be the executive officer of the board. (Alaska state constitution, 1959).

* *Ballot initiatives.* Traditionally, the task of passing laws governing a state's schools has been the province of state legislatures. However, in recent times, citizens dissatisfied with the laws—or dissatisfied with legislators' failure to address educational problems—have submitted legislative initiatives directly to the voters by placing proposed educational changes on the ballot at election time. For example, in 1998 in California a bilingual education program that

the state legislature had mandated 30 years earlier was eliminated by voters at the polls by a margin of 61% to 39% (Annis, 1998). Two years later, a similar bilingual education program in Arizona was dismantled as a result of a ballot initiative that passed 63% to 37% (González, 2000).

- *State legislative acts.* I've placed legislatures' decisions lower in the hierarchy than ballot initiatives because a ballot initiative is more difficult to create than is normal legislation. In order to qualify for a place on the ballot, an initiative must be endorsed by a large number of voters. Such is not the case with a legislative proposal, which can begin with a single lawmaker, then must be approved by a legislative committee, and finally must receive a majority vote of the lawmakers. Changing legislative acts is far easier than changing a state's constitution. Thus, constitutional provisions are more lasting than legislation.

- *State regulations.* On the next step down the ladder, state departments of education issue regulations that schools are obliged to follow. Regulations are far easier to establish and to change than are laws passed by a legislature or created by ballot initiatives.

- *School district laws.* The boards of education of individual school districts within a state pass their own laws that govern the conduct of schools within their domain. And just as national laws take precedence over state laws, so also state laws take precedence over district laws. In effect, no policy or practice proposed at a lower level in the authority hierarchy can be in conflict with, or can override, policies and practices mandated at a higher level. Compared with state laws, district laws are far easier to institute and change because they require the support of only a majority of the members of a school board (with board membership usually ranging from 5 to 15 persons, depending on the size of the school district) rather than the majority of an entire state legislature.

- *School district regulations.* Individuals or small departments within a school district typically issue a host of rules treating such a variety of matters as textbooks to adopt, students' dress codes, number of days of sick leave for staff members, parking fees, conditions under which non-school groups can use the gymnasium, libraries' lending practices, administrators' travel expenses, and far more.

- *School customs.* Even narrower in scope than district rules are unwritten customs within individual schools. Such customs are practices that all veteran members of a school staff understand and are expected to adopt.   Newcomers learn the customs by observing their colleagues' and by listening to their colleagues' advice.

- *School regulations.* Principals, committees, and specialized personnel create written regulations aimed at fostering consistency of practices within their school. A principal may require teachers to attend all faculty meetings, a student-affairs committee may outlaw blouses and sweaters that expose their wearers' navels, and the bus drivers may demand that all pupils be seated before a bus moves.

- *Classroom rules.* Finally, at the bottom of the authority structure, teachers—sometimes in cooperation with students—set classroom rules about acceptable behavior, when to hand in assignments, how many points a test is worth toward a semester grade, what bibliographical form should be used on a term paper, and much more. Classroom rules apply to fewer people than do all types of laws and regulations above the classroom level, and attempts to alter classroom rules encounter less inertia than do attempts to reform laws and regulations at any higher level. A single teacher, sometimes with student participation, can accomplish the task alone.

Proposition: In general, the higher the location of a legal declaration on an educational-authority hierarchy, the greater the inertia faced in attempting to change that declaration.

The following two problem cases illustrate the application of this proposition. The cases show inertia operating at different levels of the authority hierarchy. The first case is at the school district regulations level. The second involves the national constitution and national law.

Problem case D: In a small city, a pregnant 15-year-old student tripped and fell on the concrete steps leading to the high school's front entrance. Paramedics rushed her to the hospital, where she lost the unborn child and spent the next few days recovering from the accident. A lawyer, acting on behalf of the girl's mother, filed a lawsuit against the school district, but the judge in whose court the suit was filed dismissed the charge for lack of evidence that school officials had been negligent.

This incident, along with data showing a rising rate of teenage pregnancy in the city, motivated the seven-member school board to issue a formal regulation, on a 5-2 vote, prohibiting pregnant students from attending the city's public schools. The dual intention of the regulation was to eliminate the chance that pregnant girls would be injured at school and to give girls a further reason not to become pregnant. The regulation received widespread publicity in newspapers and on radio and television news broadcasts.

Over the following months, several problems arose as a result of the ruling. First, it was obviously difficult for school personnel to tell if a girl was pregnant, particularly during the early months of pregnancy. Second, parents of pregnant girls complained that the regulation prevented their daughters from receiving an education. Third, the head of the high school's home economics department charged that the regulation was misguided. She asserted that it would not likely reduce the incidence of pregnancy and would prevent the school from making a positive contribution to the future welfare of both the teenage mothers and their offspring. In her opinion, the school should sponsor a child-care nursery school that would enroll infants whose mothers—and perhaps fathers—attended the high school. As was true in numbers of other school districts, the nursery school would be under the jurisdiction of the home economics department, which already taught courses in child development and parenting. The teenage mothers of the children in the nursery school would be required not only to attend such classes but also to serve as assistants in the nursery school in order to gain practical experience in proper child-rearing practices. Supporters of this plan also argued that prohibiting pregnant girls from attending school decreased the likelihood that they would ever complete their high school education, thus damaging their chances of ever qualifying for a good job. By thus being educationally handicapped, more young mothers would end up on the public-welfare roles.

When the nursery school plan was submitted to the high school principal, with the support of a variety of faculty members, the principal thought the plan was a good idea and took it to the district superintendent. Although the superintendent admitted that the proposal had some virtue, he judged it politically unfeasible and therefore declined to present it to the board of education. When asked why the plan was politically unacceptable, he offered two reasons. First, it would cost money to house, equip, and staff a nursery school; and the district was already sorely pressed for funds to conduct its present operations. Second, the board's ruling that prohibited pregnant girls from attending school was now a well-publicized, formal, legal regulation. The school board, in order to maintain the public's confidence, could not now admit that it had made a mistake. That is, the board could not afford to adopt a new position that not only reversed their earlier decision but seemed to approve of teenage motherhood by furnishing special facilities for student-parents. Consequently, the regulation prohibiting pregnant girls from attending school remained in effect.

Remedy options: Two strategies that might be attempted by advocates of the nursery school solution to the teenage-mother problem would be those of (a) ignoring the board's regulation and (b) publicizing the advantages of the nursery school and parenting class approach.

Stonewall. Although the high school faculty could not surreptitiously operate a nursery school, they could fail to report girls who appeared pregnant (or who admitted to being pregnant), and they could strongly urge such girls to enroll in the home economics department's parenting and child-development classes.

Publicize the nursery school solution. Proponents of the nursery school solution could provide newspaper, radio, and television reporters with information about other school districts' child-care centers and programs for educating teenage mothers—and mothers-to-be—in wise child-rearing practices. In addition, faculty members could encourage friends to write letters to newspapers in support of the nursery school proposal.

Electioneer. As the next election of school board members approached, supporters of the nursery school plan could support candidates favored the plan and who would replace the incumbents who had originally voted to prohibit pregnant girls from attending school.

Problem case E: When George W. Bush took office as president of the United States in January 2001, he made educational reform a key goal of his administration. He submitted to Congress a reform plan that included a nationwide achievement testing program, financial aid to disadvantaged schools, and a school voucher program. The achievement-testing and financial aid provisions were endorsed by Congress, but the voucher plan was rejected. Therefore, our purpose in this case is to inspect the apparent causes behind inertia that blocked the president's voucher plan and to speculate about how proponents of the plan might salvage it.

Vouchers are tuition subsidies for (a) students from public schools to attend private schools and/or (b) students who already attend private schools. The most notable publicly funded voucher programs have been conducted in the cities of Milwaukee and Cleveland. Privately funded voucher programs have been under way in a variety of places, including such major cities as Atlanta, New York, Baltimore, Baton Rouge, Boston, Buffalo, Chicago, Newark, Philadelphia, San Francisco, and Washington.

Since the first publicly funded voucher program was introduced in Milwaukee in 1990, bitter controversy has ensued over the propriety of using public funds to finance private schooling, particularly schooling sponsored by a religious denomination.

Opponents of publicly financed vouchers usually cite, as their most basic objection, the legal division in the United States between church and state, basing their argument on the first amendment to the U.S. Constitution, which—as explained in Chapter 9—asserts that "Congress shall make no law respecting the establishment of religion, or prohibiting the free exercise thereof." Traditionally, this has been interpreted to mean that tax moneys should not be used to support religious schools. However, because there has been no specific constitutional prohibition against giving public funds for private—and especially religious—schooling, in recent decades public funds have been gradually used for providing modest aid to the to students who attend schools sponsored by religious groups, such as aid to the disabled. But not until the 1990s did the issue of tax dollars being used to pay the tuition costs of students in private religious schools produce controversy that reached the courts.

In 1998, voucher supporters received a major boost when the Wisconsin Supreme Court upheld a Milwaukee program that provided tax dollars for vouchers at private schools, including religious schools. When the U.S. Supreme Court refused to hear an appeal, the Milwaukee voucher program remained intact in Milwaukee and left the future of vouchers nationwide unclear. In 1999, however, a federal court held that when a voucher system resulted in almost all recipients attending religious schools instead of public schools, the system violated the Constitution. Pardini (1999) reported that one religious school in Milwaukee, which received voucher funding, advocated "integrating faith in Jesus Christ with the content and process of all learning."

Proponents on both side of the voucher debate adduce lines of reasoning and evidence of various types in support of their cause. They argue over such matters as whether private schools are accountable for the fairness of their student admission policies, the quality of their services, and their use of funds. Voucher advocates claim that private schools produce better-educated students, with those claims countered by voucher opponents who contend that any superiority of private school outcomes is due to smaller classes and a habit of enrolling most of their students from better-educated families. Thus, the debate has gone on, with no definitive answers in sight.

At the close of 2001, both the Wisconsin (Milwaukee) and Ohio (Cleveland) programs continued to operate. But the Bush administration's nationwide voucher plan was rejected by both the U.S. House of Representatives and the U.S. Senate.

Remedy options: Because the voucher-funding problem faced by the Bush administration was a political matter—involving a confrontation between contending forces—a political solution would be required if tax money were to be spent on vouchers for private schooling.

Supreme Court decision. The most immediate help that the Bush administration could receive would be in the form of a favorable decision in the Ohio voucher case that was on the U.S. Supreme Court's agenda for 2002. The Court's decision about whether that plan violated the U.S. government's traditional position on the separation of church and state would determine—at least for the near future—whether either the Ohio and Wisconsin programs could continue and whether other states and cities that wished to introduce publicly funded vouchers would be able to do so.

The voucher case before the Court is a curious exception to our proposition about the difficulty of effecting an innovation that is contrary to an existing law or regulation. The proposition asserted that the higher the location of a legal declaration on an educational-authority hierarchy, the greater the inertia faced in attempting to change that declaration. However, how validly that proposition fits a particular case can depend on the specificity of the declaration. For example, the U.S. Constitution's first amendment (which is the first item of the Bill of Rights) reads as follows:

> Congress shall make no law respecting the establishment of religion, or prohibiting the free exercise thereof; or abridging the freedom of speech, or of the press; or the right of the people peaceably to assemble; and to petition the Government for a redress of grievances.

Therefore, the rights and limitations stipulated by the Constitution are in the form of very broad principles. It thus becomes necessary for some authoritative agency or person to interpret for any given situation—such as that of using tax money to support religious schools—how those principles apply. The agency established by the Constitution to provide that interpretation is the U.S. Supreme Court, whose assignment is to determine whether laws and practices that have come to the attention of lower courts are permitted under the Constitution. The question then can be asked: How difficult is it to reform a feature of the Constitution? In response, if the reform involves changing one of the Constitution's basic principles—such as removing or radically altering the freedom of religion or freedom of the press—then the task is very difficult, indeed, since the change would have to be approved by two-thirds of the members of Congress and by two-thirds of the nation's state legislatures. However, if a change involves only the interpretation of a principle as it applies to a particular kind of situation (public funding tuition fees for students in private schools), then the change can be effected rather easily, for it requires the approval of only a majority of the nine Supreme Court justices. Thus, five individuals, on the basis of their own personal values, can use those values to determine the outcome of a controversial issue that will affect the entire nation. Although the Constitution assigns Congress the right to create laws, it is apparent that courts (judges, juries) also *make law* by how they interpret general principles. A Court decision that represents a particular interpretation of a principle can thereafter be cited as a precedent equally applicable in future cases that appear to bear on the same principle. This observation leads to an addendum that we can attach to our earlier proposition about authority hierarchies.

> *Proposition:* In general, the higher the location of a legal declaration on an educational-authority hierarchy, the greater the inertia faced in attempting to change that declaration. However, the inertia faced by a proposed educational change may be much reduced if it requires the interpretation of a general principle rather than the direct, obvious application of that principle.

Lobbying members of Congress. If the Supreme Court ruled that taxes could be used to pay students' tuition costs in private schools, the Bush administration's problem would still not be solved. Congress would also need to pass legislation providing federal funds for whatever voucher systems might be adopted across the country. Therefore, voucher advocates would would need to urge lawmakers to vote in favor of voucher legislation.

Widespread publicity. Social pressure that could motivate members of Congress to support the Bush voucher plan might be generated by a major public relations campaign (newspaper stories, television and radio programs, speakers at Parent Teacher Association meetings, brochures mailed to householders) that denigrated public schools as inferior educational institutions and extolled private schools as high-quality centers of learning.

Conclusion

The purpose of the five cases described in this chapter has been to illustrate ways that (a) the proponents of an educational reform seek to exercise power in order to effect the reform and (b) opponents seek to prevent the reform. The two perspectives adopted for viewing the cases have been those of tradition and legality. Additional viewpoints from which to analyze inertia arising from political conditions are those of:

- *Personal obligation.* How can an individual's sense of duty or feeling of indebtedness to another person or to an organization affect the individual's support of an educational innovation that the other person or organization is advocating?
- *The location of a reform proposal.* From the standpoint of inertia, what difference can it make if an innovation is proposed by someone at the top of an educational authority hierarchy or if it is proposed by someone farther down in the hierarchy?
- *Fear of sanctions.* Under what conditions do individuals' fear of reprisals by people in positions of power motivate individuals to either support or oppose an educational reform?

- *Coalition building.* By what means can a coalition of individuals or groups be formed to support or to oppose an intended innovation?

Discussion Topics

1. What policies or rules would you recommend for guiding decisions about teaching traditional cultural conceptions of the origin of the universe and humankind, as compared to teaching present-day secular "scientific" conceptions?
2. When ethnic and religious groups seek to have their interpretation of American history represented in the schools' textbooks, what criteria or rules would you recommend for determining which, if any, of those interpretations should be included in textbooks?
3. Would you favor or oppose the establishment of a nationwide tax-supported voucher system? What arguments would you use to support your position? And what reasons would you expect your opponents to offer in support of their position?

11

Economic Conditions

Across the world, one of the most serious barriers to educational reform is the lack of sufficient funds to support development projects at an optimal level. How generously a society finances educational development depends on a combination of factors, but particularly on the strength of the society's general economy and the willingness of the controllers of money to spend funds on educational-reform efforts. These two matters are the principal focus of the present chapter. A third economic factor addressed is the competition that a proposed project faces in obtaining financial backing.

Economic Factors

- A society's economic strength
- Money controllers' preferences
- Competition for funds

A Society's Economic Strength

One of the most important determinants of how adequately educational-reform efforts are funded is the level of income of the organizations and individuals that have decision-making power over how money is spent. Those decision makers are (a) persons in governmental and private institutions that have expendable funds and (b) individuals (students, their parents, philanthropists) who manage their own funds.

The amount of money that such organizations and individuals have available depends to a great extent on the strength of the general economy in which they operate. In the United States, an often cited indicator of economic strength is a state's per capita disposable personal income, which in 2000 was $16,532 in Mississippi and $16,803 in West Virginia, but was $25,713 in New York, $25,990 in Massachusetts, and $29,598 in Connecticut (Trumbull, 2001, p. 756).   At the international level, a similar indicator of economic viability is a country's per capita gross national product, which in 2000 was $230 in Chad, $310 in Uganda, $440 in India, $980 in the Ukraine, $2,160 in Thailand, $25,580 in Sweden, $32,350 in Japan, and $34,030 in the United States (Trumbull, 2001, pp. 577-757).

A proposition deriving from these observations about economic strength is as follows.

Proposition 1: The weaker a society's ability to produce and distribute wealth throughout the populace, the more difficult it is to introduce an educational innovation that requires the expenditure of funds.

Problem case A: Because financing schools depends so heavily on property taxes, school districts with relatively low real estate assessment values face a more difficult time funding educational improvements than do ones that have higher property values. In a community composed chiefly of residences, homeowners will be obliged to pay far higher taxes to support schools than will homeowners in a heavily populated community that includes highly valued industrial and commercial holdings. An example of this contrast is the case of three school districts in Michigan. Atherton district was chiefly residential, Carman-Ainsworth was far more commercial, and Linden less so. As Lawlor (2001) has explained:

> A taxpayer shelling out $160 in extra taxes per year buys a lot more school improvements in Carman-Ainsworth than he or she would in Atherton.
>
> In Atherton, a proposal would tax residents an extra 3.32 mills* over the next 20 years, raising $9 million. The money—$160 per year to the owner of a $100,000 home—would go toward some basic renovations and maintenance.
>
> But a similar millage amount at Carman-Ainsworth—which has a tax base that includes heavily commercial Flint Township—would raise $50 million. Under that proposal, residents would be taxed an extra 3.34 mills for 25 years. The owner of a $100,000 home would pay an extra $167 in taxes per year to pay for extensive renovations at every school building.
>
> If Linden voters, meanwhile, passed a 30-year, 5.5-mill bond issue, it would raise $59 million and cost the owner of a $100,000 home $275 extra per year. If approved, the taxes would alleviate crowding and eliminate the 19 portable classrooms in the district. It would pay for a new middle school,

---

* One mill equals one-tenth of one cent.

converting the current middle school into an elementary school, and additions at other elementary schools.

Consequently, from the perspective of school finance, we could expect proposed reforms to encounter less inertia in Carman-Ainsworth than in either Atherton or Linden. Furthermore, the discrepancy between districts in the cost to homeowners becomes even more dramatic when sparsely populated districts are compared with heavily populated ones that have far more properties providing the tax base.

Proposition 2: The amount of funds available for financing education can drop suddenly as a result of unexpected events in the broader society, thereby increasing the inertia suffered by educational reform projects.

Problem case B: As noted in Chapter 10, the newly inaugurated United States president, George W. Bush, in 2001 made the improvement of education a central goal of his administration. He adopted the motto "No Child Left Behind" and sent Congress proposed legislation featuring his four pillars of comprehensive educational reform: accountability, local control and flexibility, expanded parental choice, and doing what works.

Traditionally, the conduct of education had been the responsibility of individual states and local school districts, not only for financing schools but also for determining curriculum contents and instructional methods. However, beginning with the administration of President Lyndon Johnson in the mid-1960s, the federal government increasingly furnished funds for special programs in the schools, particularly for reforms to improve learning opportunities for disadvantaged students—those from poverty backgrounds, those from homes in which a foreign language was spoken, those with physical or mental disabilities, and the like. Between 1965 and 2001, an estimated $147 billion in federal moneys had been spent for such purposes (Colvin, 2001). But not until the Bush presidency in 2001 did the federal government assume a more active role in determining specific instructional and assessment practices in the nation's public schools.

Three key provisions in the legislation that the Bush administration urged Congress to adopt were (a) a nationwide achievement-testing program, (b) a specific method of teaching beginning reading that emphasized phonics, and (c) a particular approach to teacher education. To implement the reading program, the Bush bill was to include $5 billion to be spent over the next five years, although some observers said that far more than $1 billion per year would be needed for providing weak readers with intensive, high-quality instruction (Colvin, 2001).

Congress accepted all three of the above provisions and was readying the final version of the legislation for the president's signature when, on September 11, terrorists crashed airplanes into the World Trade Center towers in New York and the Pentagon Building in Washington. This event, along with an already declining national economy that was hastened into recession by the terrorist attacks, forced the diversion of some funds from the proposed educational reforms to disaster relief and military preparedness. The attention of the Bush administration, which had focused strongly on the intended educational reforms, now was diverted to solving the problems caused by terrorist activities. Consequently, in the White House, one domestic policy adviser and a deputy or two in the Office of Legislative Affairs were the only staff members paying any attention to the school legislation (Sobieraj, 2001). By 2002, the prospects of implementing the testing, reading, and teacher-preparation reforms in their original form appeared rather dim.

Remedy options: Five potential ways to cope with the government's problem of financing the reform plan are those of:

Transferring. Part of the fund allocations for other government agencies could be transferred into the education budget.

Reducing. The federal education plan could be trimmed down to include fewer schools or less money for each portion of the program, thereby rendering the plan less expensive.

Delaying. The intended innovations could be deferred until the government was in a stronger financial position.

Appealing. State governments could be asked to bear at least part of the expense of the federally planned reforms.

Recommending. Rather than funding the reforms, the government could send each school district and teacher-education institution a detailed description of the aims of the reforms and of ways to implement the plan—in the hope that the districts and institutions might be able to carry out the reforms within their usual budget allocations.

Money Controllers' Preferences

The financial support of educational development depends not only on the amount of money available in the economy but also on the degree to which the controllers of money are willing to spend funds on education—and particularly on educational innovations—in comparison to allocating funds for other purposes. In the case of a national government, those "other purposes" can include national defense, highway construction, the regulation of immigration, price supports for farm products, scientific research, and more. For a state legislature, "other purposes" can be welfare payments to the indigent, the cost of collecting taxes, the improvement of water supplies, the monitoring of sanitary conditions in food-processing facilities, the promotion of tourism, and the like. Among individual citizens, "other purposes" can be such necessities as basic food and clothing or else luxuries—a new house, a new car, stylish clothes, travel, entertainment, and hobbies.

Proposition: The lower on their list of spending priorities that controllers of money place education, the greater the inertia faced by educational reforms that require funding.

Problem case C: A school-financing lawsuit that had wended its way through state courts over a 10-year period ended with the state's supreme court (in a 4-3 decision) ordering the governor to provide public schools sufficient funds to raise their quality to a standard consistent with the state constitution's commitment to furnish all children a proper education. The suit had been brought against the state by a coalition of schools that charged the state with failing to fulfill its constitutionally mandated financial responsibility.

Proponents on both sides of the controversy—the schools' coalition and the governor's staff—agreed that reforms designed to bring the quality of schools up to standard would cost around $1.2 million annually. Consequently, if the court's order were to be obeyed, the governor and legislators would need to select from among a variety of unattractive alternatives (Welsh-Huggins, 2001).

Remedy options. The following are among the alternatives the state government might adopt to implement the mandated school-improvement reforms.

Tax increases. The state income tax rate could be increased or new types of statewide taxes could be created, such as service taxes on hotels and restaurants and use taxes on trucks that drive on state highways. School districts could be urged to increase property taxes. However, any move to raise taxes would be opposed by the people who would have to pay those increases.

Closure of tax loopholes. Exemptions in existing income tax regulations could be rescinded, so that, for example, tax payers would no longer be allowed to deduct contributions to political campaigns as was currently permitted. Resistance to such a solution could be expected from the people who have profited from the loopholes.

Federal grants. Applications for federal funding could be sent to Washington. However, it seems unlikely that block grants, not specified for particular projects, would be provided. The success of this attempt would appear to depend on the amount of influence wielded by the state's representatives in Congress, influence affected by the committee positions those representatives held in the Senate and House of Representatives.

Budget shifts. Within the existing state budget, money could be transferred into the education fund from the allotments to other state agencies (highway maintenance, tourism, agricultural assistance, and more). However, bitter opposition could be expected from employees and supporters of those agencies.

Delayed action. The governor's staff and legislators could try postponing the implementation of the Supreme Court's directive by such delay tactics as appointing a solution-review committee, assigning lawyers to file briefs focusing on details of the directive, conducting public hearings across the state, and ordering a research study of measures adopted in other states to solve similar problems.

Problem case D: Individual citizens' decisions about how much of their income they are willing to spend for educating a community's children—and for supporting reforms—is typically reflected in voters' decisions at the polls during school elections. For example, in one district that had a public school enrollment of 66,000 students, the superintendent was forced to halt further across-the-board expenditures, the hiring of new personnel, and the funding of extracurricular activities after voters defeated a 10-mill tax increase. As a result, any innovations designed to improve the quality of education in the district had to be either discarded or set aside for the present (Alabama cuts taken to court, 2001).

Remedy options. Two measures that district officials could attempt for obtaining school-improvement funds would involve hunting for outside sources of money and mounting a vigorous publicity campaign to convince voters that a 10-mill property tax increase was well worth their support.

Outside funding sources. Money could be sought from the state government, philanthropic foundations, or corporations. In applying for grants, the school district would need to specify the reform activities and explain why those ventures were innovations, because grants are usually provided only for special educational-improvement projects and not for routine operating expenses.

Tax increase. The tax campaign could emphasize the discrepancy between (a) the quality of education that the school district it is able to provide with its present funding and (b) the far better learning opportunities furnished by other districts that are better financed. The campaign could also illustrate specific improvements that would result from a tax rate increase.

Problem case E: In the United States, schools that are operated by private organizations have traditionally been denied public funds, so they have been obliged to depend on individuals, philanthropic foundations, and corporations for financial support. (In many other nations, including

Canada, private schools receive public funds.) Therefore, private schools in the United States have depended on tuition fees and gifts to pay for both their routine operating expenses and innovations. During times of economic hardship in a community or when individuals' allegiance to a school or its sponsoring body diminishes, the inertia faced by reform proposals increases. Such was the situation in the opening years of the 21st century for numerous schools sponsored by religious orders.

A case in point is the problem of attracting and retaining teachers in one of the largest Roman Catholic archdioceses in America—the Chicago archdiocese. According to Carol Fowler, president of the National Association of Church Personnel Administrators, the 6,000 teachers in Catholic schools within the archdiocese were paid about half the salary of teachers in the public schools. Thus, the needed reform was an increase in the compensation received by teachers in Catholic schools. However, whenever there is a serious move on the part of church authorities to increase salaries, Fowler said, "we come up against the question of how many schools will we have to close" in order to furnish more equitable compensation to the teachers in the schools that remain open. "But it is more likely that school closings will come when there are no longer teachers willing to work for low pay. We're not going to survive unless we do something about it," she added (Fowler, 2001, p. 7).

This problem in the Catholic school system was exacerbated by inconsistency across dioceses in the amount and forms of teacher compensation. Thus, a further proposed reform in addition to increasing teachers' salaries was that of increasing the uniformity of practices from one diocese to another, particularly by reducing the wide discrepancies in pension plans across regions.

> Many [dioceses] still operate on the outdated assumption that female employees will not be dependent on their own pensions but are "second-income women" whose retirement will be funded mainly by their husbands' pension plans. (Fowler, 2001, p. 7)

Remedy options. Attempts to solve private schools' financial difficulties can include comparable-compensation plans, school-fee increases, fund-raising appeals, fund-raising projects, and school-voucher programs.

Comparable-compensation plans. One proposed solution to the variation in pension policies from one diocese to another was the introduction of a uniform "defined contribution plan" to which both the employer and employee contributed but which stayed under the control of the employee. Another suggestion was to make pension plans portable from one diocese to another. However, according to Fowler, "Dioceses don't want to lose control of millions of dollars in pension plans" (Fowler, 2001, p. 7).

School-fee increases. A customary argument in support of raising school fees is that the cost of education should be borne chiefly by the persons who profit most directly from that education—meaning the students and their parents. But a serious weakness of higher fees as a solution to the school-finance problem is that many of the families which parochial schools hope to serve cannot afford high fees. Consequently, children from families with low or modest incomes could be denied a religion-based education.

Fund-raising campaigns. A traditional way of obtaining money to support private schooling has been that of appealing to individuals, fraternal organizations, philanthropic foundations, and corporations for funds. In the case of church-operated schools, the money is often collected for the church's work in general and then dolled out to the schools by church authorities. However, sometimes an appeal is made specifically for supporting a particular school. The success of such campaigns depends to a great extent on the number of controllers of money who are willing to sustain the school and the amount of funds they control. In regions where dedication to church causes has weakened in recent times, the appeals can fail to garner the funds needed for both routine operating costs and reforms.

An example is the case of Our Lady of Lourdes elementary school, an Atlanta inner-city school operating since 1912 for African–American children. In 2001, when the archdiocese could no longer afford to furnish the supplementary funds the school needed for the upcoming academic year, a group of parents and parishioners launched a campaign to raise the necessary money. The group managed to collect $600,000, but that amount was still $262,000 short of the $862,000 required to keep the school open. As a consequence, Our Lady of Lourdes was forced to close after 89 years of operation (O'Neill, 2001).

Fund-raising projects. To finance modest innovations, schools often carry out special fund-raising activities in which students, faculty, and parents participate, such as the sale of baked goods, candy, toys, children's books, or holiday cards. Money is also raised from athletic contests, circuses, plays, movies, excursions, and exhibitions.

School-voucher programs. An opportunity for private schools to receive public funds has developed with the advent of school-voucher programs that obligate a state or city school system to give parents money for sending their children to private schools of the parents' choice. Voucher plans usually permit parents to send their children to schools sponsored by religious orders. The desirability of vouchers as a means of providing families a wider range of educational choice has continued to be a much debated issue over the past three decades. As mentioned earlier, in 2001 President George W. Bush's proposed steps to reform schooling in the United States included a voucher plan, but Congress eliminated that portion of the legislation. Similar to voucher programs are tax-credit plans that give families a tax reduction that helps parents defray the expense of sending children and youths to private schools. Opponents of vouchers and tax credits charge that furnishing tax funds to church-sponsored schools violates the separation of church and state required by the nation's constitution. They further claim that voucher programs deplete the funds needed to sustain and improve public schools. As a consequence of such opposition, from 1978 through 2001 legislation establishing voucher and tax-credit plans had been defeated in 35 states (Christie, 2001). The U.S. Supreme Court agreed to review the constitutionality of voucher plans in its 2002 session.

The spread of the existing tax-credit programs to more regions would help private schools, such as those in the Catholic archdiocese of Chicago, improve teachers' salaries and finance other reforms. However, in general, the reluctance of voters and legislators to authorize voucher systems continues to sustain the inertia parochial schools face in financing reforms.

Competition for Funds

Educators constantly face competition in their efforts to obtain the funds needed to conduct their programs. A state or county education system must compete for the available tax money against such agencies as the social welfare department, the police, firefighters, the road maintenance division, and more. Then, within the education system itself, individual schools compete with each other for the school system's available money. Furthermore, within a school, the science department competes with the English and physical education departments for the funds the school controls. Finally, the proponents of an innovation must contend against the defenders of already established programs to finance the innovation. Our recognizing this competitive nature of financing educational innovations can lead to the following proposal.

Proposition 1: The weaker the arguments that proponents of an educational reform muster in their efforts to outdo competitors for available funds, the more difficult it will be to implement the reform.

A second proposition, closely allied to the first, concerns the kinds of evidence on which sponsors of an educational reform ground their arguments. People often differ in the kinds of evidence they find convincing. Some individuals are persuaded by statements from religious documents, some are convinced by the opinions of people in positions of authority, some require data from empirical studies, and others respect still different sources. From Chapter 10, you may recall that in 1999 the issue of who determines science curricula in schools pitted biblical creationists against evolutionists when the Kansas state board of education prohibited any mention of Charles Darwin's theory of evolution on state achievement tests, thereby effectively eliminating the theory from the course of study (Marcus, 1999, p. 32). This act left open the opportunity for certain Christian educators to promote the biblical version of human beginnings as the true version of creation (God created the first man and woman, Adam and Eve, in the same mature human condition of modern-day adults). In effect, the members of the Kansas board of education accepted a document from past ages, the book of Genesis, as authentic evidence. In contrast, in 2001 the Hawaii state board of education struck down a proposal that would permit the Judeo-Christian biblical version of the world's creation to be taught in science classes as a proper theory of human beginnings along with Darwin's theory of evolution (Hawaii board, 2001). Thus, the Hawaii board members accepted the evidence from evolutionists' studies as more persuasive than the biblical account.

In view of these differences among people in the kinds of evidence they accept as warranting the financial support innovators seek for their reform projects, our second proposition is as follows.

Proposition 2: The less that providers of funds agree with the evidence on which applicants for funds base their arguments, the greater the inertia suffered by the applicants' proposed educational innovations.

Both of the following cases, designed to illustrate the foregoing two propositions, concern charter schools as efforts to improve the conduct of education. In recent years, institutions labeled *charter schools* have been established by groups or individuals as alternatives to traditional public and private schools. Charter schools, like regular public schools, are funded by tax money but are exempted from many of the regulations that public schools are obliged to follow. In the United States, the charter school movement began gradually in the latter years of the 20th century, then expanded at a rapid pace until an estimated 518,000 of the nation's 50 million school children were enrolled in charter schools by 2001 (Thomas, 2002). As one part of this movement, some private and public educational organizations began creating *cyber charter schools* that furnished lessons to students who stayed home to work at desktop computers that were linked to the cyber school's headquarters via the Internet. By 2001, more than 50 charter and public school cyber programs had been established in at least 30 states (Cyber schools, 2001).

Problem case F, in addition to illustrating the foregoing pair of propositions, also demonstrates the operation of a third tenet.

Proposition 3: The farther the implementation of an educational reform falls short of the expectations set for it at the beginning, the more likely funding to support the reform will be reduced or eliminated. This precept might be dubbed "the broken-promises proposition."

Problem case F: Typically, in order to establish a charter school, the school's sponsors must receive the permission of the board of education of the district in which the school is to be located. Furthermore, only a limited number of charter schools will be authorized in a district. This means that competition can arise among organizers of charter schools if several groups are hoping to set up a school in the same district.

In one state, the chairman of a group that hoped to start a charter school (kindergarten through grade 12) learned that three other applications were currently being sent to the district board of education, and no more than one charter school would be authorized. Applications were to be submitted to the board of education in two forms—as a written document specifying the nature of the intended school and as an oral presentation to the members of the board. To maximize the chance that his proposal would win the board's approval, the chairman adopted the following strategies in both his written and oral applications. He

- Committed the school to accept students of all levels of ability, of any ethnic backgrounds, and of any sort of social behavior (thereby counteracting the criticism that many charter schools rejected students of lower academic aptitude, those from certain ethnic minorities and those with a record of problem behavior)
- Predicted that his charter-school students would average 10 or more points higher on standardized math, reading, language, social-studies, and science tests than students in the district's public schools
- Stressed the importance of a special moral-education class that would be included in the curriculum, with the promise that behavior problems (fighting, drug and alcohol use, theft, vandalism), both in school and outside, would be far fewer than in public schools
- Described the superior physical facilities, equipment, and supplies planned for the school

At the opening of his oral presentation to the board, the chairman placed a pile of books and academic journals on the table before him. From time to time he pointed to the publications, contending that scientific studies confirmed the soundness of each element of his plan.

As the chairman had hoped, his plan proved more compelling to the board members than the plans of his competitors. The envisioned school thus became a reality. Initially the school was housed in an abandoned warehouse and equipped in a minimum fashion until the intended permanent structure was completed. Pupils were enrolled in grades 1 to 5, with the expectation that more grades would be added as the years advanced. During the first year, at the request of the charter-school's principal, pupils were excused from participating in the state achievement testing program because textbooks had arrived late. At the beginning of the second year, the school was still located in the warehouse. Although the principal displayed on his office wall an architectural drawing of the intended permanent structure, the final choice of a building site had not yet been made. About this same time, two families complained to the district school board that they had attempted to enroll their children in the charter school because the children "had not adjusted well to the public school." However, their applications had been turned down on the grounds that classes were full, even though the school was in the midst of a campaign to recruit new pupils. In the middle of the second year, the district school board insisted that the charter school participate in the annual achievement testing program, and an evaluation team was sent by the board to assess of features of the school.

The test results and the team's appraisal revealed that the charter school failed markedly to fulfill the expectations set in the chairman's original application. Test scores were below the average of public schools, only a few of the teachers held state-authorized credentials, the warehouse facilities were far inferior to the standard of the public schools, the incidence of misbehavior among the students appeared worse than in most public school classrooms, and enrollment had dwindled.

Remedy options: From the board of education's perspective, the solution to the charter school's problems would be to rescind the charter and to cease furnishing the school any public money.

From the viewpoint of the school's pupils and their parents, the remedy would be to enroll the pupils in a public or private school or to teach them at home.

From the viewpoint of the charter school's sponsors, a lesson to be learned was that offering extravagant predictions in order to defeat rivals in the competition for financial support might be a successful strategy in the short run but could eventually prove disastrous. The ostensibly "scientific evidence" that the sponsoring group's chairman had used to buttress his original presentation to the school board had been of a type well suited for convincing board members of the virtue of his application. However, his exaggerated claims for the school's achievements ultimately defeated his purpose. He apparently had felt caught in a bind. If he set modest but realistic expectations for the school, his application might not be chosen over those of his competitors. But if he set extravagant expectations for the school and then success-fully argued that such expectations were realistic in light of "scientific evidence," he might get the charter, although the school would not be able to fulfill the commitment. Yet, since any possible outside evaluation of the school's performance would come only at some distant date, the chairman apparently felt it was worth the risk at present to make exag-gerated promises for the future.

Problem case G: In 1997, a state legislature authorized the establish-ment of publicly funded charter schools. In 2000, entrepreneurs—fre-quently representing school districts—began availing themselves of the 1997 legislation to set up cyber charter schools that were advertised as tuition free and particularly suitable for individuals who were home-schooled, suspended from a regular school for discipline problems, pregnant, ill, holding down jobs, or in jail. Students enrolled in a cyber school remained at home to receive their lessons from a distant studio by means of a computer connected to the Internet by a telephone line or a communication satellite. Some cyber schools publicized their programs as appropriate for people who wished to accelerate their high-school progress, desired challenging academic fare, wanted to take college courses, sought flexibility in their daily schedule, or felt uncomfortable in a traditional school setting (Miller, 2000).

Parents who were enthusiastic about the cyber-school innovation withdrew their children from local public schools and enrolled them in one of the state's several cyber charter schools. In addition, children who were already being homeschooled by their parents or friends often joined a cyber school.* The 1997 legislation had ruled that charter schools were entitled to receive from each student's school district the same amount of funds per student that the district provided to public schools. Furthermore, the state was obligated to furnish free computers, printers, and textbooks for students in charter schools. The operators of the new cyber charter schools took advantage of this provision by pro-viding equipment and supplies to their students, then charging the costs to the state or to the school districts in which the students resided.

Therefore, as cyber schools began to operate, public school districts started receiving bills assessing the districts the amounts that the dis-

---

* In 2001, over 850,000 (1.7%) U.S. school children studied at home under paren-tal guidance. About 18% of homeschoolers were also enrolled in regular schools part time, 11% used books or materials from a public school, and 8% followed a public school curriculum (Homeschoolers, 2001).

tricts spent per student in the public schools. As one example, the superintendent of a district that had 11 children enrolled in a cyber charter school received a bill for $70,000. But he refused to pay, contending that (a) the bill included charges for pupils who were already being home-schooled, and the district had never been obligated to pay for home-schooling, (b) he had no way of judging the quality of cyber students' progress nor even discovering how often they "attended" cyber school, and (c) schooling via the Internet entailed far lower operating costs than did schooling conducted on campuses and in buildings.

Soon other districts were also ignoring the bills sent by cyber schools. Thus, if enough districts refused to pay, the cyber charter schools would be seriously weakened or out of business—unless, of course, parents would be willing to bear the expense of their children's Internet lessons.

In summary, regular school districts became engaged in bitter competition with cyber charter schools for the tax money available in those districts. The inertia that the cyber-school innovation suffered was due in large part to school districts' resistance to paying the fees charged by cyber schools.

Remedy options: In their attempts to resolve the funding conflict generated by the advent of cyber charter schools, both the advocates and the opponents of cyber schools could adopt the same options. The adversaries on both sides could file lawsuits against each other so that the issue would be adjudicated in court. Both sides could urge legislators to refine the 1997 law in order to clarify whether cyber charter schools were entitled to the public funds they sought. Within each school district, the adversaries could attempt to convince the board of education and the district administrators of the virtue of their position. They could also urge editorial writers to represent their position favorably in newspapers and on television and radio broadcasts.

In each of these efforts to settle the conflict, if the arguments against the public funding of cyber charter schools were accepted as more persuasive than those in favor of such funding, then the cyber charter school as an educational reform movement would have suffered a serious setback.

Conclusion

The influence of economics on the inertia confronting an educational reform has been illustrated in this chapter in terms of three factors—a society's economic strength, money controllers' preferences, and the competition for funds. Other factors that may also influence inertia are:

- *Inflation.* If an expenditure on an educational innovation is postponed until some future date, will the increased cost of the innovation at that time be worth the advantages of the postponement?
- *Comparative implementation methods.* What is an efficient way to identify different methods of implementing an innovation and to determine which of the ways will be the most cost effective?
- *Sources of funds.* What are good ways to discover (a) which potential donors (government agencies, foundations, individuals) are willing to fund which sorts of educational-reform efforts, and (b) what strategies are most effective for obtaining the financial support of those donors?
- *Cost/benefit computation.* What is an efficient system for calculating and comparing the costs and benefits that can be expected from an educational reform?

Discussion Topics

1. What do you see as the advantages and disadvantages of providing tax money for private schools in the form of either vouchers or services (aid for disabled pupils, bus transportation, lunches for children from poor families, health care)?
2. Are you in favor of paying cyber charter schools the same amount per pupil of tax money as is paid per pupil in public schools? If so, why? If not, why not?
3. A dual crisis (the September 11 airliner terrorist attacks and the spread of anthrax) that demanded billions of dollars in unexpected government expenditures caused the federal government problems in financing the education legislation. Earlier in this chapter, the five remedy options proposed for coping with this problem involved (a) transferring funds from other agencies, (b) reducing the magnitude of the federal program, (c) delaying the implementation of the plan, (d) asking the states to bear part of the funding burden, and (e) furnishing school districts details of the plan in the hope that districts would implement it without requiring outside funds. Which of these solutions—or which combination of several—do you believe would be the most desirable? What line of reasoning has led you to such a conclusion?

Part V

A Practical Use for Inertia Theory

The way inertia theory can be used for analyzing the complete or partial failure of attempted educational reforms has been illustrated throughout this book. However, systematic steps to follow for applying the theory to a particular case have not yet been described. That task has been left to Chapter 12, in which steps are defined and applied in the analysis of inertia that might be expected in a classroom effort at educational innovation.

12

Applying Inertia Theory to Education

As illustrated in Chapters 1 through 11, the scheme labeled *inertia theory* can serve as a vantage point from which to analyze attempted educational reforms that have fallen short of expectations. This final chapter describes in detail one systematic approach (a) to predicting ahead of time the likely causes of inertia that a contemplated educational innovation might face or (b) to understanding the sources of resistance suffered by a reform that is already under way. The approach consists of a series of decision-steps or stages, each defined by a question about an intended or in-progress reform. For a stalled or failed innovation, answering the questions can help suggest what went wrong and what remedies might be applied.

The following discussion is divided into two parts. First, the sequential decision-steps are listed in the form of questions to be answered. Second, the steps are applied in the analysis of a simple hypothetical classroom innovation that a teacher is contemplating.

The Decision-Steps

1. *The nature of the change.* How does the innovation differ from past practice?
2. *The purpose of the innovation.* What good is the innovation supposed to do? What is it intended to accomplish?
3. *Specific changes needed.* Exactly what changes are required?
4. *Barriers to change.* What factors or conditions might serve to frustrate or retard the needed changes? That is, for each element of the innovation, what forces might contribute to the inertia experienced in the attempt to change that element?

5. *Remedy options.* For each element, what remedies might be attempted for preventing or reducing the potential inertia?
6. *Selection criteria.* What standards or criteria can be used as guides to choosing which remedy options would likely be best for combating the expected inertia?
7. *Remedy selection.* Which remedy option—or combination of options—is the most desirable as judged by the selection criteria?

A Simple Classroom Application

Step 1. *The nature of the change.* In a city high school, the teacher of tenth-grade world history (four classes ranging from 29 to 33 students per class) wants students to learn how to write a research paper using a personal computer that provides access to the Internet. Students are already able to write research papers by hand, using information from books, periodicals, and interviews. Now they will learn to compose research papers on a computer, using information from the World Wide Web.

Step 2. *The purpose of the innovation.* The aim of the assignment is to equip students with the skills of (a) writing on a computer and (b) finding information on the Internet and using the information in composing a research paper.

Step 3. *Specific changes needed.* The students already know the purpose of research papers, the desired form (an introductory abstract, the body of the paper, a final summary, references), and how to cite references in the body of the work and in the bibliography.
  3.1 *New skills* required by the innovation include those of:
      3.1.1 Composing a paper directly on a computer (rather than first writing a draft by hand).
      3.1.2 Efficiently searching the World Wide Web for information relevant to the writer's topic.
      3.1.3 Accurately listing Internet sources in the bibliography.
  3.2 *Equipment and supplies* required by the innovation include:
      3.2.2 Enough personal computers to enable all students to work efficiently.
      3.2.3 Internet access for the computers.
      3.2.4 A word-processing program in the computers.

Step 4. *Barriers to change* and Step 5. *Remedy options.* For each needed change in Step 3 above, barriers to that change and potential remedies are considered together in this section.

4.1 New skills:

4.1.1 Composing on a computer

Barrier: Weak word-processing skills. Students' word-processing skills vary greatly within each class, so the least expert students take an inordinate amount of time to write their papers.

Remedy 1: Training sessions. Special training sessions in word processing can be arranged for students whose skills are deficient. The sessions may be conducted outside of regular class time (lunch periods, after school, study hall periods) in the school's computer laboratory, under the guidance of a teacher or a student adept at word processing.

Remedy 2: Home practice. Students who have computers at home can be assigned to practice there. A note or phone call to parents could alert them to the assignment so that they could monitor the practice.

4.1.2 Searching the Web

Barrier: Lack of experience. Students' vary greatly in their knowledge of how to find information on the World Wide Web.

Remedy 1: Teacher demonstration. With the aid of computer projection equipment, the image on the computer screen can be projected onto a large screen at the front of the classroom so that all students can witness the process of searching the Web for information about a topic as the teacher explains the steps in the process.

Remedy 2: Computer file. A file that is stored in the computer a student uses in school (or is available on a computer network) can contain the teacher's step-by-step explanation so any student can access the explanation anytime that she or he needs it.

Remedy 3: Peer teaching in class. A student who is already proficient at using the World Wide Web can aid a classmate who is yet a neophyte searcher. They can hunt together for information that the neophyte needs for his or her research paper.

Remedy 4: After-school tutoring. Students who need help with their search skills can be aided after school by either the teacher or an experienced student.

Remedy 5: Printed guide sheet. A Web-search guide sheet can be prepared by the teacher and distributed to class members. The sheet explains the step-by-step procedure to follow in hunting for information about sample topics on the World Wide Web.

4.1.3 Internet sources list

Barrier: Lack of experience. Most students have had no chance to learn the proper method of citing Web sources in the body of their paper and in the bibliography.

Remedy 1: Teacher demonstration. Either by writing on the chalkboard or by projecting computer-screen images onto a large screen at the front of the classroom, the teacher can compare (a) the typical way that printed sources (books, book chapters, articles in periodicals and newspapers) are cited in research papers with (b) the preferred way to cite sources from the World Wide Web.

Remedy 2: Computer file. The comparison in Remedy 1 can be reproduced as a computer file that is available to students anytime they need it in computers or on a network.

Remedy 3: Printed guide sheet. The teacher can prepare and distribute to class members a guide sheet showing how to cite references in the body of a research paper and in the bibliography.

4. 2 Equipment and supplies

4.2.1 Enough computers

Barrier: Computer shortage. There are between 29 and 33 students in each of the classes doing the Web-based research paper. There are only four computers in the classroom.

Remedy 1: Scheduled use. The teacher can set up a schedule that allows students to take turns using the classroom's four computers. Each student would be able to use a computer for a set length of time, such as 15 or 20 minutes.

Remedy 2: Mobile laboratory. The school owns a mobile computer laboratory, commonly referred to as a "cow" (computers on wheels), that consists of a large cart in which 25 laptop computers are stored. The cart can be wheeled from one classroom to another and then a computer can be placed on each student's desk. The computers have wireless Internet access so there is no problem of wiring each computer into a network to enable students to reach the World Wide Web. The mobile laboratory could be brought to the social studies classroom when students were working on their research papers.

Remedy 3: Home use. Students who have a computer at home can do much of their research after school, thereby permitting students with no home computer to use the four classroom machines.

Remedy 4: Students bring own computers to school. Students with laptop computers at home may be asked to bring them to school on days that the class is working on the research assignment.

Remedy 5: Other classrooms' computers. After school, students could be permitted to use computers in classrooms that have idle computers.

4.2.2 Internet access

Barrier: No server at home. It is necessary to have an Internet Service Provider (ISP) in order to access the Internet and its World Wide Web. The ISP may be a commercial company that charges a monthly fee for such service (such as America Online, Yahoo, or ATT) or it can be some other organization, such as a school district. Some students may have a computer at home but cannot afford the monthly fee that a commercial provider charges.

Remedy 1: School server. The school district might be willing to give such students free access to the ISP that the district controls.

Remedy 2: Philanthropy. An organization (the school's Parent Teacher Association; or a local Rotary, Lions, Kiwanis club; or an individual philanthropist) could be asked to pay the ISP charge during the period of the research project for students who cannot afford the expense.

4.2.3 Word-processing program

Barrier: Incompatible programs. All computers, both those in school and ones students use at home, are equipped with word-processing programs. The only problem likely to arise is with incompatibility between the program on a student's home computer and the program on the school computers. Thus, if students work on their paper both at school and at home (and transfer the composition from one machine to another by means of a diskette), they may experience problems of formatting, even though present-day word-processing programs can usually translate material rather easily from one version to another.

Remedy 1: Tutoring. The teacher or a knowledgeable classmate could show a student how to transfer material written on one program to a different program and adjust any formatting changes that the transfer required.

Step 6: *Selection criteria* and Step 7: *Remedy selection.* With the expected barriers and remedy options now in hand, we are ready to identify which remedies to adopt so as to avoid or reduce inertia. This task is efficiently accomplished if we first consciously state the criteria on which to base our judgments rather than merely choosing among the options on the basis of somewhat vague intuition. The process involves (a) stating the potential cause of inertia (the barrier), (b) proposing criteria, and (c) describing which remedies best fit the criteria.

—Composing on a computer. *Barrier: Weak word-processing skill.*

Selection criteria. The remedy should (a) increase students' substandard word-processing speed and accuracy (b) in an economically efficient manner, from the viewpoint of the students' time investment, and

(c) without retarding their classmates' progress on their own research papers.

The remedy choice. The best remedy would be that of *special training sessions* outside of class time. This could be supplemented by *home practice.*

—Searching the Web. *Barrier: Lack of experience.*

Selection criteria. The remedy should (a) equip students to find desired information on the World Wide Web (b) in an efficient manner—meaning with increasingly fewer visits to irrelevant, unprofitable websites—and (c) provide students help with their search as soon as they need the help.

The remedy choice. The best choice would appear to be a combination of *teacher demonstration, printed guide sheet,* and *computer file.* The teacher could introduce the searching process to the entire class by demonstrating the procedure in a computer-projected demonstration. Then a printed guide sheet explaining the search steps could be distributed to class members and also be included as a file on the classroom computers. Students could also be encouraged to seek the help of classmates as a way to get immediate aid with a specific search problem.

—Internet sources list. *Barrier: Lack of experience.*

Selection criteria. The remedy should (a) equip students to distinguish among ways of citing (in the body of the paper and in the references list or bibliography at the end) sources of material from the Internet (e-mail, chat groups, World Wide Web) as compared with citing such traditional sources as books, chapters in books, periodicals, interviews, and the like, and (b) make those distinctions readily available to be consulted during the process of collecting information and writing the research paper.

The remedy choice. As in the case of searching the Web, the best solution would probably be a combination of *teacher demonstration, printed guide sheet,* and *computer file.*

—Enough computers. *Barrier: Computer shortage.*

Selection criteria. The remedy should (a) allow each student to work on a computer for as much time as the student needs in order to do a proper job of the research paper and (b) immediately provide each student the needed support resources (word-processing program, Internet access, printer, diskettes on which to store work).

The remedy choice. The closest approach to fulfilling these criteria would appear to involve the *mobile laboratory* and *scheduled use of the classroom computers,* supplemented by *home use, students' own computers,* and *other classrooms' computers.* The computer shortage problem probably could not be solved perfectly. The mobile laboratory, plus the four classroom computers, could serve 29 students at a time, but in the larger classes some students would need to wait for a turn, bring computers from home, or work on their papers after school or at home. There might also be a problem scheduling the use of the mobile laboratory, since other classes—science, English, health education—might request to use the laboratory during the same hours that the four social studies sections meet. Therefore, the social studies teacher should have other constructive activities available for students who do not have a computer to work on at the time they want it.

—Internet access. *Barrier: No server at home.*

Selection criteria. The remedy should provide the student access to the Internet whenever the student needs it and at an affordable cost.

The remedy choice. Providing students home access to the *school server* is probably the better choice. Asking an outside agency or individual to pay for an ISP during the brief time of the research project, and going to the trouble of setting up the ISP for such a short time, could be more bother than it's worth.

—Word-processing program. *Barrier: Incompatible programs.*

Selection criteria. The remedy should equip the student to transfer material written with one word-processing program to another word-processing program as quickly and painlessly as possible.

The remedy choice. The single option described for solving this problem is that of *tutoring* by the teacher or by a knowledgeable student.

Conclusion

I fear that the above illustration will appear to readers to be no more than a laborious academic exercise. Therefore, I should explain that its purpose has not been to suggest that such a formal written analysis is either needed or desired in most instances of educational innovation. Instead, the purpose of the foregoing example has been to trace a pattern of thought—a series of mental steps—that I find useful for identifying causes of inertia and for generating ways to deal with those causes. Therefore, it's the pattern of thinking about inertia and not the formal way of expressing such thinking that's important. In effect, I think it's worthwhile to "keep in mind" the steps and apply them informally when seeking to identify and overcome inertia in school reforms.

Only in cases of complex educational reforms is it likely advantageous to trace the steps in the formal manner shown in our example. Such complex reforms might be those of (a) shifting responsibility for curriculum development from a school district's central office to individual schools (site-based curriculum planning), (b) equipping schools with the most modern electronic technology, or (c) replacing a school district's entire budgeting and procurement system.

Discussion Topic

For practice in applying the seven-stage thought pattern illustrated in the social studies research-paper case, (a) select a classroom, school, or school district with which you are acquainted, (b) suggest a reform or innovation that might be attempted, and (c) use this chapter's seven-step process as the guide to identifying how each step of that process could be used for analyzing the reform you have in mind.

References

Alabama cuts taken to court. (2001, March). *American Libraries, 32* (3), 22.

Alaska state constitution. Online. Available: http: //www.gov.state.ak.us ltgov/akcon/art07.html

Aldington, R. (Ed.). (1941). *The Viking book of poetry of the English-speaking world* (vols. 1 & 2). New York: Viking.

Alexander, M. (2001, May 31). Education professor says senior slump is rational—but preventable. *Stanford Report.* Online. Available: http: //www.stanford.edu/dept/news/report/news/june6/kirst-530.html

Anderson, N. H. (1991). Moral-social development. In N. H. Anderson (Ed.), *Contributions to information integration theory: Volume 3: Developmental.* Hillsdale, NJ: Erlbaum.

Annis, S. (1998, June 5). Despite massive opposition campaign, Proposition 227 sweeps to landslide victory. *One Nation.* Online. Available: http: //www.onenation.org/pr060598. html

Arrow, K. J. (1971). *Essays in the theory of risk-bearing.* Chicago: Markham.

Ashley, J. S., & Jarratt-Ziemski, K. (1999, Summer). Superficiality and bias. *American Indian Quarterly,* p. 49.

Bible and Darwin supported. (2000, July 29). *Portrait of America.* Online. Available: http: //www.portraitofamerica.com/html/poll-1092.html

Christie, K. (2001). Stateline—Deja Vu All Over Again, *Phi Delta Kappan,* 82 (5), 346.

Colvin, R. E. (2001, September 19). Education bill getting closer to completion. *Los Angeles Times.* Online. Available: http://www.latimes. Com/

Cooper, M. (2001, September 18). Wilhoit says too many schools not letting go of old methods. *Messenger-Inquirer.* Online. Available: http:// www.messenger-inquirer.com/news/kentucky/3570096.htm

Crévecoeur, M. G. J. de. (1957). Letter III. In *Letters from an American farmer.* New York: Dutton.

Cyber schools: Convenience or burden? (2001, May 29). *CNN.* Online. Available: http://fyi.cnn.com/2001/fyi/teachers.ednews/05/29/cyber.schools.ap/

Diver-Stamnes, A. (1995). *Lives in the balance—Youth, poverty, and education in Watts.* Albany: State University of New York Press.

Elmore, R. E. (1997). The origins and problems of educational reform in the United States. In W. K. Cummings & N. F. McGinn, *International handbook of education and development: Preparing schools, students, and nations for the twenty-first century.* Oxford: Pergamon.

Entwistle, N. J. (1985). Cognitive style and learning. In. T. Husen & T. N. Postlthwaite (Eds.), *The international encyclopedia of education* (Vol. 2, pp. 810-813). Oxford: Pergamon.

Exodus. (1930). In *Holy Bible* (King James authorized version). Philadelphia: John C. Winston. (Original work published 1611.)

Fowler, C. (2001, March 23). Too-low salaries will force school closings, workshop told. *National Catholic Reporter, 37* (21), 5.

Fullen, M. (1991). *The new meaning of educational change.* London: Cassell.

Gert, B. (1970). *The moral rules—A new rational foundation for morality.* New York: Harper & Row.

González, D. (2000, November 20). Arizona win encourages bilingual-ed opponents. *Arizona Republic,* p. 1.

Guilford, J. P. (1967). *The nature of human intelligence.* New York: McGraw-Hill.

Guilford, J. P., & Hoepfner, R. (1971). *The analysis of intelligence.* New York: McGraw-Hill.

Hall, M. (2001, September 6). Officials examine childcare education. *Augusta Chronicle.* Online. Available: http//augustachronicle.com//

Harper, D., Hardy, J., & Thomas, R. M. (1999). *Curriculum guide: Generation www.y.* Eugene, OR: International Society for Technology in Education.

Harrison, S. (2001, September 21). Special-education students are shortchanged, audit says. *Miami Herald.* Online. Available: http://www.miami.com.herald/content/news/local/broward/digdocs/107188

Hawaii board gives unanimous thumbs down to creationism. (2001, August 4). Online. Available http://wew.atheists./flash. line/evo 16.html.

Hofstede, G. (1980). *Culture's consequences: International differences in work-related values.* Beverly Hills, CA: Sage.

Homeschoolers estimated at 850,000. (2001, August 1). Online. Available: United States Department of Education, http://www.ed.gov

Jalil, N., & McGinn, N. F. (1992). Pakistan. In R. M. Thomas (Ed.), *Education's role in national development plans* (pp. 89-108). New York: Praeger.

Kansas rejects theory of evolution. (1999, August 11). *BBC News*. Online. Available: http://news.bbc.co.uk'hi/English/world/Americas/news id417000/417996.stm

Kansas restores evolution standards for science classes. (2001, February 14). *CNN*. Online. Available: http://www.cnn.com/2001/US/02/14/kansas.evolution.02/

Kirst, M. (2001, May). Executive summary: Overcoming the senior slump. Online. Available: http://www.highereducation.org/news/news_0511sum.shtml

Lawlor, J. (2001, September 23). Value of a mill can vary by a mile—Schools: All is not equal in quests to fix buildings. *Flint Journal*. Online. Available: http://fl.mlive.com/news/index.ssf?/news/stories/20010923f23a3schoolbondpreview.frm

Lincoln, G. (1998). Lack of true American Indian history in textbooks. In S. B. Andrew & J. Creed (Eds.), *Authentic Alaska: voices of its Native writers* (pp. 91-95). Lincoln: University of Nebraska Press.

Marcus, D. L. (1999, August 30). Darwin gets thrown out of school. *U.S. News & World Report, 127* (8), 32.

Miller, R. (2000, December 29). Cyber charter school in works. *Post-Gazette*. Online. Available: http://www.post-gazette.com/region/state/20001229cyber6.asp.

Moilanen, R. (2001, September 28). More districts using computers, but maintenance money is scarce. *Daily Breeze*. Online. Available: http://www.dailybreeze.com/content/bln/nmcompfix30.html

New England primer: Or an easy and pleasant gide to the art of reading. (1836). Boston: Massachusetts Sabbath School Society.

O'Neill, P. (2001, August 10). Atlanta elementary school to close, *National Catholic Reporter, 37* (36),10.

Pardini, P. (1999). False choices—Vouchers, public schools, and our children's future. *Retinking Schools, 14* (2). Online. Available: http://www.rethinkingschools.org/SpecPub/voucher.htm

Pesznecker, K. (2001, September 18). Sex book getting close look. *Anchorage Daily News*. Online. Available:http://www.and.com/alaska/story/692815p-734905c.html

Piaget, J., & Inhelder, B. (1969). *The psychology of the child*. New York: Basic Books

Robinson, B. A. (2001, August 5). *The Ten Commandments: Recent legal developments re: Posting them in public schools and government offices*. Ontario Consultants on Religious Tolerance. Online. Available: http://www.religioustolerance.org/chr10c3html

Shakespeare, W. (1987). *Tragedies and poetical works.* In *The complete works of William Shakespeare.* Secaucus, NJ: Wellfleet.

Shastri, Y. S. (1994). *The salient features of Hinduism.* Ahmedabad, India: Yogeshwar Prakashan.

Sobieraj, S. (2001, September 20). As Bush leads nation into war, a 'new normal' White House emerges. *Courier News.* Online. Available: http://www.suburbanchicagonews.com/couriernews/htm

Tarrow, M. B. (Ed.). (1987). *Human rights and education.* Oxford: Pergamon.

Thomas, R. M. (1976). *Assessing the English-language writing skills of pupils in American Samoa.* Pago Pago, American Samoa: Department of Education.

Thomas, R. M. (1988). A Hindu theory of human development. In R. M. Thomas (Ed.), *Oriental theories of human development.* New York: Peter Lang.

Thomas, R. M. (1993). Nationalism in North American education. In K. Schleicher (Ed.), *Nationalism in education* (pp. 79-105). Frankfurt: Peter Lang.

Thomas, R. M. (1997). Multicultural curriculum planning as a political activity (pp. 209-220). In K. Watson, C. Modgil, & S. Modgil (Eds.), *Power and responsibility in education.* London: Cassell.

Thomas, R. M. (2001a). *Applying risk theory to educational development.* ERIC File/(in press).

Thomas, R. M. (2001b). *Folk psychologies across cultures.* Thousand Oaks, CA: Sage.

Thomas, R. M. (2002). Education. *Encyclopaedia Britannica 2002 book of the year.* Chicago: Encyclopaedia Britannica.

Title I Amendments to the elementary and secondary school act of 1965. Online. Available: http://www.ed.gov/legislation/ESEA/ sec1001.html

Trumbull, C. P. (2001). *Encyclopaedia Britannica 2001 book of the year.* Chicago: Encyclopaedia Britannica.

Undang-undang dasar (constitution). (1945). Jakarta: Republik Indonesia.

Undang-undang No. 12, tahun 1954, tentang pernjataan berlakunja undang-undang No. 4, tahun 1950, dari Republik Indoensia dahulu tentang dasar-dasar pendidikan dan pengajran sekolah untuk seluruh Indonesia (Law no. 12, year 1954, concerning the ratification of the earlier law no. 4, year 1950, of the Republic of Indonesia regarding the foundation of education and instruction in schools for the entire nation). (1954). Jakarta: Republik Indonesia.

Undang-undang Republic Indoensia nomor 2, tahun 1989, tentang system pendidikan nasional (Republic of Indonesia law no. 2, year 1989, concerning the national education system). (1989). Jakarta: Republik Indonesia.

Ware, J. R. (1955). *The sayings of Confucius.* New York: Mentor.

Welsh-Huggins, A. (2001, September 14). Governor considers price tag on education reform. *Tribune-Chronicle.* Online. Available: http://wwwtribunechronicle.com/

White, L. A. (1994). The concept of culture. In *Encyclopaedia Britannica* (Vol. 16, pp. 874-881). Chicago: Encyclopaedia Britannica.

Whitehead, C. (1997). The role of teachers in educational reform. In K. Watson, C. Modgil, & S. Modgil (Eds.). *Power and responsibility in education* (pp. 41-48). London: Cassell.

Index

**CORWIN
PRESS**

The Corwin Press logo—a raven striding across an open book—represents the happy union of courage and learning. We are a professional-level publisher of books and journals for K-12 educators, and we are committed to creating and providing resources that embody these qualities. Corwin's motto is "Success for All Learners."